THE COMIC MODE IN ENGLISH LITERATURE

Also available from Continuum

Aesthetics and Literature, David Davies
How to Read Texts, Neil McCaw
Studying English Literature, Edited by David Higgins and Ashley
    Chantler
The Essential Guide to English Studies, Peter Childs
The Poetry Toolkit, Rhian Williams

THE COMIC MODE IN ENGLISH LITERATURE

FROM THE MIDDLE AGES TO TODAY

MURRAY ROSTON

continuum

Continuum International Publishing Group

The Tower Building	80 Maiden Lane
11 York Road	Suite 704, New York
London SE1 7NX	NY 10038

www.continuumbooks.com

British Library Cataloguing-in-Publication Data
A catalogue record for this book is available from the British Library.

ISBN: 978-1-4411-9588-3 (Hardback)
978-1-4411-1231-6 (Paperback)

Library of Congress Cataloguing-in-Publication Data
A catalog record of this book is available from the Library of Congress.

Typeset by Fakenham Prepress Solutions, Fakenham, Norfolk NR21 8NN
Printed and bound in India

Haste thee nymph, and bring with thee
Jest and youthful Jollity,
Quips and Cranks, and wanton Wiles,
Nods, and Becks, and Wreathed Smiles,
Such as hang on Hebe's cheek,
And love to live in dimple sleek;
Sport that wrinkled Care derides,
And Laughter holding both his sides.

Milton, *L'Allegro*

CONTENTS

Chapter One: Introduction   1
Chapter Two: Late Medieval   37
    a) *The Second Shepherds' Play*   37
    b) Chaucer, *The Canterbury Tales*   42
    c) Medwall, *Fulgens and Lucrece*   52
Chapter Three: The Renaissance   61
    a) Shakespeare, *A Midsummer Night's Dream*   61
    b) Falstaff   75
    c) Donne, *The Flea*   90
    d) Marvell, *The Garden*   97
Chapter Four: The Restoration and Eighteenth Century   107
    a) Restoration Comedy   109
    b) Pope, *The Rape of the Lock*   121
    c) The Vogue of Sentiment   128
    d) Sterne, *Tristram Shandy*   140
Chapter Five: The Nineteenth Century   155
    a) Austen, *Emma*   155
    b) Dickens, *The Pickwick Papers*   166
    c) Poking Fun at the Establishment   176
    d) Wilde, *The Importance of Being Earnest*   188
    e) Jerome K. Jerome, *Three Men in a Boat*   197
Chapter Six: The Twentieth Century   205
    a) George Bernard Shaw   205
    b) Stella Gibbons, *Cold Comfort Farm*   217
    c) Beckett, *Waiting for Godot*   222
    d) Kingsley Amis, *Lucky Jim*   226
    e) Malcolm Bradbury, *The History Man*   233
    f) Helen Fielding, *Bridget Jones's Diary*   245

CONTENTS

Notes	253
Works Cited – on the Comic	267
Works Cited – General	271
Index	275

CHAPTER ONE

INTRODUCTION

In contrast to tragedy, comedy requires no Aristotelian definition to determine which productions belong within its category, as the evocation of laughter provides an infallible criterion. But there exists a marked disparity between the ease of identifying the genre and the problems involved in determining how it functions, in defining how that strange phenomenon laughter is evoked. One especial difficulty derives from the extraordinary range of its forms which, as Harold Nicolson has noted, include:

> the ludicrous, the ridiculous, the quaint, the droll, the jocular, the facetious, the waggish, the bantering, the farcical. We have wit, irony, satire, sarcasm, fancy, mockery, joke, quirk, pun, tomfoolery, clowning, glee, the burlesque, the mock-heroic ...[1]

Critical investigation of that theme has, in fact, reached a deadlock. Robin Haig, after examining over 100 theories of the comic, concludes that not one has proved satisfactory; John Morreall opens his study with the categorical statement, '... we are still without an adequate general theory of laughter', while psychologists have extended that negative view by declaring that so complex a mode can never be defined, since it consists of 'a whole composite of different behaviours rather than a single one'.[2] Those definitions that have been posited, even by the most respected theorists, have been accorded either outright opposition or only limited approval.

This present study makes no claim to deal with the manifold forms of the comic listed above – it focuses exclusively upon the literary versions, upon emanations of comedy in drama, poetry and prose. Yet before addressing the literary form, it may be advisable to summarize, however briefly, the weaknesses or failings of the major extant theories on comedy at large, with the assumption that readers interested in a more detailed account will consult the numerous critical assessments that have been published.[3]

The theories may be grouped conveniently into three main categories, based upon elements of Superiority, Incongruity and Relief.[4] Leading the first is Hobbes' widely quoted designation that laughter arises '… from some sudden conception of some eminency in ourselves, by comparison with the infirmity of others …'[5] that we are amused by a patronizing sense of an advantage we possess over the person ridiculed. Some instances do indeed include that response: we laugh with condescension at Mrs Malaprop's inept reference in Sheridan's *The Rivals* to 'allegories on the banks of the Nile'; but, as Francis Hutcheson noted when challenging Hobbes' theory in 1750, a sudden recognition of superiority does not in itself produce humour.[6] A wealthy man meeting a starving beggar would, he pointed out, indeed experience a sudden patronizing sense of personal eminency, but there would be nothing amusing in the meeting without some additional component; and it is clearly that unmentioned ingredient that creates the laughter – a factor that we shall need to identify. There is, moreover, a disturbing aspect to the theory, since Hobbes added an element of cruelty to his definition, claiming (as have so many other theorists) that it involves '… the apprehension of some deformed thing in another, by comparison whereof they suddenly applaud themselves' – a definition that includes laughing at a blind man or ridiculing the mentally retarded. That view had been widely approved in the Elizabethan era, Thomas Wilson's *Art of Rhetorique* (1553) maintaining:

> The occasion of laughter and the mean that maketh us merry … is the fondness [i.e. foolishness], the filthiness, the deformity and all such evil behaviour as we see to be in other … Sometimes we laugh at a man's body, that is not well proportioned, and laugh at his countenance if it be not either comely by nature, or else he through folly cannot well see it.[7]

Hobbes recognized the deplorable aspect of such laughter, defining it as a despicable ingredient of human behaviour '… incident to most to them, that are conscious of the fewest abilities in themselves; who are forced to keep themselves in their own favour, by observing the imperfections of other men',[8] adding that laughter at the defects of others is a sign of pusillanimity. But he does include such cruelty as a major element in all instances of the comic. That is, to my mind, a remarkably sour conception of the genre. As Congreve rightly commented: 'Sure the Poet must both be very Ill-natur'd himself, and think his Audience so, when he proposes by shewing Man Deform'd, or Deaf, or Blind, to give them an agreeable Entertainment; and hopes to raise their Mirth, by what is truly an object of Compassion.'[9] How far Hobbes' argument can be taken is evidenced by John J. O'Connor's extraordinary claim that Richard III's hunchback in Shakespeare's play renders that character '... almost inevitably comic', when there is not a hint of humour in Shakespeare's sinister portrayal of him, nor in the attitude of other characters towards him.[10]

In line with the Superiority theory, Henri Bergson saw laughter as a social corrective, a means of preventing non-conforming individuals from separating themselves from society by their idiosyncrasies. The normal person, he argued, animated by a creative *élan vital*, deplores any individual whose actions attract attention to the physical elements of human behaviour by wearing grotesque clothes or walking peculiarly, so that, as he puts it, humour is aroused when 'something mechanical is encrusted on the living'. But he too adds to that definition an essentially malicious impulse, claiming that in such laughter, 'we always find an unavowed intention to humiliate'.[11] That view of the comic as being essentially sadistic has been amply summarized in the article devoted to the topic in the *Encyclopaedia Britannica*, an article regarded as so authoritative that it has been reprinted in a succession of editions up to and including the most recent. It claims that cruelty is an essential ingredient in *all* forms of humour, that laughter cannot be evoked without an element of sadism:

There is a bewildering variety of moods involved in different forms of humour, including mixed or contradictory feelings; but whatever the mixture, it must contain a basic ingredient that is indispensable: an impulse, however faint, of aggression or apprehension. It may appear in the guise of malice, contempt, the veiled cruelty of condescension, or merely an absence of sympathy with the victim of the joke.[12]

Where in such an approach are we to place those cheerful quips that make life pleasant and that seem entirely free of a desire to humiliate? Frequently, we recount amusing stories against ourselves, recalling a moment of forgetfulness or misunderstanding, and I can see no malice or any desire to mortify in that type. Yet both Hobbes and Bergson remain among the main sources for current theories of the comic, with their insistence that all instances are motivated by cruel impulses, Maurice Charney, closer to our own time, typifying that view by defining comedy as 'by its very nature destructive and anarchic'.[13]

The second category, the Incongruous, has as its major proponents Kant and Schopenhauer, who assume that an element of mismatching or incompatibility is to be found '... in everything that is to excite a lively laugh'.[14] As the word 'everything' indicates, the definition claims to be all-inclusive. The sight of a tall man walking with someone short of stature may elicit a smile from some viewers (by no means from all), but there are too many instances of incongruity that fail to arouse mirth, and that therefore contradict the attribution of humour to that factor. Salvador Dali's painting *The Persistence of Memory*, depicting a clock draped meltingly over a tree branch, is as incongruous an image as can be imagined, but only an incompetent would regard it as humorous. As a depiction of the flexibility of subjective time, its incongruity is profoundly serious, a factor that again suggests that incongruity is not in itself the cause of laughter, that it must be accompanied by some other element for it to amuse. Yet the theory of Incongruity has retained a major position among subsequent critics, such as Michael Clark, M. W. Martin, John Morreall and, more recently, Elliot Oring, each suggesting certain emendations yet accepting that element as being the common denominator for all instances of the comic.[15]

There is indeed one aspect of Kant's theory that is effective, at least in part: that laughter results from disappointed expectation. 'The understanding, missing what it expected, suddenly lets go its hold, with the result that the effect of this slackening is felt in the body by the oscillation of the organs.' There is, it is true, always an element of suddenness or unexpectedness in humour. Even wit, which may take a moment or two before its effect is felt, relies upon the abruptness of the eventual perception; but again we must apply the acid test, namely, are there instances in which sudden, frustrated expectation does not arouse humour, in which case that cannot be in itself the source of the laughter. We are not amused on opening the mail to discover that an urgently awaited letter has failed to arrive, nor when a flight is suddenly cancelled or a budding relationship is ended abruptly.

The final major category is that of Relief, the idea that laughter serves as a safety valve, offering a release of excessive or suppressed energy. Herbert Spencer, on the basis of his 'hydraulic' theory whereby excitement and mental agitation produce energy that must expend itself, argued that all laughter provides a needed discharge of pent-up forces.[16] Muscular activity, he maintained, is normally purposeful, but since the contraction of the facial muscles and the expenditure of air from the lungs in the process of laughing have no practical objective, those quasi-convulsive contractions must represent a release of superfluous energy, the need to expend a repressed force that has found no other outlet. That theory too has met with considerable opposition since, if the humour arises from some suppressed energy on the part of the narrator of the humour, it would not account for the response of a listener who has not experienced that repression. Spencer's theory was later developed with considerable sophistication by Freud, who shifted the focus from suppressed physical energy to psychological repressions, but I would like to leave his view aside for the moment.

The above is intended only as the very briefest summary of the weaknesses in the theories offered so far. But those studies, it should be noted, have raised a number of broader questions that have remained unanswered. The first problem is the restriction of laughter to humans, a fact that Bergson notes but for which he offers no reason.[17] The laugh of the hyena is, of course, no more than a resemblance in sound, not a response to an amusing situation, and there is no confirmed evidence of any creature other than humans experiencing laughter. Robert Provine, a behavioural neuroscientist, has argued that a form of panting among apes may be considered a form of laughter, but even that dubious identification occurs, he admits, only in response to physical stimulus, to their being tickled, and not to a humorous notion or situation.[18] Any theory offered would therefore need to involve some element specific to the human condition. Then there is the difficulty that a baby gurgles with laughter in response to a game of peek-a-boo long before it has developed the intelligence requisite for appreciation of humour. That fact too must be included or in some way answered in any effective explanation of the phenomenon of laughter. Furthermore, as many have noted, if laughter is so essential an ingredient of human behaviour, how are we to explain that the Bible, a literary collection that seems to cover so many aspects of the human condition, contains not a single instance of the comic and, indeed, appears deliberately to exclude it? Where the term 'laughter' does occur, it is only in the sense of scorn, never of response to humour, as in Sarah's bitter incredulity at learning she is to give birth at an advanced age (a lack of faith preserved in the naming of her son, Isaac)[19] or in such contemptuous disparagements of the foe as, 'He that sitteth in the heavens shall laugh: the Lord shall have his enemies in derision' (Ps. 2.4). There have indeed been attempts to read humour into the Bible, attempts such as those by William Whedbee and Conrad Hyers, but they are far-fetched and unconvincing.[20] Whedbee, for example, has argued that, since Dante employed the word *comedy* to indicate an event that ends happily irrespective of whether it provokes laughter, the biblical account of Creation is 'comic'. If that is the criterion, it has nothing to do with humour. The book of Jonah, with its solemn warning that even prophets designated to rebuke sinners must learn mercy, Whedbee defines as 'a huge theological and practical joke' (p. 217) because of the story of the fish, which is in fact related there with undisturbed gravity. He admits that many will dismiss as 'downright crazy' his terming the book of Job a comedy, but he proceeds to do so on the grounds that 'comedy can be profoundly serious' (p. 224), once again employing a criterion that has no connection with the evocation of laughter, the theme of this present book. Not one of the many instances adduced by him to argue for the existence of comedy in the Bible proves convincing to me, especially as such vague terms as 'ironic twist' and 'comic rhythm' are used repeatedly to veil the absence of any real humour. At all events, these three problems – the restriction of laughter to humans, a baby's ability to laugh before attaining to the perceptive discrimination demanded by humour, and its total absence from the Bible – will need to be confronted in any definition proposed.

It should be stressed once again that this book is restricted in theme to the literary forms of the comic. Although this opening chapter will include examination of certain non-literary forms, their inclusion is intended solely as preparation for the focus upon drama, poetry and prose in the subsequent chapters. That said, within the literary forms, there can, I believe, be discerned a common denominator, an underlying unity to which two past theorists have pointed, if only in very general terms. Henry Fielding, in the preface to *Joseph Andrews*, declared that 'the only source of the true Ridiculous (as it appears to me) is affectation'. It was a statement never developed theoretically, although it was to serve as a major element in his own comic writings.[21] That view reappears in George Meredith's long, rambling essay on that theme, although there it is merely one of many suggested factors. The Comic Spirit, he maintained, is aroused whenever human beings

> ... wax out of proportion, overblown, affected, pretentious, bombastical, hypocritical, pedantic, fantastically delicate; whenever it sees them self-deceived or hoodwinked, given to run riot in idolatries, drifting into vanities, congregating in absurdities, planning short-sightedly, plotting dementedly ...[22]

The most significant item in that lengthy list is the trait to which Fielding pointed, when the person serving as the object of laughter is filled with a sense of self-importance or vanity, when he or she is pretentious – although we shall need soon to modify that statement.

To begin with an ancient instance, in a wonderful scene in Aristophanes' comedy *The Clouds*, Socrates is depicted as being cranked down in a basket from the heavens while haughtily explaining to a puzzled spectator how essential it is for him as a philosopher to leave earth and to live in the skies above:

> *Socrates*: I have to suspend my brain and mingle the subtle essence of my mind with this air, which is of the like nature, in order clearly to penetrate the things of heaven. I should have discovered nothing, had I remained on the ground to consider from below the things that are above; for the earth by its force attracts the sap of the mind to itself. It is just the same with watercress ...[23]

Here is the essence of comedy. For the point lies not, as has so often been claimed, in the 'humiliation' of Socrates, nor simply in a sense of superiority in the audience, but in a more subtle response, the puncturing of Socrates' patronizing claim that only philosophers such as himself see the true light, all others being deceived by shadows. His repeated declaration that he knew nothing was, of course, only a ploy, an opening gambit, as he began systematically to demolish the beliefs of others, usually in public; and it was the annoyance he frequently aroused by playing the gadfly, posing questions seemingly simple but carefully designed to trap his inter-locutors and to establish his own intellectual superiority that was being countered in *The Clouds*.[24] The humour here consists, as in so much humour within literature, in *the deflating of human pretensions*, a derogation of anyone attempting to assert self-importance or to claim dictatorial rights, the moment of laughter occurring as the onlooker suddenly perceives, with some relief, the vulnerability of the assumed superiority.

Such definition, it should be noted, reverses the normal interpre-tation, since the sense of superiority assigned by Hobbes and others to the person laughing (experiencing 'a sudden conception of some eminency in ourselves') is here transferred to the object of laughter, mirth being aroused by the assumption of superiority on the part of the person being lampooned. An essential ingredient in the theory is the gratifying sense on the part of the amused that they are free from the claim or presumption that is being deflated, a euphoria that temporarily releases us from the pressures of life itself. In that scene in *The Clouds*, the audience experiences the pleasant thought that the lofty claims Socrates thrusts so confidently upon us are not as binding as we had believed, that it is preferable, in fact, to remain on terra firma than to soar into abstract imaginative speculations, as the gap is observed between such pretensions and the reality of the human condition.

That principle needs, however, to be modified; for the comic occurs not only when the self-aggrandizement of an individual is punctured but also when some authority or established social principle attempts to impose itself imperiously upon us. Hence our amusement at flaws in sternly worded notices in foreign hotels, such as 'Guests should leave their values at the front desk'. Its autocratic tone is quashed, the unintentional error robbing the notice of its force and leaving us happily free of its dictates. Moreover, in contrast to the continual harping upon sadistic impulses in humour, almost all instances we shall be examining in literature are essentially genial, not repre-senting any final disqualification of the object being burlesqued. Aristophanes was not denying the value of philosophy, merely targeting Socrates and the sophists for exaggerating their claims (tradition has it that Socrates, present in the audience on its first performance, rose for a good-natured bow); and in our discussion below, analysing the various forms of humour, the transitory quality of the deflation will emerge as a distinguishing factor – in contrast, indeed, to mordant satire which aims at permanent disqualification of the behaviour being targeted and which, as we shall see, rarely evokes laughter, eliciting at most a sardonic smile.

Although the ramifications of the theory demand some delicacy in application, the principle lies here. Let us begin from the crudest instance evoking laughter, when a person slips on a banana skin, an instance that highlights the necessity of including in the definition some degree of self-importance on the part of the person lampooned. We do not laugh if the individual who has fallen is an infirm elderly lady crossing the road, however 'superior' we may feel to her. We laugh only when some dignitary about to receive an honour, walking across the podium with his nose in the air, slips and lands on his rear in public; or when a schoolmaster, the symbol of authority, has his chair collapse beneath him in the presence of his pupils. In such instances, there is a warm feeling that we need no longer feel envious of the elevated, that we prefer remaining in the world of actuality, being immune (at least at that moment) to the dangers of eminence, pride or magisterial dignity.

In dealing with these cruder instances and before moving on to more subtle examples, it may be helpful to notice three factors relating to the problems mentioned above, and the ways in which the proposed definition may help to provide answers. First, why only humans laugh – because humans alone experience the lofty pretensions or claims to superiority that evoke laughter. A cow has no philosophical ambitions, no exalted principles, no self-importance or fantasies. A cockerel in the roost may appear to strut arrogantly among his hens, but that description only holds true when it is considered in human terms, as a Chanticleer. He is in fact engaged in the very serious task imposed upon him by Nature, asserting his territorial rights in order to drive away potential rivals. The exclusiveness of laughter to the human race may thus be seen to arise from the very quality that distinguishes us from the beast, the ability to project our thoughts above and beyond the material, to soar imaginatively into higher realms, and to pride ourselves on our achievements.

The second point arises from the comforting aspect of the situation, the pleasure we have in perceiving, however briefly, our own imperviousness to lofty aspirations. That feeling of satisfaction or euphoria links us with the baby's smile of content. The connection between adult laughter and the baby's smile lies not in any shared sense of humour but in the fact that the physical processes that produce the phenomenon we term laughter, a tightening of facial muscles and the expelling of air, have a more general function than response to humour, serving also to indicate a feeling of pleasure or satisfaction.[25] We smile, for example, when someone praises us, or when we meet a friend, even when those events involve no humour and signify only gratification. A baby, too, smiles in response to being coddled, and in peek-a-boo, to the reassurance of seeing a familiar face return after a worrying absence. In each instance, the feeling of contentment serves as the coordinating factor, the shared quality that produces those bodily responses that characterize smiling and laughter. Accordingly we need to distinguish between general indications of gratification and the physically similar response produced by wit and humour.

That element of gratification is relevant also to certain research suggesting the possibility of animal laughter. It has been pointed out that apes, after being frightened, squeal with relief in a manner resembling the human laugh; but that response among animals belongs, it would seem, in the same category as the baby's smile at peek-a-boo or at being tossed in the air and then caught, the animal's squeal indicating not humour but cessation of disquietude.

Lastly at this point, we may appreciate the absence of laughter in the Bible, whose aim is to nurture precisely those factors that comedy burlesques, namely elevated ideals and authoritative commands. In that respect biblical literature marked a substantial contrast to the classics, which nurtured comedy not only upon the Attic and Roman stages – for in Homer's epic too, the heavens resound to the laughter of the gods as Mars and Venus, confident that they have deceived Vulcan, are caught compromisingly in his net. The purpose of classical literature, however, was not to inculcate moral principles, the gods on Olympus being far from models of ethical propriety, Jupiter and his peers often descending to earth to rape innocent maidens. For the Bible, however, any lampooning of its moral or spiritual ideals would have countered its primary educative purpose. It is true that both Judaism and Christianity would later condone the mirth-making celebrations of Purim and the Lenten carnival as concessions to human needs; but the texts themselves formulating the principles of the faith could offer no place for jesting. Jesus himself, as medieval canonical works frequently noted, is never recorded as having either laughed or joked. When the Bible is exposed to laughter, the process inevitably verges upon blasphemy, as in Dryden's sly justification of Charles II's sexual improprieties on the analogy of King David scattering 'his Maker's image through the land', an account containing, in the description of the monarch's fathering of Absalom, a remarkably irreverent image of heavenly participation in human affairs:

> Whether, inspir'd by some diviner lust,
> His father got him with a greater gust ...

An anonymous folksong interprets the scriptural stories no less flippantly:

> Solomon and David lived immoral lives,
> They spent their time a-chasing
> After other people's wives.
> But at the end their consciences
> Began to give them qualms,
> So Solomon wrote the Proverbs
> And David wrote the Psalms.[26]

Those are attitudes whose irreverence the biblical text could by no means tolerate. The very absence of comedy in the Bible would thus seem to confirm that the purpose of humour is indeed to puncture authoritative claims and, for that reason, is entirely excluded from the canon.

The deflating of the presumptuous, usually in terms of a bathetic descent from the lofty to the mundane, includes the discrediting of inordinate flights of fancy which either ignore or attempt to transcend actuality. Hence James Thurber's delightful sketch of Walter Mitty, fondly imagining himself as the commander of a ship heroically battling a storm, or as a brilliant surgeon coolly performing an impossibly complex operation, only to be recalled to earth by his wife's sharp query whether he had remembered to purchase puppy-biscuits. Or the fairy tale of the frog that follows the beautiful princess into the palace, hops on to her bed and, on being kissed upon the forehead, is transformed into a handsome prince lying beside her – to which is added the note that her parents, entering her bedroom at that moment, refused to believe her story. We are suddenly jolted back from the dream-world of magic and fantasy to the real and everyday, and laugh at ourselves for having been temporarily deluded. So too, when there is a sudden disclosure of humankind's attempt at self-aggrandizement, concealing from itself unsavoury aspects of its own behaviour – as may be illustrated by an incident that occurred to the present author some years ago. When taking my 4-year-old daughter for a walk, I saw ahead that a student at the edge of the sports field had dressed as a bear, the university mascot. Concerned that she might be frightened, I assured her that it was not a real bear but a man wearing a bearskin. She pondered the information for a moment and then asked pointedly, 'So what's the bear wearing?' The veil decorously hiding the less admirable elements of human actions is abruptly torn aside to reveal the mundane reality, contrasting the fondness for animals implicit in the choice of the mascot with the actuality of our treatment of them.

The requirement that we have defined for comic portrayal, the sense of complacency, pride or imperiousness in the person or authority targeted, excludes, unless that aspect be present, all instances of laughter at physical deformity or mental disability so frequently adduced by Hobbes and others. There have been times when, as in the eighteenth century, people visited mental asylums and laughed uproariously at the unfortunate inmates. Today that seems appalling (a point to which we shall return), but it does conform to the theory, since what people were laughing at was not the mental deformity as such but the pretensions of the inmates so markedly contradicting their actual condition, as is evidenced in Hogarth's contemporary depiction of Bedlam. At one side a naked figure with paper crown and sceptre is convinced of his royal status, another gazes through a makeshift telescope in the fond belief that he is an astronomer, while a third has placed a makeshift mitre on his head imagining he is a bishop.[27] The requirement of affectation applies equally to the instance of Mrs Malaprop's misuse of words. Were she simply an uneducated or mentally handicapped woman with a confused vocabulary, there would be no humour. It is her claim to sophistication, her attempt to impress others with her verbal dexterity and superior learning that provides the element missing in Hobbes' theory. His terms are far too sweeping, and too negative to function as an effective definition. We laugh at monkeys in the zoo not because we feel superior to them but because, by a certain grimace or gesture, they remind us of a pompous uncle or a complacent acquaintance whom we suddenly see reduced in dignity by the similarity.

Plato, in his *Philebus*, might seem to share this suggestion that pretentiousness is the major cause of humour when he mentions that we laugh at those people suffering from a 'vain conceit of beauty, of wisdom, and of wealth'. But that is a misunderstanding of the passage. Socrates was not offering there a definition of the comic. In the process of contending that wisdom and knowledge are preferable to the pursuit of pleasure, he argued that pleasure frequently arises from pain or envy, and merely cites laughter as an instance. His focus was not on the pretensions of the person ridiculed but on the pain or envy experienced at viewing a person's weakness:

> *Socrates*: The three kinds of vain conceit in our friends which we enumerated – the vain conceit of beauty, of wisdom, and of wealth, are ridiculous if they are weak, and detestable when they are powerful: May we not say, as I was saying before, that our friends who are in this state of mind, when harmless to others, are simply ridiculous?
>
> *Protarchus*: They are ridiculous.
>
> *Socrates*: And do we not acknowledge this ignorance of theirs to be a misfortune?
>
> *Protarchus*: Certainly.
>
> *Socrates*: And do we feel pain or pleasure in laughing at it?
>
> *Protarchus*: Clearly we feel pleasure.
>
> *Socrates*: And was not envy the source of this pleasure which we feel at the misfortunes of friends?
>
> *Protarchus*: Certainly.
>
> *Socrates*: Then the argument shows that when we laugh at the folly of our friends, pleasure, in mingling with envy, mingles with pain, for envy has been acknowledged by us to be mental pain, and laughter is pleasant; and so we envy and laugh at the same instant.[28]

I can see no hint of envy, nor of pain, in our amusement at the tale of the princess and the frog cited above.

We have added to the pretentiousness of individuals the imperiousness of authoritative rulings and social imperatives. The humorous puncturing of authority, especially by revealing unintended ambiguities or discrepancies in dogmatic commands, has a long history. Enid

Welsford records the incident of a medieval buffoon-parson sternly ordered by his bishop to dismiss his attractive young housekeeper on the grounds that the minimum age permitted for such domestics was 40. The parson promptly obliged, hiring two girls, each aged 20.[29] We delight with the parson at his exploitation of unguardedness in the bishop's statement and the consequent deflating of authority. And that same principle underscores the more general function of the Fool in both medieval and Elizabethan times, where his purpose was often to expose fallacies in peremptory decrees. Hence the tale of one such jester who, after having offended the king, was condemned to permanent exile, never on pain of death to tread on English soil. His blithe return a few months later astonishes the court, whereupon he removes his footwear and, to their amusement and eventual forgiveness, reveals his shoes to be filled with French soil. That function is paralleled in *Twelfth Night*, in Feste's reproof of Olivia for her excessive mourning, her seven-year vow of celibacy and isolation intended to impress others with her sisterly devotion but, as the jester perceives, revealing a self-righteousness sorely needing deflation:

> *Feste.* Good madonna, why mourn'st thou?
> *Olivia.* Good fool, for my brother's death.
> *Feste.* I think his soul is in hell, madonna.
> *Olivia.* I know his soul is in heaven, fool.
> *Feste.* The more fool, madonna, to mourn for your brother's soul being in heaven.

Such instances help us to understand Aristotle's cryptic comment that comedy represents people as worse than they are, tragedy as better.[30] Taken literally, the statement is patently false – Macbeth is in no sense better than normal people, nor are Beatrice and Benedick worse. But the comment holds true in the sense I am using it here, namely, that the genre of tragedy accepts as valid the noble aspirations and ideals of humankind – the selfless love of Desdemona, the romantic notions of Othello and the sacrosanctity of monarchy against which Macbeth so egregiously offends – thereby representing people as better than they normally are, while comedy prefers to expose the foibles and delusions of humankind, deflating their unwarranted *amour propre*, as in Olivia's mourning pose. One would be tempted to correct Aristotle's phrase by stating that comedy

presents people not as worse than they are but precisely as they are;
but comedy does indeed tend to exaggerate the foibles in the process
of highlighting them, focusing on the weaknesses of humans rather
than their virtues.

In poetry, which can be absorbed at a more leisurely pace than
staged drama, humour is at times very subtle, as in the lines from
Pope's *Rape of the Lock* describing Belinda as she first emerges into
view:

On her white Breast, a sparkling Cross she wore,
Which Jews might kiss, and infidels adore.

The description, ostensibly in praise of the dazzling beauty of
Belinda, the heroine of the tale, contains a hint carefully inserted that
entertainingly counters the surface impression. The balanced lines of
the heroic couplet create a rhythm that chiastically attaches the word
kiss to *Breast* as well as *Cross*, implying that her admirers are more
attracted by the location of the symbol than by its religious implications. That sly hint not only exposes the erotic element concealed in
the supposed piety of her admirers (a hint culminating in the double
meaning of *adore*, with its devotional and amorous denotations),
but at the same time suggests that Belinda's wearing of the cross
may, by its placing, have had a more practical intent on her part, to
attract the admiring glances of the men. Her display of religiosity is
thus neatly undermined by that implication. One should note also
that the momentary pause before we grasp the concealed allusion
is the distinguishing element of wit as opposed to other forms of
the comic, namely its demand for some mental effort on the part of
reader or listener, the requisite pause augmenting the effectiveness
of the eventual apprehension of the humour. But essential for an
understanding of the source of the wit is the reader's amusement at
the delicate detraction from the supposed piety both of Belinda and
of her suitors, and its replacement by a more earthy implication.

A major form of literary humour is, of course, parody or burlesque,
which fits the definition closely since, in almost all instances, both
forms make fun of the pomposity implicit in the original, the sense
of elitism displayed there. Longfellow took himself very seriously
not only as a poet but also as the preserver of American myth, the
repetitive trochaic metre he employed in *Hiawatha* aimed at creating
the effect of a lofty epic incantation:

He it was who carved the cradle
Of the little Hiawatha,
Carved its framework out of linden,
Bound it strong with reindeer's sinews;
He it was who taught him later
How to make his bows and arrows ...

An anonymous parody robs it of its dignity, lampooning both the solemnity and the detailed itemizing of the original:

When he killed the Mudjokivis,
Of the skin he made him mittens,
Made them with the fur side inside,
Made them with the skin side outside,
He, to get the warm side inside,
Put the inside skin side outside
He, to get the cold side outside,
Put the warm side fur side inside ...[31]

A major theorist whom we have neglected so far is Freud, whose *Jokes and their Relation to the Unconscious* has occupied a central place in most recent studies. Adapting Herbert Spencer's theory of laughter as being a needed release of unused energy, he transferred the impulse to a psychological setting, seeing it as a safety valve for the release of repressed emotions, in most instances hostile or sexual. The process he defined as one of 'displacement' or substitution, extending to comic theory his famous explication of dreams. There he had argued that suppressed ideas emerge from the subconscious during sleep in altered form, a circumvention that avoids confronting the suppressed notion by means of transference reliant upon verbal similarity, such as alliteration or assonance. Thus a dislike of Jones will create a dream about 'bones', or hostility to Robert will produce the nightmare of being 'robbed'. Humour, he believed, depends upon a similar process of 'indirect representation', whereby one idea or phrase is substituted for another, a process of condensation occurring in both instances. Incidentally, we may well wonder at this point if, as Freud claimed, dreams and humour so closely parallel each other, why dreams themselves are not comic; but Freud did not raise that question.

The main instance he offers (and the one cited most frequently by critics) is the account of two men who, having achieved great wealth, commission portraits of themselves for a joint public unveiling. At that event, one visitor, gazing at the two portraits, asks, 'Where is the Saviour?', referring of course to the Crucifixion between two thieves. On the basis of his general theory, Freud attributes the humour to the fact that the criticism is expressed obliquely or allusively, the New Testament reference functioning as a substitute for a direct accusation of thievery. His explanation deserves to be quoted at length (the lacuna marks a reference to previously discussed jokes and omits nothing of significance to his analysis):

We at once recall where we have already come across allusion – in connection, namely, with double meaning. When two meanings are expressed in one word and one of them is so much more frequent and usual that it occurs to us at once, while the second is more out of the way and therefore less prominent, we proposed to speak of this as 'double meaning with an allusion'. In a whole number of the examples we have already examined we remarked that the technique was not a simple one, and we now perceive that the 'allusion' was the complicating factor in them ... In the American anecdote we now have before us an allusion without any double meaning, and we see that its characteristic is replacement by something linked to it in a conceptual connection.[32]

The fact that the speaker was not explicit in connecting the men being honoured to the two thieves is, Freud argues, the source of the humour, whereas, in our terms, that indirectness is merely the element that transforms the remark from humour to wit, with its demand for a moment's thought before the point is grasped; but the substitution is not in itself the source of laughter.

Identification of the humour in the tale is, one suspects, far simpler. The two wealthy men, like the dignitary slipping upon a banana skin, had, in commissioning the portraits and in organizing the public unveiling, planned to bask in acclaim for their notable achievements. The questioner abruptly exposes the gap between their claim to kudos and the reality of their situation, puncturing their self-aggrandizement with a reminder of the unsavoury means whereby they had accumulated their wealth. We laugh with the comfortable feeling that their pride is, after all, unfounded, that the attainment of riches generally involves the committing of sordid acts, and hence that their assertion of superiority is baseless.

Noel Carroll has written interestingly on the philosophy of joke theory and he too regards Freud's explanation as unsatisfactory. But I find in Carroll's own analysis a similar tendency to complicate the simple. He relates the following story: 'A young priest runs into his abbot's office shouting "Come quickly, Jesus Christ is in the chapel." The abbot and novice hurry into the church and see Christ kneeling at the altar. The young man asks "What should we do?" to which the wise old abbot replies, whispering, "Look busy."' After correctly commenting that the abbot regards Jesus as an employer rather than his saviour, Carroll proceeds to offer the following explanation of the way the humour functions:

> What the listener must do at the end of a joke is to provide an interpretation, that is, make sense of the last line of the text in light of the salient elements of the preceding narrative or riddle. This may involve reconstruing or reconstructing earlier information, which initially seemed irrelevant, as now salient under the pressure of coming up with an interpretation. For example, in the joke about the two priests, the narrative 'field' is reorganised in such a way that it becomes very significant that the abbot is 'old' and 'wise' (cagey) and that he is 'whispering' (a signal of furtiveness), given our interpretation that he believes the boss (rather than the Savior) has arrived on the scene for a surprise inspection.[33]

In fact, no such subsequent 'reconstruing' is necessary, the joke being equally effective without mention of the abbot's wisdom or age; for the humour again relies on bathos. Even if we are in the mood for a joke and are expecting this to be one, the narrative does begin on an elevated plane, the recounting of a religious visionary experience, so that the abbot's reply amusingly plummets us into the mundane contemporary setting of business procedures, the dismay of employees at the boss's unexpected arrival.

Although the theory offered here is in itself very simple and may, once defined, seem self-evident, its application to some of the more puzzling instances can be very revealing. One such area is the verbal pun, a genre that has remained unexplained in the numerous studies that have appeared so far.[34] Freud admitted, as have so many others, that the humour involved in wordplay is difficult to analyse and, perhaps because of his inability to define it, he described it dismissively as the lowest form of wit. Robert Martin, recalling how often puns have been seen as the most baffling of all evocations of laughter, summarized the general view in stating that the pun 'has had to skulk like a pariah around the fringes of comedy'.[35] Mention of puns usually leads to citation of Samuel Johnson's attack upon Shakespeare's addiction to them and his own dislike of the entire genre. An investigation of his dislike can indeed prove illuminating, especially as it needs to be seen within the context of a contemporary cultural phenomenon. 'A quibble,' Johnson wrote, using the contemporary term for the pun,

> ... is to *Shakespeare* what luminous vapours are to the traveller, he follows it at all adventures; it is sure to lead him out of his way, and sure to engulf him in the mire. It has some malignant power over his mind, and its fascinations are irresistible ... A quibble, poor and barren as it is, gave him such delight, that he was content to purchase it by the sacrifice of reason, propriety, and truth. A quibble was to him the fatal *Cleopatra* for which he lost the world, and was content to lose it.[36]

Although in this passage Dr Johnson was referring to Shakespeare's indulgence in amusing puns, he was equally opposed to any serious exploitation of verbal ambivalences, condemning also the practice of Metaphysical poets whereby 'the most heterogeneous ideas are yoked by violence together'. We are entitled to ask (as I have seen no one yet ask) why Johnson was so vehemently opposed to the genre, seeing it as contrary to reason, propriety and truth. Was it mere personal dislike or was it part of a broader eighteenth-century phenomenon?

What, indeed, is humorous in comic wordplay? In that genre, it is not the overconfidence of a person that is targeted, but the imperiousness of language itself. In contrast to Humpty Dumpty's declaration, words are not supposed to mean whatever one wishes them to mean, but to have clearly defined, specific import. Our pleasure at the best type of pun (and there are bad puns, just as there are poor jokes) lies in the sudden, amused perception of a flaw in the supremacy of language, the realization that words can mislead or point simultaneously in two or more directions. Hence the introduction of the Mock Turtle in *Alice in Wonderland*, with the entertaining recognition that in the familiar term 'mock-turtle-soup', the word *mock* can be applied to the turtle instead of the soup. We are gratified to see the dominance of words challenged. At a more sophisticated level, with that momentary pause necessary to grasp the point which distinguishes wit, we have the double meaning of *port* in the gibe at the classicist Richard Bentley, a previously contentious scholar but now retired and bibulous:

Where Bentley late tempestuous wont to sport
In troubled waters, but now sleeps in port.[37]

Charles R. Gruner, in line with the Superiority theory, has argued that all humour, including verbal, results from the ridicule directed at the person responsible for the unintended ambiguity,[38] but both above instances contradict that reading, since the puns there are so obviously intentional.

The reason Johnson was so opposed to puns lies in the cultural setting of his period, a time when the rise of science and the emergence of the encyclopedists had made it imperative to specify the exact meaning of words, to classify and identify ideas with precision. The establishment of the Royal Society in 1662 had changed the nature of scientific language. As Thomas Sprat, the Secretary of the Society, recorded, its members rejected the amplifications, digressions and swellings of style inherent in previous writings, insisting instead on purity, brevity and exactness of vocabulary. They adopted '... a close, naked, natural way of speaking; positive expressions; clear senses; a native easiness: bringing all things as near the Mathematical plainness, as they can'.[39] Instead of the term 'heart trouble', which could refer to problems with a delinquent lover as well as the blockage of an artery, the more precise term 'cardiac' was now introduced, restricted to the physical organ that pumps blood. In the context of that new rationalist approach, there emerged a general desire for precision in language and hence a condemnation of wordplay that was seen as blurring the distinctions. Well before Johnson's attack, the dislike of wordplay had, from the time of the Royal Society, become general. Dryden, in his *Defence of the Epilogue* (1672), objected to the 'wresting and torturing' of a word into another meaning, and in 1711 Addison devoted an entire essay in the *Spectator* to that theme, claiming: 'There is no kind of false Wit which has been so recommended by the Practice of all Ages, as that which consists in a Jingle of Words, and is comprehended under the general Name of *Punning*.' Puzzled that some of the great authors of the past, including Aristotle and Cicero, had approved the practice, Addison assumed that, gifted as they were, they 'were destitute of all Rules and Arts of Criticism; and for that Reason, though they excel later Writers in Greatness of Genius, they fall short of them in Accuracy and Correctness'. Precision, therefore, was the new criterion, such quibbles, he added, having been 'entirely banished out of the Learned World'.[40]

Who, we may ask, was more likely to resent wordplay than the great lexicographer himself, the person who marked the culmination of that trend, authoritatively providing precise definitions of words? Inevitably, Johnson viewed with distaste attempts to derogate from the stability of language, claiming that such indulgence marked a 'sacrifice of reason, propriety, and truth'. Ideas, he and his era believed, should be classified, separated into their categories and confined there, not jumbled together. Transgression of such defined categories included the exposure of the instability of language implicit in puns and was anathema to him.[41]

In contrast, Shakespeare, the object of Johnson's attack on 'quibbles', had lived at a time when writers were fascinated by words, not least by the plurality of words that could be applied to a single idea, and that, I believe, for an identifiable reason. During the early part of the sixteenth century, before Shakespeare appeared on the scene, writers had complained repeatedly of the poverty of the English language, of its inability to cope with the sophisticated ideas and philosophical discussions arising in the Renaissance. Where the Italian language contained a rich vocabulary inherited in unbroken succession from Latin, and where French had long served as the sophisticated language of diplomacy, the English language was deplorably poor. As a result, there was in the early sixteenth century an urgent need to expand the available vocabulary, with new words being imported from Greek, Latin and French. Some writers objected to the influx of so many 'inkhorn' terms, Thomas Wilson complaining in 1553 that the innovators were seeking 'so far for outlandish English that they forget altogether their mother tongue'. But the process continued unabated. As a result, by the year 1600 the process had reached an extraordinary level, every third word in the language being an importation. And writers delighted in the new linguistic variety. Hence the appearance of works such as Lyly's *Euphues* in 1580, not only employing an extravagant vocabulary but relishing such impressive synonyms as *lineaments* for *features*, *comely* for *handsome*, *counterfeit* for *false*. He writes of

> ... a young gentleman of great patrimony, and of so comely a personage, that it was doubted whether he were more bound to Nature for the lineaments of his person, or to Fortune for the increase of his possessions. But Nature impatient of comparisons, and as it were disdaining a companion or copartner in her working, added to this comeliness of his body such a sharp capacity of mind, that not only she proved Fortune counterfeit, but was half of that opinion that she herself was only current.

There was, thus, a dizzying intoxication with words. Hamlet may reprove Osric for carrying the principle to excess, parodying the flowery language of that courtier in his own entertainingly euphuistic description of Laertes:

> *Hamlet*: Sir, his definement suffers no perdition in you; though, I know, to divide him inventorially would dozy th' arithmetic of memory, and yet but yaw neither in respect of his quick sail. But, in the verity of extolment, I take him to be a soul of great article, and his infusion of such dearth and rareness as, to make true diction of him, his semblable is his mirror, and who else would trace him, his umbrage, nothing more.

But Shakespeare himself revelled in the opulence of language, as in the following light-hearted exchange with its puns on *soul* and *soar*:

Mercutio	Nay, gentle Romeo, we must have you dance.
Romeo	Not I, believe me: you have dancing shoes
	With nimble soles: I have a soul of lead
	So stakes me to the ground I cannot move.
Mercutio	You are a lover; borrow Cupid's wings,
	And soar with them above a common bound.
Romeo	I am too sore enpierced with his shaft
	To soar with his light feathers ... (*RJ* 1:4:13–20)

Romeo is, to his and our amusement, revealing the unguardedness of language, employing words similar in sound yet different in meaning. And again it is essential to note the temporary nature of such derogation. There is no desire in such wordplay to disqualify language; only to expose risibly how the new profusion of words had created ambivalent overlappings.

Freud once ascribed the love of punning among adolescents to an instinctive resistance to the logical framework being imposed upon them as they move into the adult world, and I would suggest that it is essentially that same resistance that lies behind the wordplay of adults too, the pleasure of demonstrating that language is not as rigidly definitive and logically precise as had been imagined, the exposed ambiguity producing a sense of momentary victory over its tyranny. That reaction is especially notable when an authoritative source produces a pun unintentionally. I once saw a prominent front-page headline in a major evening paper recording the movements of a military commander that read: 'MacArthur Flies Back to Front'. On another occasion, again in a respected newspaper, I found the following paragraph, intended perfectly seriously, that read: 'Owing to a strike among municipal workers, the local cemetery will be closed until further notice. A skeleton staff has been set up to deal with emergency cases.' In such instances, there is, in addition to the pleasure of the ambiguity itself, the satisfaction of catching out a respected newspaper at its moment of fallibility. The reason, incidentally, that we groan at a bad pun is easily explained once the principle is grasped; for when the wordplay is forced or far-fetched it fails to expose any real instability in language, pointing instead to the ineffectiveness of the putative punner.

What of indecent jokes? Wylie Sypher has suggested that their origin lies in the human's uneasiness concerning the 'nastiness' of the body and its relation to the animal world, but he fails to explain why such uneasiness should lead to laughter.[42] Freud argued that 'smutty' jokes arise from the libido's urge for sexual exposure of the genital organs,[43] but, if that were so, we must ask why neither the audience at a striptease performance nor the stripper regard such exposure as comical. The explanation lies elsewhere. In our own day, a euphemistic term for pornography and associated pursuits has become widely accepted. We are bombarded with advertisements for 'adult books', 'adult movies', 'adult websites', but the genre appears to be closer to the practice of adolescents who feel that they prove themselves mature or 'adult' by daring to use words, or by defiantly indulging in actions forbidden or frowned upon by their preceptors. In a society that disdains explicit references to genitalia, a group of persons exchanging indecent jokes is really creating a comforting sense of camaraderie, of living in the real world rather than pursuing the 'unfeasible purity' that society attempts to impose upon them, and whose imposition they resent.

That leads us to Bakhtin's discussion of carnival, so influential in recent years, in which he connects the sexual displays in medieval merry-making celebrations with the brazen indecencies of Rabelais. It is a theory that needs to be approached with caution. Developed long before its publication in the West but suppressed by the Communist authorities, it arose out of his own animosity towards the Soviet regime. His account of carnival was a thinly veiled version of the kind of uprising he would dearly have liked to see taking place in Russia. Instead of regarding carnival as a safety valve, releasing passions that might otherwise explode into revolution, Bakhtin argued that it actually constituted a form of insurrection. The bawdy elements in carnival he compared to Rabelais's writings, including in that category the medieval Feast of Fools, the Feast of Asses and the Boy Bishop celebration, all marking, he believed, a rebellious desire for change erupting from the lower classes and challenging restrictive impositions of discipline. The impulse resulted, Bakhtin has argued, in a grotesque and often blasphemous realism, similar to Gargantuan's stealing of the cathedral chimes in order to hang them derisively as harness-bells on his mare. The process involved, he maintained, a desire to abase, to drag down to bodily level by means of literary or theatrical parody the social principles imposed upon the proletariat and to replace them with something more amenable:

> Degradation here means coming down to earth, the contact with earth as an element that swallows up and gives birth at the same time. To degrade is to bury, to sow, and to kill simultaneously, in order to bring forth something more and better.[44]

As he remarks a little later, the aim is to hurl the dominant authority or repressive mode 'into the void of nonexistence'.

If we may accept his definition of carnival as a desire to derogate the sacred by drawing it down to an earthy level (in a manner we have suggested for comedy at large), we must disagree with what he terms its ultimate purpose, namely a rejection of the elements being derided, a revolutionary desire for their overthrow. I differ from Bakhtin not in his perception that the sacred is made earthy but in his interpretation of the impulse animating the carnival. He assumes that if the celebrants had their way they would abolish the imposed strictures – that their intent is essentially anarchic – but the reverse is true. The medieval carnival, as its name indicated, marked a farewell to the eating of meat and hence was, in a very real sense, a confirmation of the approaching period of Lent, an endorsement of the requirement to abstain from eating flesh. Without acceptance of the restrictions due to follow, there would be nothing to celebrate and hence no reason for the carnival. The joy and laughter in the festivity marked a temporary discarding of sobriety, with a full intention on the part of the celebrants to fulfil the precepts of Lent when it came due. Even those medieval revelries that were not technically carnivals – such as the Feast of Fools and the Boy Bishop celebration – were not only tolerated by the church but had the clerics themselves participating enthusiastically.

There were of course objections by some ecclesiastics aimed at supposed excesses, but no serious action was taken by the church to ban the festivities. A letter from the Faculty of Theology in Paris in 1445, although in the form of a complaint, confirms the degree of clerical participation: 'Priests and clerks may be seen wearing masks and monstrous visages at the hours of office. They dance in the choir dressed as women, panders or minstrels … and rouse the laughter of their fellows and the bystanders in infamous performances, with indecent gestures and verses scurrilous and unchaste.'[45] Parodying, even of the most sensitive of religious beliefs, was, we should recall, endemic in the Middle Ages even among leading members of the church. The so-called Wandering Scholars or Goliardic poets – among whom was numbered the famed theologian Peter Abelard – composed light-hearted variations on well-known hymns, songs in praise of love and wine, in which, as in the *Carmina Burana*, the classical goddess of love often replaces the Virgin Mary:

Quidquid Venus imperat labor est suavis,
Quae nunquam in cordibus habitat ignavis.[46]

Like most humour, then, these activities were intended not to annihilate authority but to provide a temporary respite from discipline before resubmission to the framework of religious obedience; and, in the sexual aspects of the carnival, they represented a celebration of the physical before returning to the church's endorsement of the spiritual and its encouragement of the celibate.

Political cartoons can indeed be vicious (the vicious ones usually inducing sardonic mockery rather than laughter); but the amusing ones are generally milder. By means of caricature, by enlarging a facial feature or placing the politician in a discomfiting situation, the dignitary is momentarily reduced from the pomposity of office to a more human level.

Clowns traditionally sport bright red noses and particoloured clothes to contrast them from the first moment with any concept of man as a sober, dignified individual, but the laughter they evoke is mainly from children, no doubt because the gap is indicated in so obvious and simplistic a manner. Yet clowning can function at a more sophisticated level. The outstanding silent comic of our era was Chaplin. The laughter evoked by famous scenes in his movies has been attributed by a leading caricaturist, Al Capp, to 'man's delight in man's inhumanity to man', that being, he claims, the source of all humour. We experience, he argues, a sense of cruel superiority in recognizing that, while the Chaplin character is starving, we shall be returning home to a full meal.[47] That thesis, as I suggested earlier, I find both distasteful and invalid, since one major aspect of Chaplin's technique is to arouse a deep sense of sympathy from the viewer, not sadistic pleasure.

The humour lies elsewhere, a primary source being traceable to his appearance, to the outfit he chose at the beginning of his career and that remained associated with him. Attention has usually been drawn by theorists to the 'incongruity' of his large shoes or, as one critic put it, to his reliance upon 'absurd, ill-fitting clothes, a flat-footed shuffling walk'.[48] His choice of apparel should be seen, however, as far more astute, instantaneously creating, in a manner very different from that of the usual clown, an awareness of the gap between pretension and reality which lies at the core of humour. For where the tramp or hobo of that time normally wore the ragged clothes of a labourer (as do his fellow-tramps in these movies), Chaplin's costume was that of the wealthy businessman – bowler hat, black jacket, waistcoat, striped trousers, bow tie, even a carnation in the buttonhole and a cane to twirl – but with the clothes dusty and worn, as befits his penniless status. Merely to glance at him, therefore, was to perceive the vulnerability of mortal achievement, the discrepancy between the ideal of wealthy comfort and the reality of the human condition. Moreover, the contrast was even more subtle, and here lay his genius. For deprived of the material means for a life of leisurely sophistication and exquisite manners, the tramp that Chaplin created acts at all times with the delicacy, sympathy and refinement of the gentleman at his best. Characteristic was the polite raising of his hat to any lady he meets, or in apology to anyone over whom he trips. We are confronted therefore at every moment with the contrast between the gracious living to which humankind aspires and the limitations imposed by its material needs.

In a famous scene in *The Goldrush*, he and his companion (a boor with whom he is contrasted), sheltering in a hut in a howling blizzard far from civilization, become so desperate for food that they boil and eat one of his leather boots. In itself, the situation is closer to tragedy, especially as the film was based upon the gruesome Donner incident of the 1840s when a group of waggoners travelling west met their deaths in the harsh winter storms.[49] The humour arises neither from the setting nor from the recourse to a boot, but from the manner in which the boot is eaten, Chaplin treating it throughout as if he were participating in a formal dinner at a ducal palace. With the air of a gourmet, having confirmed that the boot is boiled just to taste, he carefully wipes a plate to ensure that it is spotless, places the boot upon it and proceeds with the full ceremony of sharpening the knife and 'carving' the boot as if it were a Christmas turkey. From his own portion he delicately removes the shoelace, twirling it upon his fork with the expertise of a diner handling spaghetti; and, swallowing it decorously, he dabs his mouth in a manner reminiscent of Chaucer's Prioress who 'leet no morsel from hir lippes falle, / Ne wette hir fingres in hir sauce depe'. Each of these movements sequentially renews and revitalizes our perception of the disparity between the exquisite table manners designed to elevate man above the animalistic and the sordid pangs of hunger shared with the beast of the field. Jonathan Miller has argued, in a manner close to the Incongruity theory, that humour arises when we experience 'alternative situations', scenes different from the norm, and he suggests that in this instance we laugh because a boot is normally regarded as inedible.[50] Would the scene have evoked laughter – since a boot is normally on a foot – if Chaplin had offered an alternative situation by balancing the boot on his head? The effect of the scene as he presented it is surely more subtle.

One of the most delightful moments in the film occurs when Chaplin, waltzing with a lady, senses that his trousers are beginning to slip down. Surreptitiously hoisting them with the head of his cane, he manoeuvres his way to a side-table, and seizing a rope he sees lying there, ties it around his waist with obvious pride in his resourcefulness and dexterity – only to discover a moment later that the other end is tied to the collar of a large dog hidden beneath the table. One need not elaborate on the sudden fall from grace, his satisfaction at his resourcefulness collapsing as the dog, in hot pursuit of a passing cat, drags him ignominiously along the floor before the astonished eyes of the lady he was trying to impress. While we laugh at Chaplin, we are really laughing at ourselves, as he makes us aware of the human propensity for pride or self-congratulation that turns out, only too often, to be unwarranted.

An area that has proved particularly puzzling to analysts is the meaningless joke or 'shaggy dog' story, which evokes laughter despite its pointlessness, one popular instance being: 'How does an elephant get into a Volkswagen?', the answer being: '*Very* carefully!' By now, the analysis will be obvious enough to the reader, but we should recall how previous critics, including the most famous of them, resort to such concepts as Incongruity, Relief or Expenditure of Compressed Energy. There is, in fact, a subtle variation here on the pattern we have outlined. For the butt of the humour in this instance is not another individual whose pomposity or self-assurance has been exposed but our own previous self, who a moment before had dutifully expected an answer conforming to the rules of logic but was precipitated into a play-world where logic ceases to command. There is no humiliation, but there is a rueful recognition that we have been tricked because of our confident reliance on logic. Those responding to shaggy-dog tales with annoyance are usually objecting, whether consciously or not, to having had their dignity impugned.

And now to the theatre, which takes us closer to the literary theme. Northrop Frye suggested long ago that stage comedy rests on the archetypal pattern of seasonal change, its primitive motivation being a farewell to the hardships of winter and the hopes for a coming period of fertility and growth in the spring. Young lovers, blocked by some elderly person representing hoary winter, must overcome such opposition to achieve the marriage they desire, the play usually ending with a celebration of wedlock and, by association, of fertility.[51] All this is true in identifying the plot outline, but, important as his comment may be, it does not in itself explain the source of the humour. One could conceive of a play fulfilling all those require-ments that would be far from comic, such as *Romeo and Juliet* with the parents bitterly opposed to the marriage but eventually becoming reconciled on Juliet's awaking from her supposed death. It would be a play containing the lovers' overcoming of hoary opposition and concluding with fertility, but would in itself be devoid of humour.

The essence of stage comedy lies not in the archetypal or struc-tural pattern but in the way the representative of hoary winter is overcome – the outwitting of an *overconfident* parent, guardian or elderly husband convinced that they hold the reins of power through possession of dowry or legal right, or by securing the young lady behind a locked door. It is the puncturing of their self-assurance by means of a clever trick that causes us to laugh. Machiavelli's *La Mandragola* (with indebtedness to Plautine comedy but itself setting off a long series of imitations in the West, including the libretti of Donizetti's *Don Pasquale*, Rossini's *Barber of Seville* and a host of plays) provides us with an elderly husband closely guarding the attractive young wife from whom he is anxious to obtain an heir. An ardent lover, eager to win the young lady's favours, has the good fortune to possess a resourceful friend who persuades the husband, Nicea, to purchase from him a potion guaranteed to produce the son he longs for, but with one serious drawback – that the first person to sleep with the wife after she has drunk the potion will die. The friend assures Nicea that there is a young man newly come to town whom no one will miss, and the play ends with a vision of the husband ushering the young man into the bed of the wife he has so carefully guarded, where the lovers can now arrange their future assignations. The object of humour is the *senex*, convinced that he is in full control but beautifully outflanked by the lively intelligence of the young.

Important as that theme of deflating overconfident opposition may be, in stage comedy it is by no means focused exclusively upon a dislikeable character, the fault sometimes occurring no less amusingly in an attractive hero or heroine. The young king in *Love's Labour's Lost*, swearing together with his friends to abstain for a full three years from all love affairs in order that they may devote themselves to scholarly pursuits, offers the perfect instance of the lofty ideal of celibate study undercut by the earthy, natural impulses they had disregarded. At the arrival of a beautiful princess and her ladies-in-waiting whose visit had been forgotten in the midst of their determination to concentrate on their learning, we are presented with the delightful picture of young men desperately trying to conceal from their male friends the sonnets they have secretly inscribed to their new-found lady loves in defiance of their vows. The comedy of *Much Ado about Nothing* depends upon this same pattern of excessive self-assurance needing to be exposed. While Beatrice and Benedick are supremely confident that they are not in love and boast that they never will be, those about them perceive what they are incapable of acknowledging, their suppressed attraction to each other, the audience waiting expectantly for their fall. Benedick, told teasingly that even the savage bull comes in time to bear the yoke, dismisses the possibility with scorn:

> *Benedick*: The savage bull may; but if ever the sensible Benedick bear it, pluck off the bull's horns and set them in my forehead, and let me be vilely painted, and in such great letters as they write 'Here is good horse to hire,' let them signify under my sign 'Here you may see Benedick the married man.'

Beatrice, denominating Benedick as the most unlikely candidate of all, rejects with equal certitude her uncle's hope that she will one day marry:

> *Beatrice*: Not till God make men of some other metal than earth. Would it not grieve a woman to be overmaster'd with a piece of valiant dust? to make an account of her life to a clod of wayward marl? No, uncle, I'll none (2:1:62f.).

We delight, therefore, in watching them tricked by their friends into acknowledging the submerged affections, the natural impulses they had been too opinionated to recognize. And the figure of the clown in that play evokes laughter on the same principle, Dogberry being in no doubt that he is both an ideal officer of the law and a person of superior intelligence, yet revealing at every word the hollowness of that belief:

Dogberry: I am a wise fellow; and which is more, an officer; and which is more, a householder; and which is more, as pretty a piece of flesh as any is in Messina, and one that knows the law, go to! and a rich fellow enough, go to! and a fellow that hath had losses; and one that hath two gowns and everything handsome about him. Bring him away. O that I had been writ down an ass!

The bathetic drop can be effected from the side, as when Jack, in *The Importance of Being Earnest*, thrusts into the hands of Miss Prism the handbag in which he was found as a baby. Everything at that moment – his origins, his right to marry Gwendolen, his social standing – hinges upon the ex-governess's reply as she examines it closely:

> *Miss Prism*: The bag is undoubtedly mine. I am delighted to have it so unexpectedly returned to me. It has been a great inconvenience being without it all these years.[52]

Abruptly we descend from concerns with aristocratic lineage and the merging of noble families to the trivial and the mundane. Indeed, no clearer instance of such puncturing of pretentiousness could be offered than the suggestion provided by Stephen Potter in his theory of 'one-upmanship', a theory that greatly amused Britain in the 1950s, his advice on how to avoid being humiliated by the expert. If at a social gathering one member is holding forth dogmatically on a subject of which the rest, including oneself, are entirely ignorant, warning, for example, of the dangerous emergence of left-wing activists in Tanganyika, Potter recommends that the listener quietly interpolate: 'Yes, but not in the south!' – a remark requiring no expertise yet guaranteed to halt the speaker in his tracks and risibly undermine the confidence of his discourse.[53]

These instances do indeed contain elements that analysts of humour have pointed to – incongruity, relief that it is not we who have erred, a sense of superiority towards the victim – but as so many critics have noted, there are too many exceptions to those definitions for the theories to be valid as defining the cause of humour, negated as they are by instances that meet the criteria but are in no sense comic. The definition adopted here as a basis for examining literary humour, whether applied to situations, to verbal puns or to stage comedy, does seem to function effectively, namely, a sudden delight in perceiving the vulnerability either of individual pretension or of authoritative principles that society attempts to impose.

There are two final points of considerable importance for a study of literary humour. The first concerns the popular term 'comic relief' applied to humorous or entertaining insertions in serious works, the belief that, in tragedy or other genres, intervals of relaxation are required for the purpose of refreshment. While there is some truth in the theory, namely the need to relieve sustained tensions, one must not ignore the ever-present danger that such insertions are liable to break continuity, creating a jocular mood that can inhibit effective re-imposition of the grimmer theme. Sir Philip Sidney, writing before the appearance of Shakespeare's plays, roundly attacked those contemporaries who, 'mingling kings and clowns, not because the matter so carrieth it … thrust in the clown by head and shoulders to play a part in majestical matters with neither decency nor discretion'.[54] In fact, such interpolations, when inserted with discretion, preserve the major mood subliminally, by means of thematic association – a principle specifically articulated by Shakespeare. Annoyed by William Kempe's unscheduled clowning at a vital moment in a performance (an act that lost Kempe his place in the company), he delivered through Hamlet the solemn warning to the players:

> And let those that play your clowns speak no more than is set down for them. For there be of them that will themselves laugh, to set on some quantity of barren spectators to laugh too, though in the mean time some necessary question of the play be then to be considered. That's villainous and shows a most pitiful ambition in the fool that uses it.

That warning was intended not only to ensure that the actors adhere strictly to the script but also, and perhaps primarily, to instruct audiences to be on their guard, to realize that, embedded within a seemingly light-hearted comic scene, there would be 'some necessary question of the play' then to be considered whose omission or disregard could damage the carefully planned structure of the drama. Within the same play he offered a striking example. The gravedigger scene is truly comic as, to the audience's delight, an uneducated plebeian repeatedly outwits an intellectually sophisticated aristocrat:[55]

> *Ham.* Whose grave's this, sirrah?
> *Clown.* Mine, sir.
> *Ham.* I think it be thine indeed, for thou liest in't.
> *Clown.* You lie out on't, sir, and therefore 'tis not yours.
> For my part, I do not lie in't, yet it is mine.
> *Ham.* Thou dost lie in't, to be in't and say it is thine. 'Tis for
> the dead, not for the quick; therefore thou liest.
> *Clown.* 'Tis a quick lie, sir; 'twill away again from me to you.
> *Ham.* What man dost thou dig it for?
> *Clown.* For no man, sir.
> *Ham.* What woman then?
> *Clown.* For none neither.
> *Ham.* Who is to be buried in't?
> *Clown.* One that was a woman, sir; but, rest her soul, she's dead.

For all the humour, the audience is aware throughout that the grave is Ophelia's, so that there exists a tragic throb beneath the light banter. Moreover, the scene's integral relationship to the main theme is amply evidenced in the discussion between the two gravediggers prior to Hamlet's entry, a discussion which, droll as the pseudo-legal jargon may be, focuses on the central problem of the play, the problem that is driving Hamlet to near-madness, the conflict between his longing to end his life with a bare bodkin in the admired tradition of the Stoic and his fear of the eternal damnation prescribed by the church for committing suicide when of sound mind.[56]

> *Clown.* Is she to be buried in Christian burial when she wilfully
> seeks her own salvation?
> *Other.* I tell thee she is; therefore make her grave straight. The
> crowner hath sate on her, and finds it Christian burial.
> *Clown.* How can that be, unless she drown'd herself in her own
> defence?
> *Other.* Why, 'tis found so.
> *Clown.* It must be *se offendendo*; it cannot be else. For here lies
> the point: if I drown myself wittingly, it argues an act; and an act
> hath three branches – it is to act, to do, and to perform; *argal*, she
> drown'd herself wittingly.

Other. Nay, but hear you, Goodman Delver!
Clown. Give me leave. Here lies the water; good. Here stands the man; good. If the man go to this water and drown himself, it is, will he nill he, he goes – mark you that. But if the water come to him and drown him, he drowns not himself. *Argal*, he that is not guilty of his own death shortens not his own life.

One purpose of this present study in its specific concern with literature will be to watch, in the event of such comic insertions, the skill with which writers prevent such scenes from damaging the work's overall seriousness and ways in which the interpolation can, despite the seeming contradiction, contribute significantly to the graver effect of the main theme.

The second point concerns the changing cultural settings and their effect upon the humour of the time. Dr Johnson remarked that 'Men have been wise in many different modes, but they have always laughed in the same way.' The basic elements that produce laughter are indeed universal, but there is an important reservation to be made. Johnson himself possessed a ready sense of humour, Boswell recalling many evenings of merriment in which 'I never knew a man laugh more heartily', and quoting a comment by a friend that the lexicographer laughed 'like a rhinoceros'.[57] Yet if laughter is universal, Johnson's statement is to some extent belied by his own disgust at the puns that had delighted Shakespeare's audiences. The pattern of humour may, as he argued, remain the same, but the setting of the time can affect the response. Emotions or ideals may function so strongly in certain eras as to overcome the tendency to laugh. We are no longer amused at the pretensions of the mentally disturbed, racist humour is taboo and feminism has, happily, ruled out those myriad jokes at women's supposed incompetence or frivolity. There exists a striking instance of such contemporary imposition, the well-known advice of Lord Chesterfield to his son and, even more so, its remarkable conclusion: 'Having mentioned laughing, I must particularly warn you against it … I am neither of a melancholy, nor a cynical disposition; and am as willing, and as apt, to be pleased as anybody; but I am sure that, since I have had the full use of my reason, nobody has ever heard me laugh.'[58] The ideal of rational restraint that dominated the early eighteenth century prompted him to suppress his natural response.

Even the mode of presenting humour may change radically from generation to generation. The nineteenth-century cartoons in *Punch* often leave us wondering how they could have amused the reader of that time. Especially alienating are the cumbersome captions which for modern readers negate the immediacy of response so essential for wit and humour. The joke may still be valid, but the elephantine explanations smother the effect. One cartoon displayed a stout matron seated on a bench beside her charming daughter and addressing a young man seated opposite, below which appeared the following caption:

PUTTING THE OTHER FOOT IN IT
Mother: 'Ethel is the very image of what I was at her age.'
He: 'Really! I shouldn't have thought it possible!'
Mother (coldly): 'May I ask why?'
He (seeing his error, and striving to rectify it): 'Oh – er – I was forgetting what *a long time ago* that must have been!'

The reader of *Punch* in that generation seems to have needed more guidance in the form of explanatory headings and inserted parentheses than does his modern counterpart.

I have cited these instances of altered assumptions because such discrepancies are likely to prove of considerable value to the historian.[59] Once one perceives how central to humour is the process of deflating pretensions or elevated ideals, analysis of the jokes, quips, wit or comedy prevalent in each generation can offer substantial insights into the nature of the contemporary philosophical, moral or sociological values being targeted. Even from a negative fact, such as Dr Johnson's dislike of puns, we may deduce much concerning the concepts of his time. The purpose of this present study will thus be threefold: a) to test out the thesis by examining in chronological sequence how humour functions in leading works in the literature of England; b) to investigate the interaction between humour and the cultural configuration of the time; and c) where comic insertions appear in serious works, to perceive the means devised by the author to prevent them from damaging the main theme. The works to be discussed have been selected on the basis of two criteria – as being characteristic of the comic mode of each era and as offering insights into the contemporary concepts or social imperatives that were being lampooned.

CHAPTER TWO

LATE MEDIEVAL

a) *The Second Shepherds' Play*

Within the solemn series of plays enacting in sequence the main events recorded in the Bible – the 'mystery cycles'[60] performed on Corpus Christi Day, first within the cathedral and later in waggons circling the town – there is a rare instance of comedy. The original *Shepherds' Play* in the Towneley cycle had been, as in the other cycles, a solemn dramatization of the account in the Gospels, where some simple shepherds guarding their flocks are visited by an angel informing them of the birth due to occur in Bethlehem, after which they set out, arriving in time to witness the Nativity. In the Towneley version performed in the city of Wakefield from the mid-fourteenth century onward, the *Second Shepherds' Play* has, added to its opening, the lively tale of Mak the thief. Having stolen a lamb while the shepherds were asleep, he carries it to his hut where, with his wife's assistance, he dresses it in swaddling clothes and places it in a cradle to deceive the pursuers. The highlight of the play occurs when, on the arrival of the suspicious shepherds, Mak's wife disingenuously swears the oath:

> I pray to God so mild,
> If ere I you beguiled,
> That I should eat this child
> That lies in this cradle.[61]

The trick works splendidly, and the disgruntled shepherds leave the hut empty-handed. But, recalling that they have omitted to leave a gift for the newborn, they return to the hut where one shepherd, attempting to kiss the infant, suddenly cries:

> What the devil is this? He has a long snout! ...
> Will you see how they swaddle
> His four feet in the middle.
> Saw I never in a cradle
> A horned lad ere now.

All is revealed. The play concludes with Mak promising never to trick them again, the shepherds toss him in a blanket to teach him a lesson, and we are returned to the scriptural setting with the shepherds again lying down to sleep, soon to be awakened by the angel's *Gloria in Excelsis* and the continuation of the Gospel story.

The humour conforms closely to the pattern outlined in the introductory chapter. The shepherds, aware in the opening scene that Mak has '... an ill nose / For stealing of sheep', are confident they can protect their charges, warning each other on his approach to be on their guard – 'If Mak come on the scene, look well to your things' – so that they are, in that respect, much like the *senex* sure that he can guard his wife from intruders. But Mak and his wife ingeniously outwit them, and we laugh approvingly at their success. Then the roles are reversed as Mak and his wife become the over-confident guardians, bragging that they can fool their pursuers – 'I have escaped scot-free a far fiercer fray' – and they are caught out in their turn.

Yet if the nature of the humour is clear, an intriguing question arises, namely how this comedy came to be grafted so effectively on to a devout mystery cycle without impairing the reverential aura and without arousing the ire of the church under whose auspices the play was being performed. The chance discovery in the nineteenth century of an ancient ballad, *Archie Armstrang's Oath*, that told essentially the same story as the Mak playlet led at first to the assumption by scholars that the ballad was an offshoot of this drama, a popular variation of its theme; but that view was soon disproved, for the ballad was seen to be the more complete version of the story and hence the original.[62] As its title indicated, the main point lay in the oath which is, in the ballad, triumphantly implemented when, having successfully deceived the shepherds, the thief and his wife do indeed eat the 'baby' as promised. In the playlet, however, the oath, once pronounced, is entirely forgotten, the ruse is discovered, and Mak mildly punished, since a thief could not be permitted to triumph in a dramatic cycle dedicated to moral teachings. It is clear, therefore, that the Wakefield Master saw a wonderful opportunity for inserting the comic theme of the *Archie Armstrang* ballad into the margin of the mystery cycle, attaching it to the existent shepherd playlet and thereby finding a home for his own comic genius in an age when no other theatrical stage was available.

But there is a problem even more challenging than the possible clash between a comic insertion and the solemnity of the setting; for, as has long been realized, the story itself was intimately connected to the sacred scene that followed, the allusions and reverberations being too marked to be overlooked by the Wakefield Master nor missed by contemporary audiences – namely, the parallel between the placing of Mak's lamb in the cradle and the 'Lamb of God' due to be placed reverentially within the crib, in a Nativity scene that was not only adjacent but marked the climax of the shepherd play itself. Was the Mak episode, then, as some have argued, a parody of one of the most central and most sacred scenes of the cycle and hence a disfig- urement, a detraction from the impressiveness of the *praesepe* scene? A. P. Rossiter claimed that in the medieval consciousness there existed 'two contradictory schemes of values, two diverse spirits, one standing for reverence, nobility, pathos, and sympathy; the other for mockery, blasphemy, baseness, and meanness of spirit'.[63] In the tradition of pre-Christian fertility rites which had employed forms of mirth or mockery, such comedy inserted within solemn settings constituted, he argued, a compulsive ritual defamation of elements held sacred by contemporary society. If so, we are faced with the problem whether comedy can indeed avoid damaging the elevated ideal of its setting.

The answer lies, I would suggest, in the chronology of the presen- tation; for the events of the Mak episode are carefully located in the pre-Christian world, before the granting of the shepherds' vision and the inauguration of the faith. Anything boorish, crude or comic, therefore, so far from damaging the sanctity of the Nativity scene that followed, enhanced it by contrast, depicting the harsh world of suffering, thieving and trickery before the shepherds become spiritually elevated, elected to serve as inspired messengers of the new religion with its promise of peace, love and joy upon earth. The Wakefield Master was thus free to depict the shepherds' lives

in that earlier section both with realism and with humour, not only
unhampered by the religious setting but as a means of augmenting
by dissimilitude the solemnity of the Nativity itself.

The playlet opens (as had the earlier Shepherd Plays) with
complaints at the bitterness of the weather, but here they move to
more light-hearted, amusing complaints directed at the problems
of matrimony – the hen-pecking to which these males claim they
are subjected (one can visualize the catcalls from the women in the
audience and the answering hoots from the men):

> We poor wedded men suffer much woe;
> We have sorrow ever again, it falls often so;
> Old Capel, our hen, both to and fro
> She cackles;
> But begin she to croak
> To prod or to poke,
> For our cock it is no joke
> For he is in shackles.
> These men that are wed have not their own will ...

And there follows a warning to young bachelors to ponder well
before falling into the trap:

> But young men a-wooing, on God be your thought,
> Be well warned of wedding, and think ere you're taught,
> 'Had I known' is a thing too lately you're taught;
> Much bitter mourning has wedding home brought:

There are also genuine complaints of the difficulties of their lives,
and the oppression they suffer from their haughty masters:

> We are so lamed,
> Overtaxed and maimed,
> And cruelly tamed,
> By our gentlemen foe ...

The placing of those speeches early in the play thus evokes thoughts
of the change due to occur as a result of the Nativity, the promise that
the poor will inherit the earth instead of being hopelessly crushed by
their woes, and that goodwill will prevail among all humankind, not

least within the marital fold. Then follows the comedy of Mak's ruse, his promise of reform once the trick is discovered, and the resumption of the Gospel story. However long it may be till the era of goodwill arrives, the play offers a foretaste of such joy when, at its conclusion, the shepherds humbly offer their simple gifts, glory in their newly acquired faith, and depart as its new emissaries:

> [*The Third Shepherd kneels.*]
> Hail, darling dear, full of godhead.
> I pray thee be near when that I have need!
> Hail, sweet is thy cheer! My heart would bleed
> To see thee sit here in so poor a stead,
> With no pennies.
> Hail, hold forth thy hand small;
> I bring thee but a ball:
> Have thou and play withall ...

So far, therefore, from this play in any way offending against the sanctity of the cycle or functioning as a parody of the scene that was to follow, the comic insertion highlights the disparity between the mundane realities of human existence in a world devoid of faith and the new configuration to be introduced by the Nativity, whose arrival transforms the somewhat clownish shepherds into pious believers:

> *First Shepherd*:   What grace we have found.
> *Second Shepherd*:   Come, now we are unbound.
> *Third Shepherd*:   Let's make a glad sound
> And sing it not soft
> [*The Shepherds leave singing.*]

This entertaining playlet thus employs a principle paralleling in some ways that of the Lenten carnival. That carnival, too, preceded the holy period; it marked a farewell to the secular world before the celebrants entered willingly upon the period of religious penitence and piety. So *The Second Shepherds' Play* by the Wakefield Master, earthy and humorous as it is, should be seen neither as a disparagement of, nor as a detraction from the gravity of the mystery play onto which it was engrafted. By its chronological placing before the Birth, in a world of penury and mutual mistrust, medieval audiences could enjoy to the full the lively comedy of the Mak scenes, with their outwitting of the shepherds and the subsequent exposure of an overconfident Mak, and then move from that mundane setting into the solemnity of the Nativity itself, not only without a sense of incongruity but with a deepened consciousness of the contrasts between the pre-Christian and post-Christian eras.

b) Chaucer, *The Canterbury Tales*

The relating of bawdy jokes or pornographic stories is, as was suggested above, an earthy repudiation of the refined respectability that society attempts to impose. *The Miller's Tale* and *The Reeve's Tale* rejoice in bawdry, being uninhibited accounts of sexual misdemeanours, of young men climbing in and out of women's beds with or without the latter's knowledge. And the humour of those tales follows the established pattern in two respects. First, there is the entertaining rivalry between the two narrators in which a contemptuous Miller, snubbing the Reeve's profession, has his own profession mocked in its turn by the Reeve – an instance of the biter bit. As the Reeve reminds us at the conclusion of his tale (and one notes the emphasis on the Miller's arrogance before the fall):

> Thus is the proude miller wel y-bete …,
> Lo, swich it is a miller to be fals!
> And therfore this proverbe is seyd ful sooth,
> 'Him thar nat wene wel that yvel dooth;
> A gylour* shal him-self bigyled be.'   *trickster

Secondly, the tales themselves conform to the pattern of humour. *The Miller's Tale* features the traditional *senex*, the elderly husband keeping his young, attractive wife under lock and key:

> Jalous he was, and heeld her narwe in cage,
> For she was wylde and yong and he was old,
> And demed hymself been lik a cokewold (3224–6).

Present too is the eager young lover devising a trick to obtain access to her. By convincing the husband that a Noah-type flood is due and persuading him to sleep in the attic in a bathtub that would keep him afloat in the event of a deluge, the assistant is left free to cavort with the wife below. In *The Reeve's Tale* there is a similar process of

outwitting the overconfident, in this instance a boastful miller who
cheats others while assuming that he himself can never be cheated.

> He was a market-beter* atte fulle.   *braggart
> Ther dorste no wight hand upon him legge,
> That he ne swoor he sholde anon abegge.
> A theef he was for sothe of corn and mele,
> And that a sly, and usaunt for to stele.

He too is outmanoeuvred by the younger generation, the tale
concluding with the lesson that the miller:

> hath y-lost the grinding of the whete,
> And payed for the soper every-deel
> Of Aleyn and of Iohn, that bette him weel.
> His wyf is swyved, and his doghter als ...[64]

There is, however, a problem concerning the setting. Where Mak's
escapade had been only a minor prank justified by its chronological
placing before the advent of Christianity, here some of the bawdiest
passages in literature are embedded in the account of a sacred
pilgrimage that Chaucer himself treats with respect, 'the hooly
blisful martir for to seke.' Both *The Miller's Tale* and *The Reeve's
Tale* delight in the youngsters' success in 'swyving' other men's wives,
the narrators employing neither euphemism nor decorous allusion:

> And up the wyndowe dide he hastily,
> And out his ers he putteth pryvely
> Over the buttok, to the haunche-bon;
> And therwith spak this clerk, this Absolon,
> 'Spek, swete bryd, I noot nat where thou art.'
> This Nicholas anon leet fle a fart ... (3802–7).

The Reeve's Tale was, of course, based upon a French *fabliau*, a genre
known for its prurience; and some of the other tales may have drawn
upon such sources. The *fabliaux*, however, like *The Decameron* with
its similar share of bawdry, were secular works, while these lusty tales
constituted a patent contradiction to the religious setting.[65] What steps
did Chaucer take to ensure that such comic elements should not, in the
final analysis, negate the seriousness of the pilgrimage itself?

That problem was responsible for a profound split in the critical interpretation of the *Tales*, a split that occurred some decades ago and that has persisted to our own time.[66] It had long been assumed that Chaucer, sympathetic to those characters rebelling against the asceticism advocated by the church, was reflecting the liberal attitudes beginning to emerge in the early Renaissance. There were obvious instances supportive of that view. The monk, casually dismissing the discipline of his order as 'nat worth an oystre' and enjoying to the full the pleasures of hunting (strictly forbidden by Canon Law), wins the unequivocal approval of the narrator:

> And I seyde his opinion was good.
> What sholde he studie, and make hymselven wood*,   *crazy
> Upon a book in cloystre alwey to poure,
> Or swynken with his handes, and laboure,
> As Austyn* bit? How shal the world be served?   *St Augustine
> Lat Austyn have his swynk to him reserved! (Gen. Prol. 183–8).

after which the text describes, as if in continued endorsement, the fur-lining of the monk's sleeve and the love-knot with which the hood was fastened, items so inappropriate to one in holy orders.

Some years ago D. W. Robertson Jr caused a considerable fluttering in the critical dovecotes when he rejected this approach, challenging the general assumption that the *Tales* reflected a tension between the church's advocacy of religious asceticism and the growing desire in the early Renaissance to celebrate worldly pleasure. That, he claimed, was a modern misreading of the work. Chaucer, he insisted, was essentially medieval in outlook, committed to the church's condemnation of self-indulgence and sexual laxity. *The Canterbury Tales*, including the passages of licentious humour, was, he claimed, ultimately a solemn, religious and morally didactic work.[67] Drawing upon the art of the period for evidence to counter the normal reading of those scenes, he argued that the entire work was a moral treatise whose culminating message was to be found in the Parson's sermon denouncing the unseemly behaviour and the scatological stories so inappropriate to a pilgrimage. In brief, the idea of *The Canterbury Tales* as a vivacious and often humorous work with sly digs at the foibles of humankind is replaced by an interpretation of it as a solemnly didactic poem.

What had begun as a fluttering in the critical dovecotes became in time a critical battle, with Chaucerians drawn up into opposed camps, those who continued to see the comic or lewd elements in the *Tales* as indicating the author's sympathy with rebellion against ecclesiastical authority and the pro-Robertsonians insisting on the overarching religious didacticism of the work. Most controversies of this type eventually work themselves out, since a close reading of the text usually provides sufficient evidence to settle the argument. But there was a dialectical cul-de-sac here that prevented any clear solution, for Robertson employed a claim that, although not conclusive, could not be controverted. Wherever evidence could be adduced to counter his view, as in the narrator's approval of the monk's behaviour, Robertson could respond that it was an example of irony, intended to imply the opposite. Since both sides acknowledged that Chaucer did employ irony, the controversy has remained unsolved, as a recent article confirms.[68] Where, moreover, is the humour in these *fabliaux*-type scenes if we are to take them seriously as moral condemnations?

We need, I believe, to apply to *The Canterbury Tales* a principle introduced during the past few decades with the advent of narratology and its awareness of the complexity of the fictional process. Where previously it had seemed sufficient to recognize the existence of a narrator, either a fictitious participant or, as in Fielding's novels, an author who interrupts the story at intervals to speak directly to the reader, such assumptions have come to be seen as simplistic. There exists, in addition to the acknowledged narrator, an implied author whom the reader senses as existing behind that figure, even when that implied author appears to be identical with the narrator. Similarly, in addition to the person actually reading the text, there exists an implied reader, as illustrated in Seymour Chatman's useful diagram of those multiple configurations:[69]

Real →	Implied →	(Narrator) →	(Narratee) →	Implied →	Real
author	author			reader	reader

Although the crux of the problem we are confronting appears to lie in Chaucer's so-called 'irony' – whether Chaucer is serious in his expression of sympathy with the monk's self-indulgence or whether, as Robertson maintained, 'tongue-in-cheek' he means the reader to condemn the monk – there exists a further possibility that goes beyond that duality and can explain what constitutes the main source of the humour.

There are in *The Canterbury Tales* three Chaucers of whom the sensitive reader is made aware. There is the fictional character, who joins the pilgrims on their journey to the sacred shrine and acts as the narrator, carefully describing his companions and recording their stories, often with a degree of naiveté. Then there is the implied narrator, a shadowy figure behind that personage, whom we shall examine in a moment. And finally the actual Chaucer of flesh and blood, the diplomat, courtier and poet whose religious or non-religious views we would love to know. Of the gap between the pilgrim narrator and the implied narrator we become acutely conscious in one of the most charmingly droll moments, when the pilgrim-Chaucer, called upon to offer his own entertaining story, proves so boringly inept that the Host interrupts him, berating him for his incompetence:

'By God,' quod he, 'for pleynly, at a word,
Thy drasty rymyng is nat worth a toord;
Thou doost nought elles but despendest tyme.
Sire, at o word, thou shalt no lenger ryme.
Lat see wher thou kanst tellen aught in geeste,
Or telle in prose somwhat at the leeste
In which ther be som murthe or som doctryne.'

The hapless pilgrim-Chaucer is thus compelled to discontinue his tale, substituting for it a prose passage that is scarcely less tedious. For the reader the humour lies, of course, in our recognition that the poetically incompetent pilgrim-Chaucer is, supposedly, the same gifted Chaucer who composed the *Tales*. If our awareness of the distinction between the Chaucers is often subliminal, it emerges incontrovertibly at that point. As in a 'shaggy-dog' tale, the humour is created by the sudden reversal of our expectation, our assumption that his story will be the most entertaining of all and the bathetic surprise reminding us that a fictional narrator should not be confused with an author.

That aspect needs to be extended, applied as a principle functioning throughout the work, not least in those passages that have aroused such controversy. The brilliance of the *Tales* lies in Chaucer's deliberate blurring of the distinction between the different Chaucers, his technique not of 'irony', nor of 'tongue-in-cheek' statements – which imply a commitment to one side or the other – but in his maintaining a poker-faced refusal to be committed. A major delight in reading his work arises from the teasing impossibility of determining with any certainty whether the remark about the monk cited above expresses the view of Chaucer the pilgrim narrator, of Chaucer the implied narrator, or of Chaucer the author. To attempt to pin his remarks down as emanating from only one is, I believe, a misreading of the text.

This enchanting ambiguity is significantly enhanced by the pattern of the work he adopted, a series of stories presented in turn and related in their own voice by individual pilgrims, so that Chaucer is, as it were, absolved of any identification with their views, indecent or irreligious as those views may be. As the narrator blithely informs us:

> But first I pray yow, of your curteisye,
> That ye narette it nat my vileinye,
> Thogh that I pleynly speke in this matere,
> To telle yow hir wordes and hir chere;
> Ne thogh I speke hir wordes properly.
> For this ye knowen al-so wel as I,
> Who-so shal telle a tale after a man,
> He moot reherce, as ny as ever he can,
> Everich a word, if it be in his charge,
> Al speke he never so rudeliche and large;

He does not mention, however, that, were he so inclined, he could have omitted the licentious tales. He does therefore bear some degree of responsibility for their narration and, most obviously, is himself relishing the amusement they offer. When he does step in as narrator, and either approves or disapproves of the storytellers' comments and beliefs, there is indeed an appearance of authorial commitment, but we are left incapable of knowing to which of the Chaucers, if any, we are to attribute the comment. If humour relies on the undermining of pretension or confidence, here it is the reader whose confidence is found to be misplaced – we laugh at ourselves for being caught out by Chaucer's elusiveness, his refusal to commit himself to any stance.

Let us view more closely an instance of this process at work, the

Wife of Bath's wonderfully entertaining speech in favour of remarriage, of earthy sexual satisfaction, and of feminine dominance
within the marital fold. In a study of Chaucer's humour, Helen
Corsa argued strangely that the comedy in this prologue derives from
'... tensions and conflicts kept in balance, the comedy of the warring
self whose very life depends upon the continual battle'[70] – although
why inner tensions and conflicts should in themselves be comic is
left unexplained, especially as such inner warfare would seem more
relevant to tragedy. If, however, we examine closely the arguments
the wife offers for challenging established authority, her questioning
of the church's insistence on chastity, the reasons for our siding with
her become clear.

For the challenge arises not merely from the pitting of her lusty
love of life, her unabashed carnality, and her frank demand for
marital dominance against ecclesiastical dictates but, more significantly, from the fact that she undercuts the church's rulings by
quoting evidence from the sacred texts themselves, the humour
relying once again on the exposure of fallacies or contradictions
in magisterial commands. Whatever theological arguments might
be adduced to the contrary (critics frequently insist that her quotations are 'garbled' or based on misunderstandings), there did exist,
as she saw sufficiently clearly, a sharp discrepancy between the
explicit command in Genesis to be fruitful and multiply and the
church's advocacy of celibacy. She notes rightly that nowhere was
the commandment in Genesis abrogated in the New Testament, nor
was celibacy explicitly enjoined there:

> 'Men may devyne and glosen, up and doun.
> But wel I woot, expres, withoute lye,
> God bad us for to wexe and multiplye;
> That gentil text kan I wel understonde ...
> Whan saugh ye ever, in any maner age,
> That hye god defended* mariage   *forbade
> By expres word? I pray you, telleth me;
> Or wher comanded he virginitee?'

Paul had merely offered a personal recommendation: 'I say therefore
to the unmarried and widows, It is good for them if they abide even
as I' (1 Cor. 7.8), but it was not a command. With regard to a widow's
remarriage, her barbs are directed at the Gospels themselves, as she

asks why Jesus, in rebuking the Samaritan woman, objected to the legality of the fifth husband (Jn 4.17–18) without specifying at what number a widow's remarriages cease to be legal:

> But me was toold, certeyn, nat longe agoon is,
> That sith that Crist ne wente nevere but onis
> To weddyng in the Cane of Galilee,
> That by the same ensample taughte he me
> That I ne sholde wedded be but ones.
> Herkne eek, lo, which a sharp word for the nones,
> Besyde a welle Jhesus, God and man,
> Spak in repreeve of the Samaritan:
> 'Thou hast yhad fyve housbondes,' quod he,
> 'And that ilke man that now hath thee,
> Is noght thyn housbond;' thus seyde he certeyn.
> What that he mente therby, I kan nat seyn;
> But that I axe, why that the fifthe man
> Was noon housbonde to the Samaritan?
> How manye mighte she have in mariage?
> Yet herde I nevere tellen in myn age
> Upon this nombre diffinicioun; (lines 9–26).

Her perception of flaws or discrepancies within ecclesiastical rulings is especially effective as the authority targeted is identified with a high level of spirituality, while the criticism emanates from a person rooted in the carnal and the mundane.[71]

The tantalizing inability of the reader to determine which Chaucer is speaking is intensified in the Wife of Bath's prologue by the realization that in real life she would have lacked the learning to quote chapter and verse for her astute arguments. Common people at that time, unable to read Latin, obtained their knowledge of the Scriptures only at second or third hand, from sermons, pictures and stained-glass windows.[72] How far this ignorance of the text held true we may learn from an incident recorded by Sir Thomas More, not, as here, of a plebeian but of a gentlewoman whose only source is that she 'heard say':

> Ye be wiser, I wote well, than the gentlewoman was, which in talking once with my father, when she harde saye that our Lady was a Jew, first could not believe it, but saide, what ye mock I wis,

> I pray you tel trouth. And when it was so fully affermed that she
> at last bileued it quod she, so help me God and Halidom I shall
> love her the worse while I live.[73]

So in this instance, one notes the careful insertions into the Wife
of Bath's speech of such phrases as, 'But me was toold, certeyn',
or 'What that he mente therby, I kan nat seyn', to preserve the
impression that we are listening to a simple, unlearned woman. But
their insertion reminds us of the misty figure behind her, adducing
arguments that she would be unlikely to formulate so effectively. We
are aware above all that the technique adopted allows Chaucer, as
it were, to hide behind her skirts, avoiding any commitment to her
claims and leaving us unsure which Chaucer is hiding there, a sympa-
thizer with her views or a dissenter.

My emphasis has been, in these two last instances, on ways in
which authors, refraining from any ultimate damage to the objects of
their humour, carefully preserved the sanctity of the Nativity and the
solemnity of the journey to a holy shrine. Such emphasis may seem
superfluous; but the normal view does not conform to that approach.
In a study of comedy in the light of postmodernist theory, Kirby
Olson, for example, states, as if the definition were incontrovertible,
that comedy is iconoclastic.[74] Comedy does certainly transgress
accepted norms and challenge assumptions, but unlike the fiercest
form of satire – the kind that Juvenal described as arising from his
fury at vice and stupidity, evoking not laughter but scorn – true
laughter is pleasurable. It subjects its target to humour but usually
without damaging it permanently, just as slapstick only proves
effective where there is no real fear of injury or death. The advantage
of animated cartoons is that, in the skirmishes between Tom the cat
and Jerry the mouse, the cat can be flattened beneath a steamroller
because we know it will bounce back a moment later. Humour in all
its forms may temporarily deflate, but in almost all instances avoids
any final disqualification. Hence my objection to the widely held view
represented by the article from the *Britannica* cited earler, which sees
malice as the basis of all laughter, or the view generally accepted in
postmodernism that it is basically iconoclastic.

So here in the Wife of Bath's prologue, because of that 'ventrilo-
quist' technique whereby the implied author, while seeming to
identify with her views, warily dissociates himself from them, her

argument emerges as finally less damaging than it appears. Although her reasoning has much to support it and we are amused at the contradictions that Chaucer points to in the scriptures themselves, the fact that the claims are made to emanate from an untutored layperson apologizing for her limited knowledge means that we do not take her too seriously. Moreover, she is never irreverent towards Christianity. She grants that virginity is indeed a 'greet perfeccioun' for those who choose to take the veil, unsuited though it may be for her. And she is, after all, participating at that moment in a pilgrimage to a holy Christian shrine. Her purpose in that journey may in part have been to indulge her love of 'wandrynge by the weye', sharing in the impulse slily hinted at in the opening lines of the poem – that it is only in the springtime, when the weather is fine, when the wind is blowing sweetly, the flowers blooming, and the birds beginning to sing, that 'Thanne longen folk to goon on pilgrimages.' Yet Chaucer's own sense of the validity of the pilgrimage is confirmed by the presence there of the nobler characters: the knight who has hastened from the battlefield to be cleansed of his sins; the clerk whose speech was ever 'sownynge in moral virtu'; the honest ploughman; and his brother the ideal parson.[75] From within the wife's own speech there emerges a clear respect for her faith and an attempt to justify, as still falling within its precepts, her indulgence in what she sees as the legitimate, God-implanted pleasures of the body. And when characters such as the Miller indulge in indecent comedy, Chaucer the narrator solemnly reminds us, as he had earlier, that he is merely repeating the words of the participants:

Blameth nat me if that ye chese amis.
The Miller is a cherl, ye knowe wel this;
So was the Reve, and othere many mo,
And harlotrye they tolden bothe two.
Avyseth yow and putte me out of blame;

Such ambivalent apology provides a perfect example of the technique employed. Whether it expresses Chaucer's real view, an attempt to dissociate himself from indecencies included solely as moral warnings, or whether he wishes us to read it as an amusing ploy – since we know he himself penned the lines attributed to the Miller and the Reeve – is left amusingly undetermined.

c) Medwall, *Fulgens and Lucrece*

After the lengthy ban on secular drama during the Middle Ages, with only the morality, miracle and mystery plays permitted on the stage, a change finally occurred. Henry Medwall's *Fulgens and Lucrece*, composed about 1497, the first secular English comedy, is interesting in many ways. It helped introduce into England the continental genre of the interlude – a term either meaning 'play between' participants or, as some philologists maintain, an 'entertainment between' the courses of a banquet. Originating in the cultivated courts of fifteenth-century Italy, one such debate is vividly recorded in Castiglione's *The Courtier*, where the presiding duchess, assigning forfeits to anyone failing to participate, called in turn upon members of the court to deliver a speech, often impromptu, on some arguable theme, such as the supposed advantage of painting over poetry, the qualities requisite for the ideal courtier or the nature of love, the speaker being judged by the company on the degree of erudition, persuasiveness or wit distinguishing the speech. In England, that continental custom was initiated in the country house of John Morton, a distinguished person due to become both Archbishop of Canterbury and Lord Chancellor, in whose home Thomas More served as a page, learning the principles of courtly behaviour. Medwall, a chaplain in the household, took the interlude an important step further than the continental variety by presenting the debate in dramatic form, his play probably being performed during the Christmas season at a banquet honouring foreign ambassadors.

The theme of the debate was Noble Lineage versus Intrinsic Worth, posing the question whether aristocratic descent was preferable to personal ability. As those capitalized terms indicate, Medwall could, in the tradition of the morality plays, have presented the dispute in terms of personifications, but he decided instead to translate it into a more human, social setting, with two characters embodying those different attributes; and he added a further spice of interest to the debate by depicting them as rival suitors between whom the lady must choose. The play, set in Rome, recounts how Lucrece, the daughter of Fulgens, is courted by two suitors – Cornelius, a wealthy, pleasure-loving nobleman able to offer her a life of ease and comfort, and Gaius, a studious young man of humble birth. Gaius, claiming that a suitor should be judged by his own qualities, not by his ancestors, offers her, in place of the luxuries promised by his rival, a life of moderate means but of greater usefulness and personal gratification. Lucrece, of course, finally chooses him. And my reader by this time is probably wondering what all this has to do with comedy.

The answer lies in a second innovation in the play, the introduction into the interlude of a subplot, an entertaining knock-about farce. Two additional characters, named throughout only as *A* and *B*, provide that sub-theme. In all probability servants in the household, they reveal a jocular familiarity with the diners, teasing them for the meat and drink they have enjoyed at their host's expense:

> *A*: Ah! for God's will,
> What mean ye, sirs, to stand so still?
> Have not ye eaten and your fill,
> And paid nothing therefore?[76]

Is the audience, they ask, waiting for some entertainment, the appearance of a 'pretty damsel / For to dance and spring'? In fact, they announce, there is indeed entertainment on the way, but in the form of a play, and they function henceforth as a sort of chorus, commenting on the action as the play proceeds as well as participating in it.

The subplot is of especial interest. *A* and *B*, on meeting Lucrece's pert servant, Joan, find her vastly attractive, immediately becoming rivals for her hand. She, however, saucily demands that her suitors first prove their worth, that they undergo a series of trials to determine their suitability. Neither, she insists,

> ... shall be assured of me
> Till I may first hear and see
> What ye both can do:
> And he that can do most mastery,
> Be it in cookery or in pastry,
> In feats of war or deeds of chivalry,
> With him will I go.

The text itself describes the trials only briefly, but in staged form they no doubt provided some amusing slapstick as the two servants attempt to demonstrate their merits. First they are to compete in singing, during which contest they accuse each other of false notes and disharmony; then comes a bout of wrestling; and finally, after they are required to don some pseudo-armour, they are to engage in a test of jousting. Since neither possesses a horse, their joust is to consist of attempting to jab each other in the rear, at the conclusion of which skirmish *A* ruefully complains that he has

> ... a great gash here behind,
> Out of the which there cometh such a wind
> That if ye hold a candle thereto,
> It will blow it out, that will it do.

Throughout the trials, each of course claims superiority over his rival, asserting his own suitability for the role of Joan's husband, their confidence being rudely shattered in due course when the time comes for Joan to decide between her suitors. Anxiously they await her judgement, but each receives for his pains only a clout on the head, as the wench laughingly informs them that she had long been engaged to another. As so often, the boastfulness of each in claiming her love – 'There is no man hence to Calais, / Whosoever be the other, / That can himself better apply / To please a woman better than I' – is punctured by the trick she plays on them.

The subplot is a patent parody of the main debate, the noble ideal animating Lucrece's testing of her suitors being relegated here to the ludicrous and earthy. Parody, however, carries with it the problem we have already found in the previous instances, especially when, as in this play, the lampooning is so carefully intertwined with the mainplot; for Joan's choice is not presented as a separate dramatic unit but is closely integrated with Lucrece's when *A* undertakes to become servant to Cornelius and *B* to Gaius, acting as advisers to their two masters, and carrying messages back and forth between them and Lucrece. Moreover, the two servants add significantly to our knowledge by providing information concerning the suitors, *B*, for example, describing Cornelius' spendthrift qualities which, while they mark for the audience a grave disqualification for Lucrece's hand, *B* sees as a potential source of future tips for himself:

> There is now late unto him fall
> So great goods by inheritance,
> That he wot never what to do withal,

But lasheth it forth daily, askance.
That he had no daily remembrance
Of time to come, nor maketh no store.

Such intertwining once again involved the danger that the seriousness
of the main plot would be undermined by the flippancy of the
sub-theme; and we need to enquire – for the last time in this present
study – how that problem was overcome.

Medwall here introduces a technique different from that operating
in the previous works examined, and destined to dominate English
comedy for many centuries. The partition he erects to protect the
moral message is a social barrier, assigning the parodic humour to
the lower class, to plebeian characters who, it is implied, are not to
be taken seriously. Segregating the comedy to that area insulates the
main plot from the danger of infringement. *A*, for example, after
expressing his astonishment that the wealthy aristocrat is about to
be rejected, readily admits that, as a commoner, his view carries
little weight, explaining: 'For I am neither of virtue excellent / Nor
yet of gentle blood.' We can therefore laugh freely at the mundane
frolicking of the servants without such laughter impinging upon the
nobler topic. In brief, where the shepherd play had protected the
sanctity of the cycle by providing a chronological separation and
Chaucer by blurring the distinctions between the real and implied
narrators, the new technique employed a separation of class to
preserve the gravity of the main plot.

That tradition was to endure in the theatre for many centuries (it
had existed on the Roman stage where in Plautine and Terentian
comedy it was usual for the slaves to be the focus of the humour),
but now its importation became permanent. George Puttenham
declared in 1589 that comedy is never to be aimed at the upper
classes, 'never medling with any Princes matters nor such high
personages, but commonly of marchants, souldiers, artificers, good
honest housholders, and also of unthrifty youthes, yong damsels,
old nurses, bawds, brokers, ruffians and parasites'.[77] Shakespeare,
with his usual flouting of established rules, does not always conform.
The comedy both of *Love's Labour's Lost* and of *Much Ado about
Nothing* focused upon members of the upper class, although one
should note that in neither instance is there a serious mainplot that
could be affected, the problem of Hero in *Much Ado* having only a
tangential connection with that of Beatrice and Benedick. However,

the pattern did hold true in general even in Shakespeare's plays. The actual clowns – Bottom, Dogberry, Gobbo and Touchstone – are obviously plebeian, often ridiculed for their ignorance. Even when Robert Armin replaced William Kempe as the jester in Shakespeare's company, introducing a more refined and intelligent wit into the part, his roles remained lower class, Feste unashamedly holding out his hand for a gratuity from Viola and accepting tips from both the Duke and Sir Toby. And comic figures of gentlemanly origin, such as Sir John Falstaff or Sir Toby Belch, forfeited their aristocratic ranking by being associated with their tavern companions in drunkenness and penury.

In later generations, the tradition continued, with the cheeky servant Tom in Steele's *The Conscious Lovers* sharply distinguished from the high-mindedness of the main characters; and there were, to follow, the illiterate, hoax-loving Tony Lumpkin of *She Stoops to Conquer* and, despite the socialist principles of its Fabian playwright, the cockney dustman, Doolittle, in Shaw's *Pygmalion*.[78] So here, both *A* and *B* are presented as illiterate servants, mangling their messages verbally, either by unintentionally transforming them into indecencies or, in a foretaste of Dogberry, misaligning the words, in both instances reinforcing the audience's awareness of their lowly status:

> *A*: Fair mistress liketh it you to know
> That my master commends me to you?
> *Lucrece*: Commendeth you to me?
> *A*: Nay, commendeth you to him.
> *Lucrece*: Well amended, by Saint Sim.
> *A*: Commendeth he to you, I would say,
> Or else you to he, now choose ye may
> Whether liketh you better ...

Lucrece smiles condescendingly at their ignorance, especially when, on her asking *A* for his name, he scratches his head, admitting that he has forgotten and promising to ask one of the company to remind him so that he can inform her later.

A further comic aspect is provided by them. In a manner remarkably early in theatrical history, they break through two conventions of dramatic presentation. Repeatedly they cross the imaginary line separating the stage from audience – a device which the modern theatre has attempted to reintroduce after centuries of formal division. As noted above, *A* speaks directly to the audience when teasing them for having indulged themselves in food and drink at their host's expense. That in itself could have meant that they were to act as a sort of chorus, as intermediaries commenting on the action. But a few moments later they disrupt theatrical convention by participating in the action, moving in and out of the inner play itself. At the beginning, on announcing that a play is to be performed, *A*, with a foretaste of what is to come, asks *B* whether he is one of the players. *B* denies it, but then decides to traverse the invisible dramatic wall in order to offer some urgent advice to Cornelius – an idea that horrifies his companion:

A: Peace, let be!
By God, thou wilt destroy all the play.

For the moment *B* is restrained but in the next scene neither can resist the impulse, and they both enter the inner play, continuing to move in and out, sometimes chatting to the audience chorically and at other times participating in the action. When *B* knocks at the hall door, *A* blithely asks a member of the audience to open it for him. Whenever an actor crosses this invisible barrier, here or in later drama, either suddenly appearing from among the audience or calling directly to the audience from the stage, there is inevitably a ripple of laughter, for that process constitutes the bathos central to humour. The lofty assumption of theatrical pretence so essential to dramatic illusionism – imagining that the actors are in Rome, in a setting distant in time or place – is amusingly breached by a sudden reminder of actuality, the audience's and the actors' physical presence in the same hall.

Their ambiguous status as being both participants in the play and commentators on the action probably arose from the convivial atmosphere of a theatrical presentation in a house where both actors and audience knew each other well and could at times dispense with the formal division into stage and audience. We know, for example, that the youthful Thomas More would '… suddenly sometimes step in among the players, and never studying for the matter, make a part of his own there presently among them, which made the lookers-on more sport than all the players beside'.[79] And there are clearly moments here when a comment ostensibly aimed at a character was also slily aimed at the audience, as when *B* scoffs at Cornelius' sartorial extravagance, the fashion of the day worn, we may assume, by several members of the audience:

> *B*: … none of them passeth the mid thigh,
> And yet he putteth in a gown commonly
> How many broad yards, as ye guess?
> *A*: Marry, two or three.
> *B*: Nay, seven and no less …
> They have wings behind ready to fly,
> And a sleeve that would cover all the body;
> Then forty pleats, as I think in my mind,
> They have before, and as many behind …
> A gentleman shall not wear it a day
> But every man will himself array
> Of the same fashion even by and by
> On the morrow after.

The play is divided in two parts or acts in order to allow the audience to continue with the main course – 'We may not with our long play / Let them from their dinner all day' – and the second half contains the serious presentations of their right to Lucrece's hand by Cornelius and Gaius, the arguments supporting their rival claims. At the conclusion, as the two men leave the stage and Lucrece declares her decision in favour of the humbler but more worthy Gaius, *A* and *B* express their disapproval of her choice, presenting the plebeian view. Turning to the audience, they ask bluntly whether Lucrece's preference for virtue over wealth accords with the way of the world. Are such lofty ideals valid in reality?

> *B*: By my faith, she said, I tell thee true,
> That she would needs have him for his virtue,
> And for none other thing.
> *A*: Virtue, what the devil is that?
> An I can tell, I shrew my cat,
> To mine understanding.
> *B*: By my faith, no more can I
> But this she said here openly,
> All these folk can tell. [*To the audience.*]
> *A*: How say ye, good women, is it your guise
> To choose all your husbands that wise?

Virtue may be preferred in philosophical debates but, in the real world, money is not to be ignored in marital choice. As comic servants, they thus align themselves with the mundane, being intrinsically divorced from the nobility of the main plot.

The play, the servants now declare, is ended. But, as they remark in conclusion, their play had involved two distinct purposes. The main aim may have been to teach a solemn moral lesson, but it was

> also for to do withal
> This company some mirth.

And that aspect they amply supplied.

CHAPTER THREE

THE RENAISSANCE

a) Shakespeare, *A Midsummer Night's Dream*

The scenes of Bottom and his crew – among the most amusing scenes in Shakespearean drama – provide valuable evidence of the ways in which comedy responds to cultural change and, in a reverse process, how a study of the comic technique prevalent in a specific generation can reveal aspects of the altered configuration of the time.

In its basic form, the comedy conforms perfectly to pattern. Bottom, by his unwarranted pride in his histrionic powers, his conviction that he can play any dramatic role with consummate success, from the piping voice of the heroine to the roaring of the lion, is seen to suffer from a pomposity fully meriting the fall to which his behaviour is leading, his transformation into the ass that he really is:

Bottom: What is Pyramus? A lover, or a tyrant?
Quince: A lover, that kills himself most gallant for love.
Bottom: That will ask some tears in the true performing of it. If I do it, let the audience look to their eyes; I will move storms; I will condole in some measure ... An I may hide my face, let me play Thisby too. I'll speak in a monstrous little voice: 'Thisne, Thisne!' ... Yet my chief humour is for a tyrant. I could play Ercles rarely, or a part to tear a cat in, to make all split ... Let me play the lion too. I will roar that I will do any man's heart good to hear me; I will roar that I will make the Duke say 'Let him roar again, let him roar again.'

Not only does he boast of his histrionic powers but assumes he should really be the producer, repeatedly interrupting Quince with his supposedly sage advice. Similarly, he imagines he possesses a sophisticated vocabulary while repeatedly misusing words, at one point urging his companions to rehearse 'most obscenely and courageously'.

There exists, however, a more profound purpose in these entertaining scenes, of which there are two aspects. On the one hand, obviously enough, they constitute Shakespeare's insertion into the text of a form of advertisement, exhorting the audience to scorn the performances of amateurs and to attend only those offered by such professional companies as Shakespeare's own. Today, with the many excellent amateur companies operating in Britain and the United States, such advice would be invidious – for if the professionals cannot outshine the offerings of the amateurs, they deserve to fall by the wayside. But at the time of the play's original performance, the idea of professional acting companies was new. The interludes in the country-homes of the wealthy such as *Fulgens and Lucrece*, usually performed by household servants, were now filtering out into the public arena, those amateurs with some degree of acting ability finding more remunerative spheres for their talents. They began performing, somewhat crudely, on village greens, as may be seen in Brueghel's depiction of such a peasant performance in his *Kermesse* of 1562. The emergence of professional acting companies at the time this play was written and the innovative move by James Burbage in constructing in 1578 the first building in England specifically designed for theatrical performances meant that the public needed to be enlightened on the difference between the unsophisticated renderings by 'mechanicals' and the high standards now being set by the professionals.

Yet that contrast between professionals and amateurs involved considerably more than acting ability. It involved a revaluation of the theatrical principles that had prevailed from the time when stage performances were revived in the medieval period, a factor central to the evocation of laughter in these Bottom scenes. The medieval stage had provided a form of drama elevated above the real world. In the morality plays, such as *Everyman*, personifications named Envy or Good Deeds lifted the audience out of tactile reality into an abstraction where, however realistically portrayed, the characters were not individuals but concepts, distillations of human behaviour – an outgrowth from the *Psychomachia* in which the various impulses of the soul, both good and evil, were seen as fighting for precedence. In the mystery cycles, there existed a similar removal from actuality, the divorce from the real world deriving from the sanctity of the scriptural scenes. Touches of realism would be introduced to intensify the horror of nails being driven into the body of Jesus, but the scenes themselves represented events of far profounder significance to the viewers than anything occurring in their own lives. They watched with awe scenes of divine significance.

An aspect that has been too often overlooked is that, in the drama previous to the Elizabethan, the mystery cycles and morality plays still being performed in Shakespeare's day, validity belonged not to the audience but to the events represented on the stage. Attention was riveted there upon the eternal verities that the audience was being privileged to witness in re-enactment, with the audiences themselves envisaged as mere mortals passing through a shadowy corridor before the Day of Judgement. In brief, the drama was at that time more real than the transitory affairs of town or village. Actors, we know, were hesitant to play the part of Jesus or Mary for fear of the sacrilege involved in a mortal personating the divine, so that at times, as in the Shepherd Play from Rouen, while other roles were performed by actors, the Virgin Mary would be represented by a constructed image. So real were those scenes believed to be that Gerhoh of Reichesberg solemnly warned anyone playing Herod or Antichrist to beware, for in taunting or scorning Jesus he would himself be guilty of the evils he was portraying.[80] Ultimate authenticity was thus located on the stage. There was no need to convince the viewers that the Nativity or Crucifixion scene they were watching had actually occurred.

As the stage became secularized towards the end of the sixteenth century, at the time when Shakespeare joined the Lord Chamberlain's Men, there occurred a major change. The performances were no longer of eternal truths but of acknowledged fictions, whether the account of two gentlemen of Verona or the dramatist's inventive reworking of a historical event, with the right to reinterpret the material freely. For the Elizabethan audience, ultimate validity had been transferred from the stage to themselves; authenticity was now located among the rowdy participants who had paid their pennies and were waiting to be entertained. Henceforth, it was the responsibility of actors and dramatists to strive to convince, to transport the audience into the fictional world and to make them believe, while watching the play, that they were in Athens or Venice, witnessing events occurring there.

In a remarkable passage, one catches Shakespeare at the moment when he confronts the new problem, disturbed at the enormous difficulty of presenting persuasively, within the confines of the small Globe playhouse or 'wooden O', a battle between two armies involving hundreds of participants, a battle that had occurred many years before and had taken place far away, across the Channel. Accordingly, he inserts into *Henry V* a prologue in which the Chorus presents a plea to the audience to suspend their incredulity and to assist the players by employing their imaginative faculties:

> But pardon, gentles all,
> The flat unraised spirits that hath dar'd
> On this unworthy scaffold to bring forth
> So great an object. Can this cockpit hold
> The vasty fields of France? Or may we cram
> Within this wooden O the very casques
> That did affright the air at Agincourt?
> O, pardon! since a crooked figure may
> Attest in little place a million;
> And let us, ciphers to this great accompt,
> On your imaginary forces work.
> Suppose within the girdle of these walls
> Are now confin'd two mighty monarchies,
> Whose high upreared and abutting fronts
> The perilous narrow ocean parts asunder.

Later in Shakespeare's career, in his maturer phase, he will have solved the problem, moving with ease in *Antony and Cleopatra* back and forth from Rome to Egypt, from Egypt to Rome without the need for choric explanations; but we see him here anxiously confronting the difficulty at the moment of the stage's transition from the old system to the new. Even the above plea is more subtle than might appear. For a dramatist to ask the audience to employ its imagination is a little like a waiter in a restaurant presenting a customer with the ingredients of the meal and leaving him to do the cooking. It is the task not of the audience but of the dramatist to create the imagined effect; and in the above passage may be perceived the method Shakespeare will adopt – the use of vivid images and powerful language to produce that magical transposition, as when, at the words 'Suppose within the girdle of these walls …', the previously prosaic text suddenly soars into the vision of two mighty monarchies parting the ocean asunder, an image that in effect carries the audience across the seas.

All this may seem to have taken us away from a study of comic technique, but it is highly relevant; for the comedy of the Bottom scenes is, I would argue, intimately linked to that moment of theatrical transition. The target of the humour here is, indeed, the older dramatic mode or, to be more precise, those actors and producers who continued to cling to obsolete theatrical assumptions. Bottom still assumes, as had held true for the mystery cycles, the audience's unquestioning belief in the authenticity of whatever occurs on the stage, imagining that an audience will accept the veracity of the events depicted just as they had accepted the validity of the New Testament scenes. There the principle had indeed held true. When, in the Chester cycle, Jesus restores the ear of Malchus that Peter had just struck off with his sword, no attempt had been made to convince the audience. Relying on the account in Luke 22.51, the scene portrays the event with utter ingenuousness, before an audience already convinced of its truth. Malchus declares simply:

A! well is me, well is me!
My eare is healed, now I see,
So merciful a man as is he,
Knew I never non.

Bottom, unaware of the change, foolishly assumes that, in his play too, the ladies will believe as authentic anything enacted on the stage. They will be terrified by the entrance of a lion or by the presence of swords, and will naively imagine that Bottom really is Pyramus. He devises, therefore, a method not of creating credibility but of destroying it, directing the actor to assure the audience that, despite his attire, he is no lion:

Bottom: Nay, you must name his name, and half his face must be seen through the lion's neck; and he himself must speak through, saying thus, or to the same defect: 'Ladies,' or 'Fair ladies, I would wish you' or 'I would request you' or 'I would entreat you not to

fear, not to tremble. My life for yours! If you think I come hither
as a lion, it were pity of my life. No, I am no such thing; I am a
man as other men are.' And there, indeed, let him name his name,
and tell them plainly he is Snug the joiner.

As if that absurd suggestion were not enough, he plans to insert a
prologue with a message precisely the reverse of that provided by
Shakespeare's Chorus:

> *Bottom*: I have a device to make all well. Write me a prologue; and
> let the prologue seem to say we will do no harm with our swords,
> and that Pyramus is not kill'd indeed; and for the more better
> assurance, tell them that I Pyramus am not Pyramus but Bottom
> the weaver (3:1:20f.).

The humour lies, therefore, in the audience's perception of the gap
between Bottom's unshakeable conviction of his theatrical sophistication and, in fact, his total ignorance of the change in dramatic
presentation that had occurred in Shakespeare's day.

The same holds true for the mechanicals' attitude to stage settings.
The Elizabethan playhouse employed, of course, almost no stage props,
only moveable stools or thrones, the settings being created imaginatively by such seemingly casual remarks as Duncan's, 'This castle hath
a pleasant seat; the air / Nimbly and sweetly recommends itself / Unto
our gentle senses ...' Bottom and his crew, judging the audience to be
incapable of conceiving any object without visible assistance, adopt a
device borrowed from the morality plays as though its techniques were
applicable to the new secular drama. The purpose of those earlier plays
in transforming the virtues and vices into human-like characters was
to make abstract concepts more intelligible to the audience, to transfer
them from the intangible to the tangible, the concept of Envy being
more effectively conveyed by a character dressed in green and wearing
a sardonic smile. What those plays had inaugurated for abstract ideas,
the mechanicals misguidedly believe should be applied to concrete
items too. Hence their risible decision to personify or (employing the
medieval term) to 'signify' physical objects:

> *Quince*. Then there is another thing: we must have a wall in the
> great chamber; for Pyramus and Thisby, says the story, did talk
> through the chink of a wall.

Snout. You can never bring in a wall. What say you, Bottom?
Bottom. Some man or other must present Wall; and let him have
some plaster, or some loam, or some rough-cast about him, to
signify wall; and let him hold his fingers thus, and through that
cranny shall Pyramus and Thisby whisper.

On that principle, the moon too could only be conceived by the
audience if an actor appeared holding a lantern and the bush of
thorns traditionally associated with it. Dramatic illusion is deserted
in favour of an absurd literalism. By ridiculing the mechanicals'
amateurism, Shakespeare endows the members of his audience with
a sense of their own sophistication, a comforting feeling that they,
better informed, were immune to such errors. What should not,
however, be missed, is the ultimate purpose of the comedy here,
the presentation of a Bottom inordinately proud of his mistaken
notions. Its purpose was to ensure that, having been entertainingly
prompted to perceive the hollowness of Bottom's histrionic self-
esteem and the inappropriateness of his confident assumptions, the
audience should henceforth realign its allegiance, identifying with
the new principles of theatrical practice. This is, indeed, an instance
of humour permanently rejecting the object being targeted; but the
satisfaction in audience response rests in their recognition that the
new system is significantly superior to the old, that the mechanicals,
so proud of their acting ability, are in fact hopelessly out of date.

There was a further process of audience edification in these scenes. In
the performance of *Pyramus and Thisbe* before the Duke and his court,
Bottom's bombastic overacting not only parodied the style of Edward
Alleyn, the leading actor of Shakespeare's rival company (again hinting
to the audience that they would be wise to patronize only the Lord
Chamberlain's Men), but poked fun also at Marlowe's 'mighty line'. In
introducing *Tamburlaine* to the Elizabethan stage a few years before,
Marlowe had in the prologue claimed, with considerable justice, that he
would revitalize the stage, replacing the pedestrian verse of such plays
as *Gorboduc* with a new type of majestically resounding poetry:

From jigging veins of rhyming mother wits,
And such conceits as clownage keeps in pay,
We'll lead you to the stately tent of war,
Where you shall hear the Scythian Tamburlaine
Threatening the world with high astounding terms.

67

Those 'high astounding terms' had served well to introduce a greater range and power to the language of the theatre, as in Marlowe's:

> *Bajazeth*: Smother the earth with never-fading mists!
> And let her horses from their nostrils breathe
> Rebellious winds and dreadful thunder-claps!
> That in this terror Tamburlaine may live,
> And my pined soul, resolved in liquid air,
> May still excruciate his tormented thoughts! ...
> [*He brains himself against the cage. Re-enter Zabina.*]
> *Zabina*: What do mine eyes behold? my husband dead
> His skull all riven in twain his brains dashed out,-
> The brains of Bajazeth, my lord and sovereign:
> O Bajazeth, my husband and my lord!
> O Bajazeth! O Turk! O Emperor! (*Tamburlaine* Pt. I, 5:1)

That declamatory mode, having indeed revolutionized the stage, now needed to be modulated; hence the parody of it in Bottom's performance:

> *Pyramus*. O grim-look'd night! O night with hue so black!
> O night, which ever art when day is not!
> O night, O night, alack, alack, alack ...

Such parody opened the way for Shakespeare's more flexible verse-patterns. Furthermore, Bottom's frequent interruptions of the play with explanations to his audience in a manner destroying any last vestige of dramatic illusion, coupled with the courtiers' withering comments as the play is in process, ensured that Shakespeare had succeeded in educating his own Elizabethan audience. The authority of the theatrical principles that had governed the medieval stage are thus made to appear outmoded, together with the grandiloquent style of his immediate predecessor.

It is time to turn from the mechanicals to the larger theme of the play. R. W. Maslen recently described the main plot as 'no less unsettling than the tragic universe of *Romeo and Juliet*', claiming that Hippolyta is haunted by the cruel destruction of the Amazons and that Puck maliciously enjoys watching the male lovers' murderous quarrels.[81] Earlier, Bertrand Evans, in his study of Shakespeare's comedies at large, was puzzled by the introduction in this play of an outside force other than Fate. Oberon, he points out, initiates the use of the magical drops yet fails to control the results; and both he and his assistant Puck are unaware of the havoc caused to the mortals by Puck's error, discovering it only when they witness the quarrel between Demetrius and Hermia. That inability to control events also applies, Evans adds, to the main participants who are ignorant of what is happening, seemingly manipulated like puppets, those fortuitous elements detracting from the play's effectiveness.[82]

Is the play as dark and as haphazardly organized as those readings suggest, with chance ruling the events? Many critics have also been perturbed by the seeming jumble of diverse plots and subplots – the marriage of Theseus and Hippolyta, Egeus' threat to Hermia, the rehearsals of Bottom and his crew, the dispute between Oberon and Titania, and Puck's mistaken disposal of the drops. John Palmer has claimed accordingly that the play consists of a 'gossamer structure, an airy fabric' only held together by the presence of Bottom in the three separate localities of court, forest and fairyland.[83]

The play is in fact wonderfully integrated, once its underlying theme is perceived. As far as the principle of comedy is concerned, the highpoint of the play, the scene in which Titania, as she wakes from sleep, declares her tender love for the grotesque figure of Bottom the ass, might seem to support the theory of Incongruity. Nothing, indeed, could be more incongruous than a delicate fairy's infatuation with this embodiment of coarseness and stupidity. As Schopenhauer claimed, 'The cause of laughter in every case is simply the sudden perception of the incongruity between a concept and the real objects which have been thought through it in some relation, and laughter itself is just the expression of this incongruity.'[84] In Schopenhauer's terms, we bring to this scene our normal conception of love as a relationship between two essentially compatible persons, and are confronted instead with a glaring disparity. The incongruity in Titania's awakening is certainly there. However, to perceive that as the main source of the humour – as if it would arouse laughter were it presented in isolation – is to miss the subtlety of the scene, which in fact marks the culmination of a theme carefully developed through the play. What, then, holds these seemingly disparate scenes together?

The magical drops that Oberon employs could well be seen, as they have so often been seen by critics, as one of those fantasy elements for which, within the mythological tradition of Midsummer Night

when elves and fairies come out to play, no justification or explanation is required. We do not enquire, in the fairy tale of Cinderella,
why her carriage should turn into a pumpkin at midnight, nor, in
another tale, why a giant should suddenly be found inhabiting a
beanstalk that sprouted overnight. Those aspects are intrinsic to
the fantasy; they are 'given' elements that we must simply accept
if we wish to read on. The theme of the miraculous drops might
appear similarly fortuitous in this play – they produce a certain
effect upon those in whose eyes they are placed, and that is all. But
that assumption needs to be re-examined if we are to appreciate the
nature of the comedy.

In Shakespeare's early romance plays, the movement into the
magical forest or 'green world' is not a form of escapism, a flight
from the discomforts of the real world. It is far more subtle,
functioning as the equivalent of the psychiatrist's couch in our own
day, the forest serving as an instrument of healing, a world where,
relieved from the pressures of city life and the harsh demands of the
law, one can relax and dream out solutions to one's problems, and
then return to the real world having learnt some profound lesson.
Viewed in that light, the events that are to occur in the forest emerge
as a wonderful commentary on, or elaboration of, the initial scene
set within the city.

The rivalry between Demetrius and Lysander, two equally eligible
suitors for the hand of Hermia, with her father Egeus insisting that
she marry the former or submit to the punishment of death, represents the youngsters' need to overcome the 'hoary' winter that blocks
their path to fertility, and in that regard it conforms to the archetypal
theory of comedy as reflecting seasonal movement.[85] But there is
more to it than that, although before moving on to that major aspect
we should note the seemingly minor element of Theseus' offer of an
alternative to the death penalty – Hermia's permanent confinement
in a nunnery if she defies her father. Leo Salingar has dismissed the
alternative as an unnecessary addition, superfluous to the plot,[86] but
it provides two elements essential to comedy. Any serious possibility
of death would damage the light-heartedness, while the alternative
of permanent chastity provides that blocking of fecundity requisite
in comedy as the impediment the lovers must overcome. The final
scene of the play, in which Oberon blesses the newly married couples,
leaves no doubt of its concern with fertility:

So shall all the couples three
Ever true in loving be;
And the blots of Nature's hand
Shall not in their issue stand;
Never mole, hare-lip, nor scar,
Nor mark prodigious, such as are
Despised in nativity,
Shall upon their children be (5:1:409–16).

To return to the underlying theme of the play, tucked into the opening scene, as if it were merely an effort on Lysander's part to support his case, is an item of central importance. Urging his own claim, he points out that Demetrius had earlier aroused Helena's love, had pledged his troth to her, and had then cruelly deserted her in order to claim Hermia as his own:

Demetrius, I'll avouch it to his head,
Made love to Nedar's daughter, Helena,
And won her soul; and she, sweet lady, dotes,
Devoutly dotes, dotes in idolatry,
Upon this spotted and inconstant man (1:1:106–10).

It is a charge that Demetrius makes no attempt to refute and whose validity is at once confirmed by the Duke. Helena herself (with her irrepressible addiction to puns) describes the desertion more emotionally:

… the boy Love is perjur'd everywhere;
For ere Demetrius look'd on Hermia's eyne,
He hail'd down oaths that he was only mine;
And when this hail some heat from Hermia felt,
So he dissolv'd, and show'rs of oaths did melt.

The message of the play lies here – that the fickle transference of devotion from one person to another, with all the pain it causes to the victim, is deplorable, the lesson being conveyed in the play by means of a wonderfully symbolic device. For the magical drops reproduce in comically exaggerated form the fickleness of which Demetrius has been guilty. Just as he had woken one day with the haughty feeling that he preferred Hermia to Helena – 'off with the old love, and on with the new' – so the drops produce in absurdly hyperbolic form the same effect, making the victim fall in love with the first object viewed on waking, however unbefitting that object may be. Hence within the forest, Titania's infatuation with a grossly inappropriate ass functions as a *reductio ad absurdum* of that process, revealing in parodic form the dangers to which such irresponsibility may lead.[87] As the crude figure of Bottom, oblivious of his own change and desiring only a peck of hay, brays his jarringly discordant song, Titania, queen of the fairies, the epitome of delicacy and refinement, murmurs sleepily:

> What angel wakes me from my flow'ry bed? ...
> Mine ear is much enamoured of thy note;
> So is mine eye enthralled to thy shape;
> And thy fair virtue's force perforce doth move me,
> On the first view, to say, to swear, I love thee (3:1:130f.).

Shakespeare had in fact inserted earlier in the play a patent hint of the symbolic function of the magic drops. Included in Oberon's poetic description of their origin, of the flower from which the drops had been distilled, is the name by which the flower was commonly known. An arrow, missing its intended target, we learn, '... fell upon a little western flower, / Before milk-white, now purple with love's wound, / And maidens call it Love-in-idleness'. That name could have served as the title of the play. That the hint has so often been missed is evidenced by the omission of those lines in the otherwise impressive 1999 film version, presumably because the producer felt them to be irrelevant.[88] Such love-in-idleness, Shakespeare suggests, will, like the drops, '... make a man or woman madly dote / Upon the next live creature that it sees'. And it is, of course, Demetrius' arrogance that needs to be deflated, his unfeeling dismissal of his past love Helena with the words: 'Tempt not too much the hatred of my spirit / For I am sick when I do look on thee.'

Of the young men, the lesson of constancy in love ought to be directed solely at Demetrius. Lysander has committed no such fault, having proved faithful to his love; but he is subjected to the same experience as Demetrius, at least temporarily, in order to univer-salize the lesson, to remind us that we are all subject to the pull of disloyalty and must learn to resist it. Moreover, the misplacing of the drops by Puck when he confuses the two male lovers underscores the general lesson Shakespeare is conveying, creating a visible example of human instability. For the foursome that had first entered the forest – Helena pursuing Demetrius who is in pursuit of Hermia and Lysander – is now entertainingly reversed, with the paired Lysander and Demetrius now pursuing Helena, and Hermia left deserted in her turn. Gazing down at this visual representation of careless infidelity, Puck comments chorically: 'Lord, what fools these mortals be!'

At the close, the lesson has been learnt, the need for responsibility in love – the kind of mature responsibility exemplified at the opening by Theseus and Hippolyta who have buried their past enmity and determined to begin a new life in amity. And exemplified also by Oberon and Titania, who serve as reminders that the pull of inconstancy does not end with marriage; that within the marital fold the same kind of maturity as they eventually achieve is needed to preserve steadfastness in love. In the final scenes, as city and green world meet in the forest, Demetrius awakes from his dream, as from the psychiatrist's couch, not quite sure what he remembers of it but happily cured – no longer claiming the love of another in place of Helena. The journey into the green world has provided the remedy for what he now sees as his earlier 'sickness':

> ... my love to Hermia,
> Melted as the snow, seems to me now
> As the remembrance of an idle gaud
> Which in my childhood I did dote upon;
> And all the faith, the virtue of my heart,
> The object and the pleasure of mine eye,
> Is only Helena. To her, my lord,
> Was I betroth'd ere I saw Hermia.
> But, like a sickness, did I loathe this food;
> But, as in health, come to my natural taste,
> Now I do wish it, love it, long for it,
> And will for evermore be true to it (4:1:168–79).

So far from being a jumble of seemingly disconnected scenes, as has been argued, there is here a unifying theme indicating how comedy at its best either reflects or burlesques the prevalent concepts of the day. For in Shakespeare's day, constancy in love, especially within the marital fold, was something of an innovation. Nuptials in medieval times had been – certainly among the upper classes – a sober matter of joining estates. Andreas Capellanus' *The Art of Courtly Love*, the most reliable source book defining the basic concepts of the courtly love tradition in the late twelfth century, stated unequivocally that, since love was impossible within marriage, it should be sought outside it. Hence the love of Queen Guinevere and Sir Launcelot in legend, and Petrarch's adoration of the married Laura in fact. It was in the Elizabethan era, as Denis de Rougement has shown,[89] that there arose a new ideal of eternal fidelity, love consummated by and continued within marriage – an ideal immortalized in Shakespeare's *Romeo and Juliet*, as well as in his sonnet's claim that love is not love which alters when it alteration finds nor bends with the remover to remove, but is an ever-fixed mark that looks on tempests and is never shaken. To confirm that new view, he chose in this play, in the duke's over-ruling of Egeus's demands, to reject the old tradition of marriage imposed by paternal authority and to lampoon those who disregard the bonds of engagement and marriage.

That principle of eternal devotion in love may seem to be contradicted by the concluding scenes of the play, the performance of *Pyramus and Thisby*. As many have noted, the situation there is in its essential aspects identical with the ending of *Romeo and Juliet*, composed at approximately the same time as this play, the lovers' suicides when they each believe their beloved to be dead. The parody involved in that performance might seem to indicate Shakespeare's desertion of the ideal. But there is no contradiction, for the humour is directed here not at the ideal itself but at the gap between the nobility of the idea and the ineffectiveness of Bottom's performance:

> *Pyramus*: O wherefore, Nature, didst thou lions frame?
> Since lion vile hath here deflower'd my dear;
> Which is – no, no – which was the fairest dame
> That liv'd, that lov'd, that lik'd, that look'd with cheer.
> Come, tears, confound;
> Out, sword, and wound
> The pap of Pyramus;
> Ay, that left pap,
> Where heart doth hop. [*Stabs himself*]
> Thus die I, thus, thus, thus.
> Now am I dead,

Now am I fled;
My soul is in the sky.
Tongue, lose thy light;
Moon, take thy flight. [*Exit Moonshine*]
Now die, die, die, die, die. [*Dies*]

The ridicule is thus directed at Bottom's inability to rise to the demands of the revered theme, not at detracting from the validity of the theme itself.

We may summarize, therefore, that in *A Midsummer Night's Dream* the laughter evoked by the Bottom scenes arises from two sources: on the one hand, the deflating of his unwarranted conviction of his histrionic talent and, on the other, a parodying of the obsolete theatrical traditions to which he and his fellow mechanicals so confidently cling. In the main plot, we are entertained by the marvellously integrated structure of the play, in which the magic drops produce, in the scene of Titania enamoured of an ass, a vastly exaggerated and hence absurd reflection of Demetrius' arrogant inconstancy, while the overall pattern of the play burlesques the still-authoritative social principle of its time, the patriarchal imposition of marriage irrespective of the wishes of the proposed bride, a principle now to be replaced by the new ideal of true and lasting love, to be preserved with maturity within the marriage setting.

b) Falstaff

Falstaff represents a fascinating anomaly. Most comic figures who arouse a degree of empathy, encouraging us to laugh with them as well as at them, are, like Dogberry, Fielding's Partridge, or Tony Lumpkin, essentially harmless, good-natured and well-meaning individuals. Falstaff is the opposite – an unconscionable liar, a glutton, a thief, a drunkard, a brotheler and a parasite. He is, one might say, the Seven Deadly Sins rolled into one enormous ball, and yet the most loveable character in the Shakespeare canon. That paradox has been frequently noted, but it has never been satisfactorily explained. Maurice Morgann's eighteenth-century essay posed the question very effectively:

> We all like *Old Jack*; yet, by some strange perverse fate, we all abuse him, and deny him the possession of any one single good

or respectable quality. There is something extraordinary in this: It must be a strange art in *Shakespeare* which can draw our liking and good will towards so offensive an object. He has wit, it will be said; cheerfulness and humour of the most characteristic and captivating sort. And is this enough? Is the humour and gaiety of vice so very captivating? Is the wit characteristic of baseness and every ill quality capable of attaching the heart and winning the affections? Or does not the apparency of such humour, and the flashes of such wit, by more strongly disclosing the deformity of character, but the more effectually excite our hatred and contempt of the man? And yet this is not our *feeling* of Falstaff's character.[90]

Unfortunately, Morgann's attempt to explain the discrepancy (an attempt that occupies his entire essay) relies somewhat perversely upon the hypothesis that, despite his reputation for cowardice, Falstaff was in fact courageous in battle. The theory is not only difficult to accept but, even if proven true, would provide no answer to the problem, since that single virtue would not outweigh his multifarious vices and would certainly have no relation to his comic appeal.

J. Dover Wilson's famous study of Falstaff, although it did not deal directly with this question, provided an insight that can serve as a starting-point for our discussion. The figure of Falstaff, he maintained, would have been immediately identified by an Elizabethan audience with characters familiar to them from the morality plays, such personifications as Gluttony and Lechery. He noted particularly the close resemblance to one such character appearing in an interlude entitled *Youth*, composed about 1520, the figure of Riot who performs there many acts that foreshadow Falstaff's. He commits robbery on the highway, jests afterwards on the subject of hanging, and invites his friends to spend the stolen money at a tavern where, he promises, 'We will drink diuers wine' and 'Thou shalt haue a wench to kyss whansoeuer thou wilte'. Riot, moreover, parallels Falstaff's joviality, bouncing onto the stage at his first entry with the cry:

Huffa! huffa! who calleth after me?
I am Ryot full of jollity.
My heart is as light as the wind,
And all on riot is my mind,
Wheresoever I go.[91]

On that basis, Wilson argues that the parallel would have created an initial sympathy with Falstaff, and he proceeds to argue, like most other critics, that Prince Hal must, in the course of the play, choose between Riot, represented by Falstaff, and the exaggerated form of Chivalry embodied in Hotspur; that he must learn to achieve a mean between those two extremes, the noble path of honour and duty that Shakespeare will build upon in presenting him in the sequel, *Henry V*.

There is clearly much truth in Wilson's linking of Falstaff to the characters familiar to the audiences from the earlier morality plays, but there is a major factor that militates against the theory – the fact that Riot and his companions in the morality plays are at all times seen as reprobates, not as attractive or deserving of sympathy, since such sympathy would contradict the explicitly didactic intention of the plays. Wilson may quote the cheerfulness of Riot's entry and parallel it to Falstaff's gaiety, but he omits to mention that the reason Youth invites Riot to join him and the reason for the latter's jollity is the opportunity it offers to serve as the declared enemy to two primary Christian virtues, Charity and Humility, Riot cruelly boasting of his readiness to thrash and pummel Humility at the first opportunity:

Ryot: Let him come if he will
He were better to hide styll
And he gyue the croked langage
I wyll laye him on the visage
And that thou shalt se sone
How lightly it shall be done
And he wyl not be ruled with knockes
We shall set him in the stockes
To heale his sore shinnes.

There is thus no hint in that parallel of the paradox within the character of Falstaff, who, although he does indeed represent the vices of riot, lechery and gluttony, manages to endear himself so effectively to his audiences up to and including the very end, when the Hostess movingly reports his demise. Whatever Falstaff owes to those earlier dramas, the affection he arouses was not indebted to them.

The most interesting essay on Falstaff is still Bradley's, although it was published a century ago. Concerned at the mingling of condemnation and empathy that Falstaff arouses, he focused upon the moment of his rejection by the newly appointed king. Why, he asks, do we so strongly resent Hal's dismissal of his erstwhile friend even though we acknowledge that such dismissal is a duty imposed by his new office? The question is undoubtedly valid, but, after a lengthy examination of possible reasons, Bradley's conclusion proves disappointing. He determines that the scene is simply a failure on Shakespeare's part, that having created so wonderful a character the dramatist was unable to produce an effective last scene. Shakespeare '... overreached himself. He was caught up on the wind of his own genius and carried so far that he could not descend to earth on the selected spot.'[92]

If we apply the principle of comedy advocated in this present study, an intriguing point emerges. In most discussions of Falstaff's function in the play, it has been assumed that he represents the antipole to Hotspur, an earthy rejection of moral principles, with, as we have noted, Hal needing to choose a median between the two, to adopt an ideal of honour that manages to avoid the excesses of Hotspur while rejecting the dissipation of Falstaff. Implicit in such a reading is the assumption that we, the audience, however amusing Falstaff may be in his ready wordplay and resourcefulness, align ourselves with the noble standards that Hal will ultimately achieve. The morality plays, and such interludes as *Youth*, do indeed preserve in us an undisturbed moral sense – we may be momentarily entertained by Riot's witty resourcefulness but are consistent in recognizing him as a Vice. But the situation here, I would argue, is far more subtle. It is true that, when Hal and his companions make fun of his huge weight and insatiable 'gormandising', we join with them, laughing from the comfortable standpoint of sobriety and moderation, and rejecting Falkstaff's epicurean indulgences. Such is our first view of him, as Hal teasingly rebukes him for his laziness, his drunkenness and his lechery. Falstaff, slowly wakening from a deep slumber, enquires:

Falstaff: Now, Hal, what time of day is it, lad?
Prince: Thou art so fat-witted with drinking of old sack, and unbuttoning thee after supper, and sleeping upon benches after noon, that thou hast forgotten to demand that truly which thou wouldest truly know. What a devil hast thou to do with the

time of the day? Unless hours were cups of sack, and minutes capons, and clocks the tongues of bawds, and dials the signs of leaping houses, and the blessed sun himself a fair hot wench in flame-coloured taffeta, I see no reason why thou shouldst be so superfluous to demand the time of the day (*Henry IV* Pt.I:2:1:1f.).

However, if, as we have argued, comedy tends to deflate authoritative, socially approved concepts, in these plays there is no single authoritative concept being deflated, for the target of the humour changes from moment to moment, oscillating between two antithetical standards, and thereby producing an alternating response in the audience. For Falstaff is far more than the butt of the humour. He is just as often the instigator of ridicule, directing the humour back at his critics, compelling us temporarily to desert our moral condemnation of his misdemeanours and to laugh instead at the solemn principles to which we had imagined we subscribed. His sallies, that brilliantly turn the tables on his detractors, give us pause, making us wonder for a moment how valid it is to condemn the standards he represents.

Let us focus on a seemingly minor point – the gluttony ridiculed in the above passage. Time after time, he is teased, insulted or mocked for his love of food and drink, his enormous girth being derisively likened to a 'huge bombard' or 'hogshead'. As Doll Tearsheet remarks scoffingly, 'There's a whole merchant's venture of Bourdaux stuff in him, you have not seen a hulk better stuffed in the hold.' Yet, so far from being offended, Falstaff delights in his girth, at one point deploring what he suspects is a minor reduction in his weight: 'Bardolph, am I not fall'n away vilely since this last action? Do I not bate? Do I not dwindle? Why, my skin hangs about me like an old lady's loose gown! I am withered like an old apple John' (Pt.I:3:3;1f.). Such pleasure in his girth takes the sting out of the ridicule, transforming the attack into a form of compliment.

But the process can go much further. Whatever our predominant view may be, including our normal advocacy of moderation in drink and diet, can one resist the powerful lampooning of sobriety and moderation in the following passage, the amusing attack upon temperance in drink, an asceticism which, he maintains, robs young men of their virility, deprives them of martial vigour, weakens their mental powers and transforms them into mere wimps:

Falstaff: There's never none of these demure boys come to any proof; for thin drink doth so over-cool their blood, and making many fish-meals, that they fall into a kind of male green-sickness; and then, when they marry, they get wenches. They are generally fools and cowards – which some of us should be too, but for inflammation. A good sherris-sack hath a two-fold operation in it. It ascends me into the brain; dries me there all the foolish and dull and crudy vapours which environ it; makes it apprehensive, quick, forgetive, full of nimble, fiery, and delectable shapes; which delivered o'er to the voice, the tongue, which is the birth, becomes excellent wit. The second property of your excellent sherris is the warming of the blood; which before, cold and settled, left the liver white and pale, which is the badge of pusillanimity and cowardice; but the sherris warms it, and makes it course from the inwards to the parts extremes. It illumineth the face, which, as a beacon, gives warning to all the rest of this little kingdom, man, to arm; and then the vital commoners and inland petty spirits muster me all to their captain, the heart, who, great and puff'd up with this retinue, doth any deed of courage and this valour comes of sherris (Pt.II, 4:3:94f.).

Similarly, Hal's upbraiding of Falstaff for his outrageous size evokes a counter-attack not only evidencing the latter's resourcefulness but suggesting also the unattractiveness of a life of abstemiousness – that starving oneself to resemble a stick or ruler's yard constitutes a form of anorexia, deplorably inferior to a healthy indulgence in meat and drink, with the richness of his insults excelling Hal's, and thereby swinging us round to empathize with him:

Prince: ...this bed-presser, this horseback-breaker, this huge hill of flesh –
Falstaff: 'Sblood, you starveling, you elf-skin, you dried neat's-tongue, you bull's pizzle, you stockfish – O for breath to utter what is like thee! – you tailor's yard, you sheath, you bowcase, you vile standing tuck! (Pt.I:2:4:242f.)

Therein lies the paradox of his loveable iniquity as he so frequently turns the ridicule back upon his ridiculers. In the scene after the Gadshill robbery, when scorned by Hal and his friends for having fled the field, his famous reply in rebutting the attack just when his cause seems lost not only leaves his detractors dumbfounded but swings us firmly behind him once again:

> *Prince*: What a slave art thou to hack thy sword as thou hast done, and then say it was in fight! What trick, what device, what starting hole canst thou now find out to hide thee from this open and apparent shame?
> *Poins*: Come, let's hear, Jack. What trick hast thou now?
> *Falstaff*: By the Lord, I knew ye as well as he that made ye. Why, hear you, my masters. Was it for me to kill the heir apparent? Should I turn upon the true prince? Why, thou knowest I am as valiant as Hercules; but beware Instinct. The lion will not touch the true prince.

The Gadshill scenes provide a perfect example of the way humour functions, evidenced in this alternating form. Falstaff's boast of having routed numerous attackers amuses because of the gap between his pretentious claims to martial valour and our knowledge of his cowardly behaviour, and we await eagerly the moment when Hal will expose the hollowness of Falstaff's bragging. The exposure does take place to the delight of the audience, but just as Hal and his friends are rejoicing in the success of their ruse, his ingenious response reduces them in their turn to the discomfited. We laugh at the sudden descent of Falstaff's detractors from confident victory to rueful admission that he has outwitted them, as they themselves become the object of laughter.

Throughout the two plays, then, Falstaff's rejoinders not only entertain but deflect the charges of cowardice and dissipation, and they do so not by denying the vices but by ridiculing their proponents, by undermining confidence in the validity of the moralists. He is both the butt of humour and the jester, as Shakespeare himself informs us, Falstaff remarking: 'I am not only witty in myself, but the cause that wit is in other men.' He makes no attempt, for example, to refute by argument the Chief Justice's solemn reprimand that he is wasting his limited resources, but rebuffs the charge by outrageous puns – transferring the word 'great' from his supposed infamy to his girth and pretending to misunderstand the word 'waste' in a manner that leaves us laughing at his sense of humour and the discomfiture of the law's representative, and hence forgetting the reprimand itself:

> *Chief Justice*: Well, the truth is, Sir John, you live in great infamy.
> *Falstaff*: He that buckles himself in my belt cannot live in less.
> *Chief Justice*: Your means are very slender, and your waste is great.
> *Falstaff*: I would it were otherwise; I would my means were greater and my waist slenderer (Pt.II, 1:2:158–61).

This is, in addition, a perfect instance of the effectiveness of wordplay, for not only is the authority of language impugned by the puns but, by association, so also is the authority of the Chief Justice, shown here to have been vulnerably ambiguous in his wording of the charge.

Falstaff even manages to justify or at least elevate his night-time thievery, in this instance too by means of puns, using a play on *night* to transform himself and his companions into *knight's* squires, into gentlemen in the service of a goddess as they justifiably 'steal' away in the darkness under her auspices. It is a claim we do not take seriously but which, by its liveliness and originality, compels us, at least momentarily, to regard with indulgence activities we would normally condemn:

> *Falstaff*: Let not us that are squires of the night's body be called thieves of the day's beauty. Let us be Diana's foresters, gentlemen of the shade, minions of the moon; and let men say we be men of good government, being governed as the sea is, by our noble and chaste mistress the moon, under whose countenance we steal (Pt.I,1:2:23f.).

The way he wins our affection and reverses our conventional assumptions could not be more clearly illustrated than in the scene in which they act out the king's admonition of the prodigal prince. Part of the fun is in the play-acting itself, with Falstaff, to the delight of an Elizabethan audience, parodying at one point (as in Pyramus' lines) the somewhat bombastic acting of Edward Alleyn of the rival company: 'Weep not, sweet queen, for trickling tears are vain' (2:4:391). In general, however, the moral inversion is at work once again. Hal, in the role of King, warns his supposed son, with considerable justice, against befriending that 'villainous abominable misleader of youth, Falstaff, that old white-bearded Satan' – statements that, despite the conviviality of the scene, ring only too true, pointing to the reform which Hal has already predicated for himself, the time when he will in due course throw off his 'loose behaviour' and the companions that foster it. Falstaff's wonderful rejoinder is not only witty but succeeds in creating in the audience that warm response that belongs to true humour as he justifies his girth with a scriptural reference that is indeed difficult to deny and that, by the biblical authority it calls upon, in effect turns Hal's strictures on their head:

> *Falstaff*: If to be old and merry be a sin, then many an old host that I know is damn'd. If to be fat be to be hated, then Pharaoh's lean kine are to be loved. No, my good lord: banish Peto, banish Bardolph, banish Poins; but for sweet Jack Falstaff, kind Jack Falstaff, true Jack Falstaff, valiant Jack Falstaff, and therefore more valiant being, as he is, old Jack Falstaff, banish not him thy Harry's company, banish not him thy Harry's company. Banish plump Jack, and banish all the world! (Pt.I:2:4:470f.)

Does anyone at that moment desire to banish plump Jack? The humour has reversed our moral allegiance.

He will, it is true, occasionally declare with due solemnity that he will reform, a declaration that might suggest his eventual acceptance of the morality he constantly derides. But the decision to reform is always conveniently postponed to some vague future occasion, a postponement that neither he nor we take seriously. Moreover, such claims contain an element of humour that a modern audience may well miss, as it employs language – and, no doubt, in the original staging, employed appropriate gestures – that parody the solemnities of the Puritan sect, so distasteful to theatregoers. In contrast to earlier church traditions, Puritans regarded spiritual conversion not as a long, slow process of repentance and self-abnegation but as a sudden revelation. Luther had set the model, recording in a famous passage how, when haunted by a terrifying vision of his rejection by Christ on the Day of Judgement, he had chanced upon the phrase in Romans: 'The just shall live by faith.' In a flash, he had felt born again – a tradition later reinforced by Calvin's claim that he too had achieved faith by means of 'a sudden conversion'.[93] Based on those precedents, Puritans came to conceive of salvation as something to be instantaneously felt, the true believer, in a surge of faith, being immediately convinced of eternal redemption. That phenomenon was as well known in Shakespeare's day as is the idea of being 'born again' in our own. Hence Falstaff's postponement of repentance until he can do so with similar abruptness:

> *Falstaff*: Well, I'll repent, and that suddenly, while I am in some liking. I shall be out of heart shortly, and then I shall have no strength to repent. An I have not forgotten what the inside of a church is made of, I am a peppercorn, a brewer's horse. The inside of a church! Company, villanous company, hath been the spoil of me.
> *Bardolph*: Sir John, you are so fretful you cannot live long.
> *Falstaff*: Why, there is it! Come, sing me a bawdy song; make me merry (Pt.I:3:3;3f.).

The final line indicates how seriously we are to regard his desire to reform.

All this has major repercussions on the central theme of the play, the theme of honour, which emerges not in the simplistic form of two antipoles – contentious Chivalry and dissipated Riot, both of which Hal must reject. That he will discard Hotspur's quarrelsome sense of honour, the continual fermenting of dispute in order to prove one's mettle, is clear enough. But Falstaff's representation of the opposite view is more complex, for it offers insights that we cannot so readily rebuff, again challenging convention. His wonderful speech devoted to honour in warfare is not simply the speech of a coward but cuts to the core of the matter. It touches upon a problem that was already disturbing Shakespeare and that was to emerge as the central theme of *Hamlet*. And here I must ask the reader's indulgence for what may appear to be a divergence but which has a direct bearing on our discussion.

Central to the Renaissance concept of the dignity of the individual was its validation of the pursuit of eternal fame, the conviction that within the grasp of each human being was the potential for achieving a noble and lasting reputation. The medieval world, accepting as axiomatic the cardinal Christian virtue of humility, had decried desire for fame, but that interdiction, despite remaining theologically valid, gradually lost its force, supplanted by a new sense of the individual's yearning to live on gloriously in human memory. Even within the heart of the church that concept took hold, with Pope Julius II planning the construction of an enormous tomb intended to preserve his memory, a tomb in which Michelangelo's massive figure of *Moses* was to form only a minor element. That concern with eternal glory was echoed in Shakespeare's own sonnet: 'So long lives this, and this gives life to thee.' But a shadow of doubt was soon to fall upon that idea, a reversion to the medieval view, the feeling that mortality wipes away all records, that a man's reputation cannot survive the grave. Donne was haunted by visions of the putrefaction of the body, by the sense that death vitiates everything attained to in this world, only the afterlife holding any permanence:

> This dissolution after *dissolution*, this *death* of *corruption* and *putrifaction*, of *vermiculation* and *incineration*, of *dissolution* and *dispersion* in and *from* the *grave*, when these bodies that have beene the *children* of *royall parents*, and the *parents* of *royall children*, must say with *Job, Corruption thou art my father*, and *to the Worme thou art my mother.*

In another passage, he vividly depicted death as wiping away all distinctions of achievement or of class, thereby undercutting the basic Renaissance faith in eternal glory:

> when a whirle-winde hath blowne the dust of the Church-yard into the Church, and the man sweeps out the dust of the Church into the Church-yard, who will undertake to sift those dusts again, and to pronounce, This is the Patrician, this is the noble flowre, and this the yeomanly, this the Plebeian bran? [94]

Shakespeare in his major phase reveals a similar disturbance, marking in his plays a transition from the validation of achieved fame to the new, more disquieting view. In the phase that followed upon *Henry V* that disturbance was to become a central concern, Hamlet being haunted throughout the play, like Donne, by the putrefaction of corpses, the stench of human decay, and the seeming purpose-lessness of life. His summary of traditional Renaissance optimism, the divine potentiality of man, is followed there by a thought that in effect undercuts or cancels out the previous claim:

> What a piece of work is a man! how noble in reason! how infinite in faculties! in form and moving how express and admirable! in action how like an angel! in apprehension how like a god! the

beauty of the world, the paragon of animals! And yet to me what is this quintessence of dust?

He is obsessed by visions of a royal body passing through the guts of a beggar, of Polonius' corpse that will be 'nosed' as they go up the stairs. Hamlet's own father had been forgotten within two months by all except his son. All worldly achievement seemed futile, Fortinbras's march to conquer a piece of Poland for purposes of self-aggrandizement now seeming an empty and vain aim. Hence it is that Hamlet, holding the rotting skull of Yorick, thinks instinctively of the figure who represented the epitome of human greatness and eternal renown, sadly asking his friend Horatio: 'Dost thou think Alexander look'd o' this fashion i' th' earth? ... And smelt so. Pah!'

Shakespeare had not adopted that view at the time of writing the Falstaff plays. There could be no prouder conviction of eternal fame than Henry's promise to his soldiers before the battle of Agincourt in the play that was to follow, that their victory on St Crispin's day would be remembered for eternity:

Then shall our names,
Familiar in his mouth as household words-
Harry the King, Bedford and Exeter,
Warwick and Talbot, Salisbury and Gloucester-
Be in their flowing cups freshly rememb'red.
This story shall the good man teach his son;
And Crispin Crispian shall ne'er go by,
From this day to the ending of the world,
But we in it shall be remembered (4:3:51–9).

That, however, was an exhortation to the troops, an encouragement for them to fight bravely. But during the night before battle, the king's thoughts were elsewhere, acknowledging that monarchal fame consists only of 'titles blown from adulation', that greatness is subject to the breath of every fool and, as he is reminded by one of the soldiers, that there is a dreadful price to be paid for the achievement of such fame:

... the King himself hath a heavy reckoning to make when all those legs and arms and heads, chopp'd off in a battle, shall join together at the latter day and cry all 'We died at such a place', some swearing, some crying for a surgeon, some upon their wives left poor behind them, some upon the debts they owe, some upon their children rawly left ... (4:1:140f.)

Shakespeare's growing recognition of this less sanguine viewpoint is, however, evidenced even in the earlier play. Falstaff's speech on 'honour' amuses us by its gross admission (when he is sure of being alone) of his own cowardice, serving to counterpoint Hotspur's madcap idea of bravery. But the speech does something more. Like so many of his previous witticisms and ripostes, there is too much truth in it for its sentiments to be airily discarded. They echo only too well the thoughts that pass through the mind of any soldier on the field of battle, thoughts that he may be able to overcome but which disturb nonetheless. Why should he be the one to lose a limb? Perhaps he should draw back and let others rush forward? Would anyone thank him for his sacrifice once the battle is over? And, most of all, would the supposed renown due to accrue for his action last beyond the grave or live on with the living?

To Hal's parting comment, 'Why thou owest God a death', he responds, once he is sure he is alone:

Falstaff: 'Tis not due yet. I would be loath to pay him before his day. What need I be so forward with him that calls not on me? Well, 'tis no matter; honour pricks me on. Yea, but how if honour prick me off when I come on? How then? Can honor set to a leg? No. Or an arm? No. Or take away the grief of a wound? No. Honour hath no skill in surgery then? No. What is honour? A word. What is that word honour? Air. A trim reckoning! Who hath it? He that died a Wednesday. Doth he feel it? No. Doth be bear it? No. 'Tis insensible then? Yea, to the dead. But will it not live with the living? No. Why? Detraction will not suffer it. Therefore I'll none of it (*HIV* Pt.I, 5:1:130f.).

The speech not only targets the conventional concept of honour but leaves it seriously impaired. The sympathy that Falstaff's humour evokes thus alters the balance of the play. C. L. Barber, in his study of the anthropological background to Shakespeare's comedies, sees Falstaff functioning as a scapegoat whom Hal, after he himself participates in the Saturnalia, must ritualistically sacrifice so that order may be restored: '... by turning on Falstaff as a scapegoat, as the villagers turned on their Mardi Gras, the prince can free himself from the sins, the "bad luck," of Richard's reign and of his father's reign, to become a king in whom chivalry and a sense of divine ordination are restored'.[95] This is a valuable insight but needs one vital modification – for a scapegoat is intended to carry off the sins, leaving the scene purified. If my reading is correct, the empathy Falstaff aroused in us as he scoffs at the claims of honour does not evaporate on his departure, but leaves its mark. To see the play as advocating Hal's choice of a mean between Hotspur and Falstaff is thus an oversimplification. Hotspur's view of honour never wins our approval, but the sympathy and partial endorsement which Falstaff's derision of honour evokes endow us, however momentarily, with a more complex view of honour, an awareness of the darker aspects to fame and glory, a concept that will begin to emerge in *Henry V* and reach its apogee in *Hamlet*.

Nor is this attack on the supposed honour of warfare confined to the above speech. The scene of Falstaff's ragamuffin platoon is uproariously funny on the stage, largely because Falstaff has so astutely utilized his commission to fill his purse, thereby outwitting his military superiors – as usual in comedy, he has followed the letter of the command to recruit soldiers while subverting its intention. However, as his speech informs us, the fault lies not so much with him as with the system prevalent at that time, a system that allowed the wealthy to redeem their sons for payment, sending others to death in their place, a practice that again makes us wonder about the supposedly honourable principles of warfare. Falstaff, it transpires, has carefully conscripted into service only those with the means to ransom themselves, pocketing the money offered and proceeding 'to fill up the rooms of them that have bought out their services' with low-life riff-raff.

The comic element in Falstaff thus functions in a manner more complex than has been thought, for it arises not only from the fact that he makes us laugh, but also – and even more so – from the fact that his joviality reveals truths that we tend to hide from ourselves, and hence endears him to us in a way differing fundamentally from a Dogberry or Gobbo. And so we return to the question of the resentment we feel at Hal's rejection of Falstaff even though we acknowledge that such rejection is indeed necessitated by new monarchal responsibilities.

The cause of our resentment lies in the totality of Hal's repudiation, the harshness and callousness of Hal's dismissal of his one-time friend. For it reveals to our dismay that Hal has learnt nothing from him, that Hal has failed to carry with him into his new life the lessons and the doubts that we, the audience, have imbibed from that jovial, plump old man in the course of the two plays. Falstaff may have been, as Hal now calls him, a gormandizing jester, but he has within those plays revealed, with a validity we cannot easily dismiss, the darker elements in the much-vaunted pursuit of renown. In larger terms, he has perceived, as Sir Toby will soon famously restate, that virtue, including dedication to the royal tasks now incumbent upon Hal, does not mean that there should be no more cakes and ale. As Falstaff approaches the newly crowned Hal, joyfully sure that his fortune is made, he is greeted with a speech that shocks us all:

> I know thee not, old man. Fall to thy prayers.
> How ill white hairs become a fool and jester! ...
> Leave gormandizing; know the grave doth gape
> For thee thrice wider than for other men ...
> ... I banish thee, on pain of death,
> As I have done the rest of my misleaders,
> Not to come near our person by ten mile.

Postmodern criticism has led us to recognize that there is often in literary works a subtext working against the main thrust of the work,[96] and that aspect holds true in this instance. In rejecting Falstaff with such contempt, Hal has rejected with him the subtext, namely everything that Falstaff represents – not only the dissipation and self-indulgence but also his awareness of the limitations to established moral concepts, his conception that life offers more than sober dedication to high-minded ideals. There is indeed truth in the statement, 'Banish plump Jack and banish all the world!' Hal, in banishing Falstaff so totally and so irremediably, reveals that his fraternizing with the taverners has taught him nothing. On ascending the throne, he should indeed have broken with his old friend, but should have done so gently, displaying gratitude for that jester's revelation of truths about life at large, including those doubts about warfare and honour of which Shakespeare himself was beginning to become aware, and that were to figure so largely in his subsequent drama.

The audience's resentment at this scene is thus not a failure on Shakespeare's part, but deliberate – the dramatist's indication that Hal has one further step to take in his advance to monarchal fitness, the lesson that he will learn during his solemn musings on the transience and flimsiness of martial glory on the night before the battle of Agincourt – although by then it will be too late for reconciliation with his dissolute, jovial, yet ultimately instructive companion who, as Mistress Quickly quaintly puts it, is by now at rest in Arthur's bosom.[97]

One last point: Tradition has it that Queen Elizabeth, impressed by Falstaff, expressed a wish for a further play in which he would figure, the result being *The Merry Wives of Windsor*.[98] That play has its moments but is, by general agreement, inferior to the two plays we have been examining. And the reason lies precisely here. For in that latter play, Falstaff is merely a clown or butt of humour, with no larger setting in which he can function to modify the major theme.[99] It is the twofold target of the humour in these *Henry IV* plays, the oscillation between our laughter at his nonchalant rejection of socially approved morality and our recognition of the inherent justice in many of his rejoinders, that cumulatively determine our final moral stance, our recognition that 'honour', while indeed a noble ideal, needs to be seen as more complex than we had imagined – that the confidence in that ideal displayed excessively by Hotspur, yet subscribed to in principle by all but the taverners, is ultimately less authoritative than had been thought. If humour deflates or modifies authoritative concepts, an awareness of that principle reveals deeper elements in the comic function of Falstaff than have been recognized hitherto, as the series of oscillating moral alignments he produces repeatedly causes the audience to question the established views of martial honour and sobriety.

c) Donne, *The Flea*

The sober Dean of St Paul's, meditating on the corruption of the flesh and of the soul's yearning for the afterlife, may seem an odd candidate for inclusion in a study of humour. In his younger days, however, although he was, even during that period, deeply immersed in theological speculation, devoting, as Walton informs us, the hours from 4 to 10 each morning to a study of the distinctions between the Catholic and Reformed churches, he produced a number of fascinating poems on secular love themes, one of which not only attests to his wry wit but also casts light on a dominant mode of the time.

For modern readers, the attraction of *The Flea* may appear to reside in its theme, the incongruity of a male lover employing an insect to persuade a young lady to grant him her favours, with the speaker proffering the claim that, since so insignificant a parasite has been permitted to roam over her naked flesh, he surely should be granted a similar privilege. In fact, the assumption is unfounded, for by the time Donne produced his version, that theme had become a tiresome cliché. An anonymous Latin poem entitled *Carmen de Pulice*, incorrectly attributed to Ovid, had inspired so many imitations in this period that by 1582, a decade or two before this poem's composition, an anthology containing 50 flea poems had been published in France by Etienne Pasquier, in each of which the lover envies the parasite's right to nestle in the lady's bosom and to 'taste' the joys of her flesh. None of Donne's readers, therefore, would have been amused by the theme as such. The popularity of his widely admired poem derived therefore from some other source, that other source having, I would suggest, more serious cultural significance than may at first appear.

The humour lies in its dazzling display of intellectual agility as the speaker moves in seemingly logical progression from point to point, trapping us into amusing absurdities. We are led to conclusions so obviously untenable that we are compelled to reject them, although the means whereby we have been trapped remain hidden. The source of the humour emanates from the repeated deflation of our confidence in our own reasoning as we repeatedly find ourselves in rueful and amused recognition that we have been tricked. This poem plays the same type of game as in the 'proof' that every cat has nine tails – a process employing the most solid and reliable of all logical patterns, the syllogism. Each statement is undeniably true, but the conclusion is patently invalid. The syllogism runs:

No cat has eight tails.
Every cat has one tail more than no cat.
Therefore every cat has nine tails.

The Flea pulsates for all its surface raillery, with an emotional energy that is hard to resist, as well as employing a deceptively firm progression. The poem opens with a statement evocative of a scientific experimenter pointing to the verifiable object on the laboratory bench about which there can be no disagreement:

> Marke but this flea, and marke in this,
> How little that which thou deny'st me is;
> Mee it suck'd first, and now sucks thee,
> And in this flea, our two bloods mingled bee;
> Confesse it, this cannot be said
> A sinne, or shame, or losse of maidenhead,
> Yet this enjoyes before it wooe,
> And pamper'd swells with one blood made of two,
> And this, alas, is more then wee would doe.[100]

There is nothing in the sequence that one can point to as incorrect, and apart from the entertaining play on 'little', referring both to the size of the flea and to the supposedly minimal request of the lover, everything appears serious. And yet by the end of the stanza we know some misdirection has taken place, that some sleight of hand has deceived us, like that of a conjuror distracting our attention to a bright handkerchief while he slyly substitutes an item on the table. The nature of the deception, however, is difficult to identify, especially as the poem moves swiftly forward, leaving no time for reflection or for the kind of leisurely analysis we can employ here.

There are, in fact, two cunning elisions, moments when we are made to slide across from one meaning to another. The first misdirection is hidden in the seemingly insignificant word *this*. In the phrase 'this flea', the referent is unambiguous; but at the end of the first line 'this' has already become equivocal, suggesting as the source of his proof the flea itself and also, more vaguely, 'this experiment'. By the fifth line – 'this cannot be said / A sinne' – the purpose of the ambiguity emerges, for while ostensibly referring to the flea's factual foraging for blood, the phrase 'our two bloods mingled be' has introduced a metaphorical image of wedlock with its implication that, as a form of marriage has already taken place in the flea, the sexual intercourse with the lady he so desires has now been fully justified. Were the reader allowed time to ponder, it would be realized that the metaphor of the mingling of bloods in marriage refers not to the mixing of two physical drops of blood as the surface meaning seems to suggest but to the merging of the 'blood' of two family lineages within the offspring of the union – an event that has certainly not occurred here.[101] Moreover, tucked away almost unobserved in the word 'pampered' is the unwarranted assumption that the lady had willingly indulged the flea, permitting it the favours denied to him, when in all likelihood she was as annoyed by the flea's attentions as she was by the lover's protestations.

The debate, as so often in Donne's poems including his most serious religious verse, is presented as a form of eavesdropping in which we hear only one side of the conversation. In this instance, however, the actions of the female disputant are entertainingly dramatized in the silent gaps between the stanzas so that, even though we do not hear her responses, her presence is strongly felt. Although she may not have perceived the nature of the logical flaw, she is certainly aware (as are we all) of the invalidity of the conclusion, but as a woman both of intelligence and of independent judgement, as Donne's fictional mistresses invariably are, she determines to trump his argument. Crushing the flea will effectively disprove the reasoning he has cleverly deduced from it, providing a pragmatic rebuttal of his philosophical theorizing. But as she raises her thumb to do so, the lover urgently interrupts:

> Oh stay, three lives in one flea spare,
> Where wee almost, yea more then maryed are.
> This flea is you and I, and this
> Our mariage bed, and mariage temple is;
> Though parents grudge, and you, w'are met,
> And cloysterd in these living walls of Jet.
> Though use make you apt to kill mee,
> Let not to that, selfe murder added bee,
> And sacrilege, three sinnes in killing three.

As with all wit, it takes a moment for us to grasp the significance of 'three lives', until two elements are grasped. First, why the speaker assumes that killing the flea will result in deaths. From the Bible, as well as other sources, the stricture against murder had been phrased as a prohibition of the 'shedding of blood', on the assumption that 'the blood is the soul'. Again Donne deliberately confuses the metaphorical sense with the literal, the Bible clearly not classifying as murder the spilling of a drop of blood that has already been removed from the owner's body. Secondly, in the word 'three' the speaker has puckishly included the shedding of the flea's blood, as if that were a crime no less grave than the murder of the two debaters. And to intensify the argument, there follows the extrapolation that, since the mingling of their bloods has already taken place inside the flea, such mingling having been established as tantamount to marriage, the lover is now entitled to speak of the flea as a 'temple' or 'cloister' thereby endowing their desired union with supposedly divine approval and legality. There follows too a sly glance at the Petrarchan tradition of the unrequited lover wasting away and dying, killed by his mistress's coldness, after which the speaker takes the earlier argument a step further, risibly suggesting that her shedding of her own drop of blood constitutes the sin of suicide.

The final stanza is a tour de force. The lady has called his bluff. Ignoring his protests, she has now crushed the flea, thereby, we imagine, destroying in one moment the pseudo-arguments he has so carefully developed:

> Cruell and sodaine, hast thou since
> Purpled thy naile, in blood of innocence?
> In what could this flea guilty bee,
> Except in that drop which it suckt from thee?
> Yet thou triumph'st, and saist that thou
> Find'st not thy selfe, nor mee the weaker now;

She has, it appears, won – but the victory is short-lived. As usual, Donne is in full control as we discover that the entire preceding argument has been a trap in which the lady has been unwittingly ensnared. She has been decoyed into rejecting his metaphors as mere fanciful aberrations, insisting instead, as she crushes the flea, on the factual and physical realities from which she refuses to be deflected. She takes the stance of an empiricist, scoffing at abstruse, metaphorical argumentation. He may, she implies, develop illusory arguments about bloodshed and suicide, but a flea is a flea, and its death, she points out, has not only left no one the worse but has effectively disproved all his fabrications.

True, points out the speaker, turning the argument on its head, but, since that is so, what is the so-called 'honour' that prevents her from consummating their love if not another fabricated metaphor, an abstract idea invented by society that has no real relevance to the physical act of love?

'Tis true, then learne how false, feares bee;
Just so much honor, when thou yeeld'st to mee,
Will wast, as this flea's death tooke life from thee.

What appears at first to be a poem of amusing amorous seduction in
fact turns out to be something very different. It is a delightful play
with ratiocination, employing the traditional flea theme, merged
with the traditional coy mistress theme, to create a brilliant poem of
wit, a series of deceptive arguments, each, like that of the nine-tailed
cat, leading to a laughable absurdity but at the same time leaving us
unsure where precisely we were led astray. But that leaves us with
the question of how the humour here relates to the theory we are
investigating. In fact, the wit in this poem does precisely the same to
logic as wordplay does to lexical definition, revealing weaknesses or
ambiguities in the contemporary authority of ratiocination. Where
puns allow one to slide from one meaning to another and thereby
disclose the existence of ambiguities in language, here the ability to
slide from one concept to another while preserving the outward form
of logic exposes the dangers in the reasoning process. However, if
punning is generally flippant, there is here a serious purpose behind
the ridicule, one related to the cultural setting of the time.

The order and harmony assumed by the Renaissance as governing
the universe had rested upon the firm assumption that the system
was held together by reason, that the hierarchy of the Great Chain
of Being with the Supreme Creator at the apex, the archangels
below, and the king or prince acting as God's representative on
earth, formed the logical pattern of creation. As Thomas Blundeville
recorded in a poem written in 1580:

Such is that Prince within his land
Which, fearing God, maintaineth right
And reason's rule doth understand
Wherein consists his port and might.

So too, Richard Hooker, Donne's contemporary, in 1591 based his
Laws of Ecclesiastical Politie upon 'the law of reason, that which
bindeth creatures reasonable in this world and with which by reason
they may most plainly perceive themselves bound'.[102]

But a counter-movement was emerging that was to gain force by
the turn of the century. In the 1580s, Montaigne as a sceptic had

already challenged that view, complaining that all philosophers and researchers, '… accept or approve nothing except by way of reason. That is their touchstone for every kind of experiment: but indeed it is a touchstone full of falsity, error, weakness, and impotence.'[103] He gave the delightful instance of relativism of viewpoint – when playing with a kitten we imagine we are indulgently amusing it, but perhaps it is we who are being indulgently played with by the kitten. No less profound a change was occurring in the religious sphere, a change we have already touched upon in an earlier mention of *Hamlet* and the play's troubled concern with mortality and the afterlife. As so often in cultural history, there was a pendular swing back to certain medieval views that the Renaissance had discarded, a renewed conception that life in this world was merely a corridor to the world-to-come, that *media vita in morte sumus*. That new direction of thought was to animate the metaphysical poets, the very name of the group indicating their dissatisfaction with reliance upon the physical world and their yearning for the *meta-physical*, for what lay beyond the tactile and visible. In art, El Greco and Tintoretto no longer attempted to depict actuality, to produce a window on to reality as in the visual perspectives of Renaissance artists. They desired to record scenes that were for them far more important, the dream-visions of a meditator ecstatically conjuring up in his mind the martyrdom or bliss of a Christian saint; hence the rejection of normal perspective in their paintings, the unnaturally elongated figures yearning upwards in a world of phosphorescent colours such as have never existed in the natural world.

Donne himself not only paralleled that movement; he served as a main exemplar. He loved logic, but was deeply conscious of its limitations. It constituted, he claimed, only a threshold to knowledge, a threshold that one must cross in order to discover ultimate truths beyond, truths only achievable by faith. '*Knowledge* cannot save us,' he wrote, 'but we cannot be saved without Knowledge: Faith is not on this side Knowledge, but beyond it. We must necessarily come to *Knowledge* first, though we must not stay at it when we are come thither.' Not only was it limited, incapable of leading him to the final stages of his spiritual search, but it was dangerous too, liable to fail or mislead the seeker at time of need. As he wrote in one of his most moving sonnets:

Reason your viceroy in mee, mee should defend,
But is captiv'd, and proves weak or untrue.[104]

What interested him most, therefore, was the limitation to logic, the paradoxical inconsistencies within nature which, by undermining confidence in empirical reasoning, could teach us to respect those spiritual experiences that seem to defy logic. In the tradition of Tertullian's famed declaration that he believed not *despite* the irrationality of his faith but *because* of that irrationality – *Certum est quia impossibile* – Donne sought for the paradoxes in this world that defy rationality and that should be seen therefore as justifying the seeming illogicalities of transcendent devotionalism. Hence such comments in his sermons as: 'I can better know a man upon the top of a steeple, than if he were halfe that depth in a well; but yet for higher objects, I can better see the stars of heaven, in the bottome of a well, than if I stood upon the highest steeple upon earth.'[105]

Seen in that context, *The Flea* is not the casual or trivial poem it might seem to be, nor is it really a poem about love or a coy mistress. It is a brilliant and amusing exercise revealing the dangers inherent in logic, employing wit and humour to demonstrate a central aspect both of the poet's beliefs and of his cultural milieu. Each sudden realization of the absurd conclusion into which we have been led evokes laughter at our own confident expectation of logicality, but at the same time awakens us to the perils embedded in ratiocination itself, in the logical processes that had seemed so incontrovertible. Humour, once again, is employed to query one of the dominant concepts of the time.

d) Marvell, *The Garden*

If Donne seemed a strange choice for illustrating the literary use of humour, the same could be said of Andrew Marvell. In his own day he was known primarily for his serious political activities. He won a reputation as a dedicated and incorruptible Member of Parliament for Hull and, as a poet, was remembered mainly for his political satires. A collection of poems discovered after his death was, when published by the person who claimed to be his widow, largely ignored, and it was only in the twentieth century that he achieved the status of a major poet, largely through the admiration aroused by his poem, *To His Coy Mistress*. While *The Garden* was also admired, it has, since that time, been almost invariably discussed with a solemnity that I believe is quite inappropriate. Shortly after T. S. Eliot drew attention to Marvell's excellence as a poet in two essays, neither of which even mentioned *The Garden*, William Empson in 1932 devoted an entire article to the poem, but discussed it with extraordinary gravity, his main concern being with the stanza that concludes:

> Annihilating all that's made
> To a green Thought in a green Shade.

That couplet, he wrote, 'combines the idea of the conscious mind, including everything because understanding it, and that of the unconscious animal nature, including everything because in harmony with it'; and he continued in the same vein, only referring briefly to the rest of the poem which, as he put it, argues 'impertinently' that nature is more beautiful than women. Frank Kermode, some 20 years later, again focused upon this poem, and again the tone was intensely serious as he analysed the references to the *hortus conclusus* and the poem's relationship to libertinism, a typical comment being that Marvell here, 'rejects the naturalist account of love, and with it that of Platonism which was associated with the delights of the senses'.[106] That such solemn reading persists is indicated by a college professor's summary recently offered on the internet for the use of students, which states that the poem 'returns to the praise of idealised Nature and contrasts it with the fallen state of things under human domination. The quest to re-imagine the un-fallen world leads the poet to a kind of *ekstasis* in which his language becomes almost nonsense: what exactly would one be thinking were one to think "a green thought in a green shade."'[107] Where in all this does one find acknowledgement of the enchanting humour of the poem which is, for me, its primary attraction and, once again, the querying of a dominant principle of the time?

Although *The Garden* also employs illogicality, the pattern of humour differs considerably from that of *The Flea*, for where Donne was targeting logic itself, leading his readers into absurdities intended to reveal the hazards of rationalism, here the humour lies primarily in the assumed role, a speaker supposedly believing in the arguments he is presenting while poet and reader are deliciously aware of the inbuilt implausibilities. The humour is aimed, therefore, not at logic itself but at the gap between the speaker's confident assertion of supposed facts and our perception, in league with the implied poet, of the discrepancies and ineptitudes in those statements. Our discussion of the principle being targeted will come a little later.

A word in preface: Any suspicion that the speaker really prefers the delights of the garden to those offered by women, that he is 'impertinently' making that claim as Empson suggests, is countered by the lines in the fourth stanza, lines that Empson seems to have overlooked:

> When we have run our Passion's heat,
> Love hither makes his best retreat.

It is only *after* making love, when one needs to recuperate one's strength, that the relaxation offered by the garden can be fully appreciated; so that the speaker's seeming preference for the beauties of nature over those offered by the ladies is revealed to be the playful teasing of one who is, in fact, fully responsive to the attractions of his female friends – an aspect, as we shall see, confirmed in other stanzas.

The poem opens with a different theme, a concern not with women but with those perspiring aspirants to renown who strive to achieve the honours accorded for distinction in their fields, the victory wreaths awarded for athletic, military or poetic distinction:

> How vainly men themselves amaze
> To win the Palm, the Oke, or Bayes;
> And their uncessant Labours see
> Crown'd from some single Herb or Tree,
> Whose short and narrow verged Shade
> Does prudently their Toyles upbraid;
> While all Flow'rs and all Trees do close
> To weave the Garlands of repose.[108]

The principal amusement lies, of course, in the idea that the wreaths such men obtain are pursued in order to provide shade from the sun's hot rays, whereas, the speaker suggests, those hard-working contenders could, free of effort, obtain far more generous protection by strolling beneath the rich foliage provided by the garden – a claim that deliberately ignores the symbolic value of the wreaths. There is, however, no attempt here, as in Donne's poem, to conceal the falsity of the logic. On the contrary, the fallacy is patent from the first, the reader being amused at the ingenuity whereby the illogicalities are constructed and by the wordplay that raises the level of sophistication. *Vainly* suggests that the efforts of these aspirants are both in vain and prompted by mere vanity; while towards the end of the stanza there is a more subtle pun in the phrase '... their Toyles upbraid'. It implies on the one hand that the wreaths only narrowly *braid-up* the victor's hair (an obsolete meaning of *toil*)[109] and at the same time that they *upbraid* or reprove the useless toils invested in their acquisition. With the aspirants to renown effectively dismissed, the speaker can proceed with his justification of the joys of verdurous relaxation.

The next stanza introduces a new theme as the speaker praises the quiet and innocence of the garden in contrast to the bustle and noise of the city. By personifying those admirable qualities as females 'dear' to him, he slily suggests the superfluity to him of mortal women, the silence and beauty of the garden being preferable to them – although his representation of those attractions in terms of women itself undercuts the supposed misogyny, suggesting that the admirable qualities of serenity and virtue are indeed attributes of femininity. He then inverts the normal view of the countryside as being boorish and uncultured by contrarily applying the term 'rude' to urban society, arguing that city life lacks the delicacy and refinement of the natural scene, the latter 'sacred' in so far as it is evocative of Eden (a hint he will develop later):

> Fair quiet, have I found thee here,
> And Innocence thy Sister dear!
> Mistaken long, I sought you then
> In busie Companies of Men.
> Your sacred Plants, if here below,
> Only among the Plants will grow.
> Society is all but rude,
> To this delicious Solitude.

Employing the standard poetic description of the complexion of English women as white and red, he pursues this dismissal of the fairer sex by claiming that the colouring of herbs and flowers is superior to theirs, the stanza concluding with an image delightful in its absurdity:

No white nor red was ever seen
So am'rous as this lovely green.
Fond Lovers, cruel as their Flame,
Cut in these Trees their Mistress's name.
Little, Alas, they know, or heed,
How far these Beauties Hers exceed!
Fair Trees! whereso'er your barkes I wound,
No Name shall but your own be found.

With the double meaning of 'fond' ('foolish' as well as 'affectionate' in seventeenth-century usage), the dismissed lovers lead him to the ludicrous conclusion that if ever he, as a nature-lover, were to be so cruel to his arboreal friends as to cut figures into their bark, it would not be to incise the usual lover's device of 'Marvell ♥ Mary' but the far nobler version: 'Marvell ♥ the Elm Tree'.

Another absurdity awaits us, this time a misreading of classical mythology, one which Marvell of course assumes the reader will immediately grasp. Where Apollo, pursuing Daphne in order to rape her, had in the original legend been bitterly frustrated when at the last moment her river-god father rescued her by transforming her into a laurel bush, the speaker suavely assumes that Apollo's interest in pursuing Daphne had been from the first solely for horticultural reasons, his desire to possess a laurel bush, thereby sharing the speaker's own preference for verdure. And to buttress his argument, Marvell adds the parallel instance of Pan's frustrated pursuit of the maiden Syrinx, supposedly because he needed a pipe to play on:

When we have run our Passion's heat,
Love hither makes his best retreat.
The *Gods*, that mortal Beauty chase.
Still in a Tree did end their race.
Apollo hunted *Daphne* so,
Only that She might Laurel grow.
And *Pan* did after *Syrinx* speed,
Not as a Nymph, but for a Reed.

Although in this poem the implausibility of the reasoning is patent, the author employing no sleight of hand to obscure the illogicalities, there does exist one similarity to Donne's *Flea* – that neither poem permits the reader to pause or ponder. We are allowed just sufficient time to perceive the anomaly before being moved swiftly on to a new point. The evidence from the rape scenes is thus immediately dropped, and we enter what seems to be no more than a laudatory description of the pleasures of the garden, until we suddenly apprehend the erotic quality of the imagery. Again, although now from a different angle, the speaker adopts the pretence of suggesting how unnecessary are mortal women when the garden can provide delights similar to, or outclassing, those offered by a female:

> What wond'rous Life in this I lead!
> Ripe Apples drop about my head;
> The Luscious Clusters of the Vine
> Upon my Mouth do crush their Wine;
> The Nectaren, and curious Peach,
> Into my hands themselves do reach;
> Stumbling on Melons, as I pass,
> Insnar'd with Flow'rs, I fall on Grass.

Marvell's supposed claim for the superfluity of women is, we realize, only a pose, for even in the period between his speaker's amorous encounters, after he has run his passion's heat and is enjoying an intermission, his imagery is redolent of the joys of lovemaking. One may assume that the speaker would not really prefer to confine his lovemaking to fondling a peach or caressing a melon.

At this point, the poem moves into its serious phase, the passage that has so intrigued critics, and we should recall how often the mingling of humour and seriousness occurs in metaphysical poetry, the humour neither detracting from nor being cancelled out by the more solemn passages.[110] The philosophical sources of these stanzas need not concern us, as our topic here is humour. It is sufficient to note their beauty, their appreciation of the inspiration the garden provides in that interval of peace and quiet, encouraging the imagination to roam, to dream of thoughts immortal, and thereby to prepare for the longer flight beyond the grave:

> Meanwhile the Mind, from pleasure less,
> Withdraws into its happiness:
> The Mind, that Ocean where each kind
> Does straight its own resemblance find;
> Yet it creates, transcending these,

Far other Worlds, and other Seas;
Annihilating all that's made
To a green Thought in a green Shade.

Here at the Fountains sliding foot,
Or at some Fruit-trees mossy root,
Casting the Bodies Vest aside,
My Soul into the boughs does glide:
There like a Bird it sits, and sings,
Then whets, and combs its silver Wings;
And, till prepar'd for longer flight,
Waves in its Plumes the various Light.

To end the poem on that serious note would cast a retrospective shadow over the light-heartedness of the previous stanzas. The speaker's thoughts therefore return whimsically to the garden itself, picking up the earlier hints of its Edenic qualities. Once again, in much the same way as he had inverted the import of the classical rape scenes, Marvell puckishly inverts the import of the story of Eden. Where the scriptural account had been unequivocal in presenting the creation of Eve as an act of kindness on God's part, granting Adam a mate through compassion for his loneliness, Marvell amusingly extracts from the account a meaning opposite to the norm while yet remaining faithful to the text itself, altering only its implications. The scriptural verse reads:

Also the Lord God said, It is not good that man should be alone: I will make him a help meet for him.

Deliberately misreading the verse, the speaker interprets 'It is not good …' to mean that it was not good for God, in his supposed jealousy of man's happiness, to allow him to continue enjoying the pleasures of solitude. And playing on the antiquated form of 'help-mate', the speaker assumes that the female forced upon him was indeed 'meet' or qualified to spoil his joys:

Such was that happy Garden-state,
While Man there walk'd without a Mate:
After a Place so pure, and sweet,
What other Help could yet be meet!

But 'twas beyond a Mortal's share
To wander solitary there:
Two Paradises 'twere in one
To live in Paradise alone.[111]

Rosalie Colie, with the gravity usual among critics of this poem, wrote of this delightful stanza: 'only monastic man could have been perfect, and when he split into another, shared his bone and being with another, his singularity became doubleness'. She saw no hint of humour.

The poem concludes with what appears to be a simple tribute to the parterre, with its clipped hedges and geometrically planned flower beds such as were common before the advent of Capability Brown and the landscape gardens of the eighteenth-century *jardin anglais*. But the final stanza is more subtle than it appears. It focuses upon a sundial, consisting of a column whose shadow falls successively upon the patches of variegated flowers encircling it:

How well the skilful Gardner drew
Of flow'rs and herbes this Dial new;
Where from above the milder Sun
Does through a fragrant Zodiack run;
And, as it works, th'industrious Bee
Computes its time as well as we.
How could such sweet and wholsome hours
Be reckon'd but with herbs and flow'rs!

Hidden within that description is a return, full-circle, to the poem's opening stanza. The 'milder' sun, its rays partly blocked by the leafy branches, reminds us of the generous shade offered by the garden in contrast to the 'narrow-verged shade' that the wreaths provide for perspiring victors. Mention of the industrious bee, however, modifies that earlier pose. For the bee reminds the speaker that energetic activity is, after all, intrinsic to the natural scene too, that within the seemingly relaxed aura of the garden there exists the same devotion to labour as animates the industrious scholars, soldiers and athletes. The final stanza, therefore, adjusts the previous argument, retrospectively admitting the validity of such efforts, but claiming at the same time the right, during intervals between such activity, to enjoy the quiet pleasures of a fragrant, verdurous garden and the relaxation that it offers.

It remains for us to suggest what contemporary tradition was being targeted in this poem of wit. Marvell, we have noted, was deeply involved in both the religious and the political events of his day, with a reputation as a powerful satirist and as a Parliamentarian respected for the seriousness and dedication with which he performed his duties. An anonymous poem of 1678 singled him out as 'this island's watchful sentinel', and he was frequently cited in the following century as a model of dedication to the causes he supported.[112] In real life, therefore, he was as industrious as any of the athletes and warriors his poem had derided, and he was himself a practitioner of poetry whose laurel wreaths he had dismissed as nugatory in the opening stanza. Moreover, there were other elements in his character and setting associating him with industriousness. As a Puritan, he subscribed to the work ethic that his sect had inaugurated, and to that sect's belief that even secular activities must be regarded as part of God's work, as 'vocations' requiring devoted effort. Marvell served for a time as personal assistant to Milton when the latter was Latin Secretary for foreign affairs under Cromwell. Apart from working closely with Milton in these administrative tasks, Marvell was an admirer of his poetry, describing *Paradise Lost* in one of his own poems as the work of a 'mighty Poet' who soared above human flight.[113] He would not, therefore, have been unaware of the lines in Milton's *Lycidas* describing the poet's dedication to his sacred task and his hope, despite the warnings of Christianity against pride and the pursuit of renown, that he would receive the 'fair guerdon' or laurel wreath in recognition of his efforts:

Fame is the spur that the clear spirit doth raise
(That last infirmity of Noble mind)
To scorn delights, and live laborious days:

Viewed in that context, *The Garden* emerges as only a momentary or passing protest against the pressures of his time, against the injunction to 'scorn delights and live laborious days'. Whimsically, Marvell employs humour to justify his own moments of relaxation, conjuring up a web of patently untenable theses, each savoured for its ingenuity. Ostensibly, he may dismiss dedication to noble aspirations, but inherent in the argument, not least in its obvious 'misreading' of both scriptural and classical tales and the modification offered in the final stanza, is the admission that his protest is only a game, that in his pretended disdain for women and, even more so, in his assumed scorn for the workaholics of this world, he is only teasing. He concludes, therefore, on a note of reconciliation, granting through his reference to the bee the validity of diligence and industry, but at the same time affirming his right to enjoy occasional retreats into the refreshments offered by the garden. His disparagement of sedulous activity had thus emanated from a passing mood. The process employed to express that passing mood is one of enchanting humour, challenging only temporarily the stern Puritan work ethic to which he was committed.

CHAPTER FOUR

THE RESTORATION AND EIGHTEENTH CENTURY

In satire, there are indeed moments of humour, satire at times merging into comedy. But the kind of satire that predominated in the late seventeenth and early eighteenth centuries was usually of the harsh Juvenal type. Even there comedy could enter, as in the witty opening to Dryden's *Absalom and Achitophel* at which we glanced earlier, but those moments are rare. The drollery in that passage functioned in much the same way as Marvell's manipulation of the biblical account of Eve's creation, a tongue-in-cheek assertion of what both the speaker and the reader knew to be untrue. Provocatively, Dryden selects as the precedent for sanctioning Charles II's promiscuity the very Bible that was so strongly opposed to such behaviour, pretending that the scriptures would have fully approved of the king's libertinism had its tolerant attitude not been negated by those later lawmakers who had instituted monogamy:

> In pious times, ere priestcraft did begin,
> Before polygamy was made a sin;
> When man on many multiplied his kind,
> Ere one to one was cursedly confined;
> When nature prompted, and no law denied,
> Promiscuous use of concubine and bride;
> Then Israel's monarch after heaven's own heart,
> His vigorous warmth did variously impart
> To wives and slaves; and, wide as his command,
> Scattered his Maker's image through the land.

The Old Testament did, of course, permit polygamy, but, as Dryden's readers well knew, it sternly restricted sexual intercourse to those wives or concubines to whom the polygamist was formally married. King David may have imparted his 'vigorous warmth' to numerous females, scattering his Maker's image through the land,[114] but, with the sole exception of the adulterous affair with Bathsheba for which he was harshly punished, his seed was imparted only to his legal consorts. Charles, in contrast, was unashamedly dissolute, consorting with other men's wives and publicly flaunting as his acknowledged mistresses such married women as the Duchess of Cleveland and the Duchess of Portsmouth, in the course of which promiscuity he imperturbably sired and acknowleded at least 14 illegitimate children. Society's continued acceptance of scriptural polygamy would have legitimized neither his liaisons nor his children. Once again, the humour relies upon the recognition by both reader and author that the scriptural text is being adroitly manipulated to suit the writer's political purpose, the result being an implied burlesquing of the Bible itself. By complaining that his generation had been 'cursedly confined' by the restrictions of monogamy, Dryden, moreover, manoeuvres the reader into experiencing with him, as in the salacious-joke syndrome, a sense of conspiratorial rebellion against the stifling morality imposed by society.

Such are the rarer instances of humour in the intellectual satire of the day. However, the moment the light-hearted wit is replaced by cruel lampooning, the potentiality for laughter ends. We may admire the forcefulness of caricature, the exposure of the victims' weaknesses, and the effectiveness of the language, but the viciousness prompting the satire removes it from the category of the comic. And since I have excluded such satire from our investigation, I should add a necessary distinction, that although Horace entitled a collection of his charmingly urbane poems *Satires*, they are not satires in our sense of the term. In the introduction to the collection he advocated tolerance of human failings and, indeed, firmly rejected any charge that he aimed to injure the subjects of his poems:

Why do you hurl this slander at me? ... Whoever backbites an absent friend, defends him not from another's accusation, who seeks to draw forth laughter around and be reputed a wit, who can invent stories about what he has seen, and can violate confidence, such a man is black of heart—shun him!

It was Juvenal's fierce anger at what he saw as human deficiencies that functioned as the model for literary satire. Thus, while Dryden's initial comparison of Charles II to King David does amuse, the moment he becomes acidulous, as in his vicious attack upon the Earl of Shaftesbury, there is room only for a sardonic smile, not laughter:

Of these the false Achitophel was first;
A name to all succeeding ages curst:
For close designs, and crooked counsels fit;
Sagacious, bold, and turbulent of wit;
Restless, unfixed in principles and place;
In power unpleased, impatient of disgrace;
A fiery soul, which, working out its way,
Fretted the pigmy-body to decay.[115]

As Addison was to complain, 'There is nothing that more betrays a base, ungenerous Spirit than the giving of secret Stabs to a Man's Reputation. Lampoons and Satyrs, that are written with Wit and Spirit, are like poisoned Darts, which not only inflict a Wound, but make it incurable.'[116] True comedy is to be found during the Restoration not in its satiric verse but upon the stage, where the barbs, less personal in aim, are alleviated by the comic situation and the witty dialogue. It is to that we should turn.

a) Restoration Comedy

Drama underwent a remarkable bifurcation during the period of the Restoration. In all genres ranging from tragic to comic, Elizabethan and Jacobean drama had shared essentially the same ideals – courage, constancy in love, honour and fulfilment of duty – from *The Comedy of Errors*, through *Twelfth Night* and *Othello*, and on to *The Duchess of Malfi*. The melancholy Jacques of *As You Like It* may scoff at the lover and the soldier but the overall message of the play confirmed those more positive notions and, in even the most chilling of Jacobean drama, such as *The Revenger's Tragedy*, the lechers and seducers were made to pay for their crimes. But a split occurred in the latter part of the seventeenth century. On the one hand, Restoration heroic drama inflated the noble tradition, its heroes constantly eulogizing as well as performing bravery, patriotism, devotion to duty and undying love. Nathaniel Lee could thus assure the Duchess of Pembroke in dedicating to her his *Theodosius* that '… your Grace shall never see a Play of mine that shall give

THE COMIC MODE IN ENGLISH LITERATURE

offence to Modesty and Virtue'. On the other hand, the comedy of the era scornfully rejected the moral codes embedded in heroic drama, dismissing them as absurd, impractical and unjustified. A lady in one of Shadwell's comedies, instead of feeling complimented, ridicules her rhapsodizing lover for declaring his eternal devotion to her, dismissing his pledge with the contemptuous comment: 'What foolish Fustian's this? You talk like an Heroic Poet.'[117]

As Ann Righter has noted, a peculiar transposition occurred on the stage of that time. The appeals to virtue and honour emanating from the noble figures in the heroic drama are in the comedies assigned to the hypocrites, to the tiresome past mistresses, or to the fops, while the cynical sentiments of Dorimant, Harriet, Freeman and other admired members of the inner circle of Restoration comedy are, in the heroic drama, assigned to the villains.[118] Lysimachus in Nathaniel Lee's *The Rival Queens* swears of his beloved Parisatis: 'I shall never quit so brave a prize / While I can draw a bow or lift a sword' and he remains true to his oath, while Etherege's Dorimant, charged by a discarded mistress with having been false to his promises, to the oaths, protestations, and vows sworn by him during their affair, soberly responds: 'What we swear at such a time may be a certain proof of present passion, but to say truth, in Love there is no security to be given for the future.'[119] Righter offers no explanation for the bifurcation of the genres, the glaring contrast in the principles espoused by the two dramatic forms, but I believe there is one.

The idea of the didactic value of literature had a long history. Sir Philip Sidney, in attempting to refute Plato's exclusion of literature from his ideal republic, argued that even comedy had a moral purpose, namely to ridicule 'the common errors of our life', to hold them up to scorn and thereby discourage their practice.[120] Ben Jonson, a theoretician as well as a dramatist, made the same point both forcefully and explicitly, insisting within his critical essays on the moral responsibilities of all authors, including the writers of comedy. In his Preface to *Volpone*, after demanding that all literary works should have the loftiest of aims, he focused primarily on comedy itself, its purpose being, he claimed, '... to informe yong-men to all good disciplines, inflame growne-men to all great vertues, keepe old-men in their best and supreme state, or as they decline to childhood, recouer them to their first strength' – in brief, comedy was to be 'a teacher of things diuine'.[121] The libertine hero of Restoration comedy not only contradicted that moral function but seemed impervious to distinctions between good and evil, the only unforgiveable crime being lack of wit.

The source of the change would seem to be located in the new concern with categorization and definition that was discussed earlier, the process instituted at the time of the Royal Society. If its primary purpose had been to improve accuracy in scientific experiment, the concept was applied very broadly in that era, creating, I would argue, the split between the dramatic genres. In a period modelling itself on Augustan Rome, Horace's definition of literature had become axiomatic, the line most often quoted in that generation, namely his statement that all writers *aut prodesse volunt aut delectare poetae*. By claiming that poets (again referring to all creative writers) aim 'either to instruct or to delight' he had probably meant no more than that at times literature was instructive, like his own *Ars Poetica* where that statement occurs, while at other times, as in his *Odes*, it was intended simply to be pleasurable. As he added in the following line – '*aut simul et iucunda et idonea dicere vitae*' – there also existed a third possibility, when both aims, the enjoyable and the useful, could be fulfilled simultaneously.

However, the new insistence upon separation into distinct categories that formed the basis of the new science led to the assumption that the alternative offered in the earlier line indicated the existence of two separate genres with a different purpose for each – that serious literature bore the task of instructing, while comedy's function was simply to amuse, that new assumption profoundly affecting the genres of the time. For the serious stage, therefore, there emerged an essentially new type of play with a high moral tone, on the assumption that its heroes should serve as ethical examples. The stern advocacy of morality implicit in that aim created a genre no longer belonging within the definition of tragedy; for its heroes were so virtuous as generally to be free from the flaw or blemish that Aristotle required, their pious pursuit of noble ideals, moreover, generally absolving them from having to die at the conclusion. Fortifying the educative function of heroic drama was its incorporation of a new principle articulated by Dryden's friend, Thomas Rymer, the concept of 'poetic justice' which required in serious literature, since it was to serve as a behavioural model, an invariable rewarding of the good characters and punishment of the villains. He claimed '... that a *Poet* must of necessity see *justice* exactly administered if he intended to please'.[122] Apart from its effect upon the heroic drama, which indeed followed that rule closely, there arose the strange practice of rewriting Shakespeare's plays in a Procrustean attempt to fit them to the new standard. Hence Nahum Tate's notorious 'improvement' of *King Lear*, in which Cordelia, who had committed no sin, must be allowed to survive at the conclusion married to Edgar; and, since by Tate's standards Lear had possessed the right as both monarch and father to divide his kingdom as he wished and had therefore been guiltless, he too was to be rewarded by being restored to the throne. Sometimes the change was more subtle but prompted by the same desire. Enobarbus, the choric figure in Shakespeare's *Antony and Cleopatra*, had been a wonderfully inconsistent character reflecting the complexity of the play itself as he swung audience sympathy back and forth, at one moment scorning Cleopatra's wiles when she appears in the ascendancy, and at the next, when she seems at a nadir, expressing in the barge speech his breathless admiration of her magnificence. In Dryden's version of that play, *All for Love*, he is, significantly, replaced by a consistently didactic choric figure, Ventidius, forever chiding Antony for surrendering to passion, urging him to follow reason and duty, and thus imposing upon the play a clearly defined and unchanging ethical stance.

The obverse of that change concerns us here, the implications derived from the second half of Horace's dictum. The statement that comedy aims to delight offered, in itself, nothing new. The innovation in this period's interpretation of the line lay in the implicit contrast that, if it was the task of tragedy or heroic drama to provide moral instruction, comedy was exempt from that purpose. Writers of Restoration comedy could therefore feel disburdened of ethical considerations. Dryden doubted accordingly whether 'instruction could be any part of [comedy's] employment'; and, if he conceded elsewhere that it did teach one useful lesson, to make folly ludicrous – 'the shame of that laughter teaches us to amend what is ridiculous in our manners' – he left unspecified the nature of the folly to be ridiculed.[123] The mockery could therefore be levelled, as it was so often in Restoration comedy, at the folly of conforming to an outdated morality.

An attempt has, in fact, been made to justify Restoration comedy on ethical grounds, citing incidents in which such plays seem to support moral behaviour, the author of that attempt, Ben Ross Schneider, stating at one point that 'hedonism never has the final say in Restoration comedy'.[124] But to take that viewpoint is to twist the comedies out of shape. The most famous scene in Wycherley's *The Country Wife* was the adoption of the term 'china' as an approved cypher, a code word for the sexual licence sanctioned by the Wits and their paramours. The prologue defines clearly enough the libertine ambience not only of this play but of the theatre at large:

> We set no guards upon our tiring-room,
> But when with flying colours there you come,
> We patiently, you see, give up to you
> Our poets, virgins, nay, our matrons, too.[125]

Moreover, Horner does have the final say in that play, glorying in the success of his ruse, his pretence of impotence in order to seduce other men's wives, and contrasting it with the stupidity of those who follow convention:

> Vain fops but court and dress, and keep a pother,
> To pass for women's men with one another;
> But he who aims by woman to be prized,
> First by the men, you see, must be despised.

It was this Restoration concept of the non-didactic, non-moralistic function of comedy that opened the way for the creation of the rake hero.

That non-moralist approach affected directly the wit that formed the predominant source of laughter in these plays. But, in analysing the peculiar sense in which that term was used during this period, it is essential to distinguish it from the wit of the preceding generation, although the same term has traditionally been applied to both forms. The wit of the metaphysical poets was rarely humorous. It was intended to surprise, even to shock readers out of their normal assumptions into a new apprehension, usually validating the spiritual over the physical. Marvell, in a more serious mood than he displayed in the poem we examined earlier, presented in dialogue form the soul's bitter complaint against the body:

> O, who shall, from this Dungeon, raise
> A soul inslav'd so many wayes?
> With bolts of Bones, that fetter'd stands

In Feet; and manacled in Hands;
Here blinded with an Eye; and there
Deaf with the drumming of an Ear.[126]

In a series of brilliant alliterative images, he overturns normal
conceptions, presenting the body not as an instrument to action
but as its obstacle, blocking the way to spiritual fulfilment. Each
corporeal member has its function reversed. The physical eye blinds
the viewer to heavenly visions, the hands, instead of ministering
to their owner, imprison him in the tactile world, and the eardrum
drowns out the sounds of celestial voices. It is the intellectual
surprise implicit in 'blinded with an Eye' that endows the poem with
its power.

The wit of Restoration comedy is, in contrast, rational, unemo-
tional and limited not merely to this world but to the conventions of
contemporary urban society. As Fujimura was the first to observe,[127]
the principles of the new comedy relied primarily on the philosophy
of Thomas Hobbes, the most influential thinker of his time. As a
rationalist scorning religious belief, he defined wit as consisting of
two elements – Fancy, which perceives similarities in things apparently unalike, and Judgement, which perceives differences in things
apparently alike. In that distinction, Fancy is the rejected instrument
of the metaphysical poets, the conceit joining the apparently unalike,
while Judgement marks the new ideal. The underlying requirement
in wit, therefore, becomes discrimination, with its affinity to the
current separation of ideas and objects into their clearly demarked
categories. The True Wit was marked out by his ability to define
accurately those elements on the borderline of such categories,
elements that might appear to belong to one group but needed to
be assigned more accurately to another. It was thus an intellectual
quality, whose purpose was not to establish some vibrant paradox
but to attain to a rational compartmentalizing of human ideas and
activities. Since Hobbes placed such stress on similarities and dissim-
ilarities, it is not surprising that much of the wit in these comedies
depends upon the use of simile, with the degree of the appropri-
ateness of such similes serving to distinguish the True Wit from the
False. Dorimant's response to the charge of inconstancy exemplifies
such use of simile at its best, as he cynically but pertinently invokes
it to justify his libertinism:

Mrs. Loveit: Is this the constancy you vowed?
Dorimant: Constancy at my years? 'Tis not a virtue in season; you might as well expect the fruit the autumn ripens i'the spring.
Mrs. Loveit: Monstrous principle!
Dorimant: Youth has a long journey to go, madam; should I have set up my rest at the first inn I lodg'd at, I should never have arrived at the happiness I now enjoy (2:1).

By surprisingly effective analogies, he has succeeded in subverting traditional morality. The inverse in these plays is represented by the False Wits, as in the scintillating exchange between Millimant and Witwoud in *The Way of the World*, where Witwoud draws parallels lacking the social pertinence and subtlety of her own well-chosen similes:

Mrs. Millamant: Oh, I have denied myself airs to-day. I have walked as fast through the crowd –
Witwoud: As a favorite just disgraced, and with as few followers.
Mrs. Millamant: Dear Mr. Witwoud, truce with your similitudes; for I'm as sick of 'em –
Witwoud: As a physician of a good air. – I cannot help it, madam, though 'tis against myself.
Mrs. Millamant: Yet again! Mincing, stand between me and his wit.
Witwoud: Do, Mrs. Mincing, like a screen before a great fire. – I confess I do blaze to-day; I am too bright.
Mrs. Fainall: But, dear Millamant, why were you so long?
Mrs. Millamant: Long! Lord, have I not made violent haste? I have asked every living thing I met for you; I have inquired after you as after a new fashion.
Witwoud: Madam, truce with your similitudes. – No, you met her husband, and did not ask him for her.
Mrs. Millamant: By your leave, Witwoud, that were like inquiring after an old fashion, to ask a husband for his wife (2:1).

The humour provided by the Witwouds, Witlesses and Foplings in these plays – and it is they who, in the best performances, evoke gales of laughter from audiences[128] – is a classic instance of the pattern we have been investigating, the deflating of pretentiousness as these fops vaingloriously imagine that they have grasped the new concept of wit or the latest innovations of fashionable dress but in fact have hopelessly misconceived them. One notes how they are always inordinately proud of their supposed intellectual dexterity, Witwoud, in the above excerpt, asking Mincing to stand between him and Millamant 'like a screen before a great fire – I confess I do blaze today', and are hence fully deserving of the derision they receive at the hands of the Truewits.

But their lack of sophisticated discrimination expresses itself in a further way, their inability to see through disguise or, to use Hobbes' phrase, to distinguish between the apparently similar. In Wycherley's *The Country Wife*, Sparkish is easily fooled by the disguised parson, while Horner, a Truewit, sees instantly that Margery has been forced by her husband to dress as a man in order to prevent her attracting paramours, and takes advantage of the situation, affectionately embracing her as Pinchwife looks on, helpless to interfere. Pinchwife, incidentally, is well within the *senex* tradition, having married a much younger wife in order (as he admits) to ensure the satisfying of his sexual needs for a longer period, as well as to save himself the cost of a mistress. And he conforms to that pattern also by literally locking her up, and forcing her to dress as a man, certain, as in the earlier versions of that tradition, that his vigilance will protect him, while yet being eventually tricked into permitting Horner to kiss and fondle her in his presence.

There is, however, one vital difference in the emergence of the *senex* theme in this play, a contrast with the way comedy had emerged in previous eras – the absence of any sense of springtime fertility due to overcome winter's barrenness. Horner's pretence of impotence arises neither from love nor from any desire to produce offspring; it is prompted by a desire to satisfy his sexual appetite coupled with the sheer pleasure of duping husbands. In this, he reflects Hobbes' view that all humans are driven by 'a perpetuall and restlesse desire of power after power, that ceaseth onely in death'.[129] The play does indeed end in a ritual dance, as did so many of the earlier 'fertility' comedies, but it consists, perversely, of a Dance of the Cuckolds led by the unfortunate Pinchwife.

The libertine setting also accounts for the charm of Margery Pinchwife, naively unaware of the new philosophy, gradually inducted into it in the course of the play, learning to trick her husband and, at the conclusion, coming hilariously close to upsetting the entire scheme. But the libertinism does not account for certain elements that tend to be underplayed or ignored in analyses of these plays, namely the subdued theme that affirms marriage despite the overt ridicule accorded to the marital state. It did not contradict the licentiousness but acknowledged that there was a sliver of hope in the idea of conjugal bliss so frequently derided on the stage.

In Wycherley's play, a very large part of the action concerns not the seduction of wives but Harcourt's pursuit of Alithea and his attempts, also by ingenious tricks, to obtain not only her love but, in contrast to the general thrust of the play, her hand in marriage. The fact that Wycherley assigned the name Alithea ('Truth') to one so obviously rejecting the Hobbesian philosophy and so opposed to the general libertinism of the play suggests that the author himself did not fully subscribe to the new mode of thinking. Alithea, although aware of the profligacy surrounding her, is a true person of honour.[130] Although it takes her a little time to discover the shallowness of Sparkish to whom she is engaged, inconstancy is anathema to her and she insists on remaining faithful to him until his behaviour, especially his inadvertent admission that he is marrying her only for her money, makes further fidelity impossible. Harcourt too, although a Truewit and in the opening of the play seemingly one of the rakes, as contemptuous in his exploitation of women as his peers, is entirely sincere in his love of Alithea and in his determination to marry her despite the scorn that these plays pour on wedlock. One suspects therefore, not only from this play, that for all the derision and scorn towards marriage the underlying impulse of these dramatists, whether or not they were conscious of it, was the libertine's search among all these promiscuous and hypocritical females for the sole honest and pure woman whom they could genuinely admire and love.

Recognition of that sub-theme opens up a somewhat different conception of the way the comedy functions. Some critics, in analysing Etherege's *The Man of Mode*, have wondered at Dorimant's strange penitence at the end.[131] But it needs to be seen, paralleling Harcourt's, as the fulfilment of his readiness, indeed his eagerness to love if only he can find a worthy, clever and beautiful woman who will, to quote Harriet, never act 'against the rules of decency and honour'. The purpose of Harcourt and Dorimant may not have been fertility – there are no celebrations of nuptial promise in these plays such as the blessings by Oberon that end *A Midsummer Night's*

Dream – but there is approval of true marriage, that theme forming a strong undercurrent both here and in other supposedly libertine comedies of the time.

That distinction is particularly relevant to the 'proviso' scene in Congreve's *The Way of the World*. The series of conditions that Mirabell and Millamant lay down before their agreement to wed has been repeatedly interpreted as a Hobbesian contract, each side stating the terms whose acceptance they insist upon before considering wedlock, and each attempting to outbid the other. Kathleen Lynch writes that Mirabell finds Miramant's 'first terms reasonable enough but her later "bill of fare" somewhat alarming', although they eventually achieve a graceful 'capitulation'; and Alexander Leggatt similarly interprets the scene as a battle in which Millamant, faced with the dreadful alternative of spinsterhood, reluctantly surrenders – a view that ignores her sense of superiority throughout, as in her final decision: 'Well, you ridiculous thing you, I'll have you …'[132] In the accepted critical view, therefore, they are essentially combatants, making quite sure that their requirements will be met before entering into a treaty of marriage. But the humour is surely more subtle and more congenial; for the provisos are aimed not at each other. Those conditions represent in play form their joint condemnation of the defects in the marriages of convenience common among their peers, forms of hypocritical behaviour that these two by mutual agreement scorn to adopt. Under the guise of a contract, their exchange constitutes an amusing parody of those husband–wife relations in the Restoration that they abhor. Each pretends to insist upon what both know that they, with their greater sensitivity and affection, will never need to demand from each other. The tone of playfulness is, indeed, set in the opening exchange:

> *Millamant*: Ah, I'll never marry, unless I am first made sure of my will and pleasure.
> *Mirabell*: Would you have 'em both before marriage? Or will you be contented with the first now, and stay for the other till after grace?
> *Millamant*: Ah, don't be impertinent … And d'ye hear, I won't be called names after I'm married; positively I won't be called names.
> *Mirabell*: Names?
> *Millamant*: Ay, as wife, spouse, my dear, joy, jewel, love, sweetheart, and the rest of that nauseous cant, in which men and

their wives are so fulsomely familiar – I shall never bear that. Good Mirabell, don't let us be familiar or fond, nor kiss before folks, like my Lady Fadler and Sir Francis; nor go to Hyde Park together the first Sunday in a new chariot, to provoke eyes and whispers, and then never be seen there together again, as if we were proud of one another the first week, and ashamed of one another ever after (4:1).

How far they are really agreed – that behind this ostensible series of demands there is already genuine love and mutual respect – may be perceived in one of Mirabell's conditions before she 'dwindles' into a wife and he be 'enlarged' into a husband, '... that you continue to like your own face as long as I shall; and while it passes current with me, that you endeavour not to new-coin it'.

Here, in this true marriage of minds, the traditional fertility theme does reappear, though veiled as a joke:

> *Mirabell*: Item: when you shall be breeding –
> *Millamant*: Ah! name it not.
> *Mirabell*: Which may be presumed on our endeavours –

And this play does conclude with a dance, this time not in honour of cuckolds but in honour of marriage, Sir Wilfull suggesting it somewhat enviously so that 'we who are not lovers may have some other employment besides looking on'.

Our constant reversion to the pattern of humour may seem a little tiresome, but as in music where there is only a limited number of notes in the scale and yet an infinite number of variations, combinations and sequences, so here the basic pattern remains the same but is applied in a fascinating variety of ways. For the drama of this period has its own distinctiveness. The puncturing of the unjustified conceit of the Witwouds and Witlesses follows the usual form, but the fact that it is expressed in terms of the specific concept of wit prevalent at that time, namely the deploring of false similitudes and of misconceived claims to fashion, lends it an originality and spice that it would not otherwise possess. The variety with which the principle can be applied is illustrated by Mirabell himself, who, although by no means a False Wit, must himself undergo the process of deflation.

Like Shakespeare's Benedick, he seems originally to have been firmly opposed to marriage, as much of a rake as his peers, admitting with no sense of guilt that he had passed off a previous mistress to another man in order to 'fix a father's name' on the child with which she is pregnant. His self-assurance seems unassailable. But a change has begun to occur. He has, of course, already determined to marry Millamant for her fortune, the reason that Fainall and most other Restoration rakes reluctantly enter into wedlock – hence Mirabell's already existent plan to trick the aunt into granting him Millamant's 'moiety' of a dowry. But beneath that seeming cynicism we are allowed to perceive his growing admiration and affection for her, and to watch how his resistance to and dislike of marriage, so confidently acknowledged in the exchange with Mrs Fainall, is gradually overcome by the one woman who knows how to handle him and who, instead of pleading for his love, constantly laughs at him – a practice that breaks down his defences and the dictates of his reason:

> *Mirabell*: You are merry, madam, but I would persuade you for a moment to be serious.
> *Millamant*: What, with that face? No, if you keep your countenance, 'tis impossible I should hold mine … [*Exit*].
> *Mirabell*: I have something more – Gone! – Think of you? To think of a whirlwind, though 'twere in a whirlwind, were a case of more steady contemplation – a very tranquillity of mind and mansion. A fellow that lives in a windmill, has not a more whimsical dwelling than the heart of a man that is lodged in a woman … To know this, and yet continue to be in love, is to be made wise from the dictates of reason, and yet persevere to play the fool by the force of instinct (2:1).

To return to the music analogy and the infinite variations available, the situation here is indeed close to that of Beatrice and Benedick as we watch Mirabell's opposition to marriage except in terms of financial advancement gradually erode; but the contrasting settings supply the originality. In *Much Ado*, marriage is socially approved, even Don Pedro, the bachelor choric figure, undertaking to plead Claudio's case with the fair Hero, charging Benedick with being 'an obstinate heretic' in his refusal to wed and, when assuring Beatrice that he will find her a husband, offering himself as a candidate. In that setting of conjugal delight, Beatrice and Benedick form exceptions to the norm, needing to be nudged and tricked by their peers into achieving connubial bliss. Contrastedly, almost all characters in Congreve's play are either opposed to marriage or reluctantly accept the yoke as the sole means of obtaining a fortune, while Mirabell and Millamant must defy the norm in order to find their way to a truly satisfying form of matrimony. In both instances, the humour arises from our pleasure in watching the hero gradually succumb, as his arrogant opposition to wedlock is sapped, but the contrasting social settings create the freshness so necessary to comedy, producing in each a humorous situation suited to contemporary norms.

b) Pope, *The Rape of the Lock*

Pope's mock epic, his attempt to reconcile two leading Catholic families after Lord Petre's misguided but well-intentioned theft of a lock of Arabella Fermor's hair, offers a splendid example of the use of ridicule to deflate pomposity, the self-importance of people standing on their dignity. However, if there were to be any hope of reconciling the families, it was essential for the poet to temper the ridicule. He took care to do so, but the underlying aim of puncturing pride remains the motive force of the work.

The literary technique implicit in mock epic so obviously conforms to the idea of pricking a balloon that that aspect requires only minimal comment before we focus on more specific elements. The epic genre was especially vulnerable to deflation. Categorized the noblest of literary forms, it was, like the Bible, committed to the loftiest of aims, so lofty that it traditionally opened with an invocation to the Muse in which the poet requests assistance in fulfilling so sublime a task. Its avowed purpose was to elevate historic events above human level, its leading characters being heroes in the Greek sense of the term, either the offspring of a union between a god and a mortal, or a mortal under the aegis of a divine power. Milton's *Paradise Lost*, the work most obviously in Pope's mind during the writing of this poem, had blended the classical with the biblical to create an epic even more ambitious than those of Homer and Virgil, its scriptural theme requiring it, as he informs us at the opening, to '… soar / Above th' Aonian Mount, while it pursues / Things unattempted yet in Prose or Rhime'. There could be no loftier aim than that, and the delight in reading *The Rape of the Lock* derives in large part from the relief it offers from the solemnity and (dare one say) the pretentiousness of the epic form itself.

The process of epic deflation and its relationship to the established forms is especially evidenced in an apparently minor scene in Pope's poem. Milton, faced with the daunting problem of describing, in terms comprehensible to human readers, the cosmic War in Heaven, the celestial battle between the loyal and the rebel angels which Christianity believed had actually taken place, had portrayed with the utmost gravity the moment when Michael, wielding the sword of God, had sheared through Satan's right side, leaving him in agony.[133] As Milton well knew, angels, even when reprobate, are by their nature immortal and hence bodily inviolate, and he therefore explains somewhat cumbersomely:

> so sore
> The griding sword with discontinuous wound
> Pass'd through him, but th' Ethereal substance clos'd
> Not long divisible, and from the gash
> A stream of Nectarous humor issuing flow'd
> Sanguin, such as Celestial Spirits may bleed ... (6:328–33)

A heavenly fluid from within, he solemnly informs us, repairs and heals the torn flesh of Satan, allowing him to return to battle. In Pope's poem, one of the Sylphs, attempting to protect Belinda's lock of hair from the scissors wielded by the Baron, finds itself in a similar predicament:

> Ev'n then, before the fatal engine clos'd,
> A wretched Sylph too fondly interpos'd;
> Fate urg'd the shears, and cut the Sylph in twain,
> (But airy substance soon unites again) ... (3:149–52)[134]

to which Pope added the mischievous footnote: 'See Milton, Book 6'. In much the same way, the mighty battle in heaven reappears here, but diminished to a card game in which an unconquerable lord, the equivalent of an Ace, sweeps the board and marches off 'a Victor from the verdant field', leaving behind, that is, the green baise that covers the card table.

It should be noted, however, that the use of the mock epic in this period had deeper roots than merely serving as a device for Pope's parody, deriving its force from a contemporary shift in sensibility; for rejection of the passionate religious beliefs and sectarianism

of the previous decades against which the Restoration and eighteenth century were rebelling led to the view, as Dryden's *Absalom
and Achitophel* had shown, that even the Bible could be treated as
a form of myth, an authority not to be taken too seriously. David
Garrick, when asked why actors in the eighteenth century moved
their audiences so much more effectively than clergymen speaking
from the pulpit, replied neatly (and, for that period, with considerable justification) that actors deliver their fictions with the warmth
and energy of truth, while clergymen '... pronounce the most
solemn truths with as much coldness and languor as if they were the
most trivial fictions'.[135] Preachers were not expected to rouse their
congregations to enthusiastic devotions, as the Methodists would
do later, but to offer rational arguments for the decorous behaviour
of good Christians. The churches built at that time for London's
expanding population reflected that secularizing of religion. Nicholas
Hawksmoor's church, St George's at Bloomsbury, was graced with
a steeple that included such pagan elements as a pyramid and a
classical mausoleum, and was surmounted by a statue not, as one
would expect, of St George, but of King George. In that context,
the task assigned to Pope's sylphs represents, in whimsical form, a
secularized substitute for the traditional angels and archangels, their
task reduced to caring for Belinda's toilet ('These set the head, and
those divide the hair, / Some fold the sleeve, whilst others plait the
gown') and to defending her, however ineffectually, from the depre-
dation of admiring suitors.

The parodying of epic magnitude functions with remarkable
effectiveness, and if Arabella and Lord Petre failed to appreciate the
reduction of the supposedly offensive crime to its due proportions,
the fault was not Pope's. Initially, both Arabella and her suitor were
indeed amused, but Arabella later felt that her dignity had been
offended, apparently reacting to the few mild barbs it contained,
such as the one cited in our opening chapter.[136] She may also have
changed her view for an entirely extraneous reason when Lord
Petre, who was assumed in the poem to be her ardent swain, became
engaged to another, but the poem remains a delight for subsequent
readers.

With humour often adapting its form to suit each era, one notes
a further shift here, a contrast with the wit of Restoration drama.
Satire, following the Juvenal model and bitterly attacking the misdemeanours or literary failures of others, does not, I have suggested,

come within the category of humour, and Pope's *Dunciad*, fulmi-
nating against the supposed dullness of his fellow poet Theobald,
was indeed in that tradition. In *The Rape of the Lock*, however, Pope
is closer to the alternative Augustan model, Horace. His attitude
is urbane and detached, reflecting (as in the title of Addison and
Steele's journal) the stance of the amused spectator, watching from
the sidelines the entertaining antics of society without becoming
emotionally involved. The choice of the heroic couplet, the metrical
form most frequently employed during the first half of the century
with its balanced, end-stopped lines, was ideally suited to that
attitude. It encouraged, on the reader's part, an unhurried savouring
of the lines, an appreciation of the symmetry of ideas and words that
represented even-handed judgement.

  That balanced, unhurried reading forms a major source of the
poem's humour. Zeugmas, for example, require a pause for their
effect to be savoured, as in the comment that Queen Anne at
Hampton Court 'Doth sometimes counsel take – and sometimes *Tea*'
(3:8). The charm lies not merely in having two nouns, one serious,
one trivial, subordinated to a single verb, with the implication that
the queen regards those two activities as of equal importance. It
employs in addition a process very close to that of punning, the
word *take* having essentially different meanings in the two contexts
adduced – to 'take counsel' meaning not to receive advice but 'to
confer with an adviser', and to 'take tea' not 'to accept a cup' but to
participate in the afternoon ritual. Similarly, 'Or stain her honour or
her new brocade' apart from its pretended equivalence in the gravity
of the two events also involves a shift from the metaphorical use of
stain to the literal. The zeugma thus creates the kind of humour that
wordplay generally produces, an amused perception of the way that
language can be effectively and purposely manipulated.

  That slow savouring of the lines permits an additional form of wit,
whose identification requires a brief detour. In the study of classical
languages that formed so major a part of the school curriculum
in Pope's day, not only was the schoolboy required to translate
Latin verse into English but also to practise the reverse, to translate
passages of English poetry into Latin verse. Since Latin verse was
quantitative, not accentual, demanding scrupulous exactitude in
the sequence of long and short syllables, its composition demanded
considerable ingenuity. A trochaic word such as *pectus*, ending in
a short syllable, has that latter syllable lengthened if the following

word begins with a consonant. The result for a composer of Latin hexameters is a complicated process of juggling words to fit them, like parts of a jigsaw, into the prescribed pattern, avoiding forbidden juxtapositions in order to produce a metrically permissible line. To the immense relief of the struggling schoolboy, there appeared in 1691 (just at the time when Pope would have been learning to write Latin verse)[137] a reference book that was to become the standard aid for such exercises. Entitled the *Gradus ad Parnassum*, it assembled in dictionary form a series, culled from the best Roman poets, of circumlocutions for common words, phrases that were metrically complete or needing only slight adjustment to fill a substantial portion of the line. Under the Latin word for *death* appears *perpetua nox*; listed under *sea* the schoolboy would find *campi liquentes*; and under *fish* the phrase *squamigera gens*. Hence the appearance in eighteenth-century English verse of such periphrases as *eternal night* for death, *liquid fields* for sea, and *the scaly breed* or *finny race* for fish. The Roman poets had employed those phrases not to solve metrical problems but in order to create a poetic diction elevated above the mundane, elegantly suited to the lofty genre of the epic, but they proved wonderfully helpful to the schoolboy.

In Pope's verse such periphrases were not required metrically; but, familiar with the technique from his writing of Latin verse, he introduced them with a twofold purpose. The first was, as with the Roman poets, in order to elevate the diction. In contrast to Wordsworth, who was later to rebel against such practice, employing in his verse 'a selection of language really used by men',[138] poets of the neoclassical period believed that verse should scrupulously avoid all vulgar or common words and phrases. Where Homer, since Greek verse was metrically more flexible than Latin, had simply mentioned the *cow-heel* that Ctesippus flung at Ulysses' head, the best that Elijah Fenton could produce when he tried his hand at translating the passage into the type of verse acceptable to the eighteenth century was the absurdly cumbersome:

and of the steer before him plac'd,
That sinewy fragment at Ulysses cast,
Where to the pastern-bone, by nerves combin'd,
The well-horn'd foot indissolubly join'd.[139]

Pope, in contrast, handles such problems with elegance. Although the scissors that Lord Petre wielded were so central to the story, they are never referred to as such. Instead, we are offered such circumlocutions as the 'two-edg'd weapon', 'the glittering *Forfex*', 'the meeting Points' and 'the little Engine on his Fingers' Ends'. But Pope's second purpose, in addition to fulfilling the requirement of elevating poetic diction, was – closer to our present topic – to supply thereby a form of wit. The *Gradus* technique provided in miniature an intellectual challenge, demanding a momentary pause before the object is identified, with readers then congratulating themselves, as it were, for having solved the puzzle and for having participated successfully in Pope's game of allusiveness. As Pope himself described the technique, periphrases must be '… so misteriously couch'd, as to give the Reader the Pleasure of guessing what it is that the Author can possibly mean; and a Surprise when he finds it'.[140] The principle was applied not only to objects but also to everyday events that needed to be refined and raised to a poetic level, their significance in a humorous poem amusingly inflated by circumlocution. He will offer the lines:

> From silver Spouts the grateful Liquors glide,
> While China's Earth receives the smoking Tyde (3:119–20).

and it is our task to decipher the couplet's meaning, to identify the 'grateful liquors' and the 'smoking tide' as tea poured into cups. In more leisurely form, the opening stanza of the third canto will, for three lines, leave us guessing, offering only hints of the building to which they refer – its towers reflected in the waters of the Thames – and defying us to solve the enigma before a broader hint is eventually provided for any reader who may have failed the test:

> Close by those meads, for ever crown'd with flow'rs,
> Where Thames with pride surveys his rising tow'rs,
> There stands a structure of majestic frame,
> Which from the neighb'ring Hampton takes its name.

If we have contrasted the relaxed, urbane wit here with the form inspired by Hobbes in Restoration drama, there is no less a contrast here with the wit of the metaphysicals. The purpose of the wit here is not to shock the reader in order to reveal some vibrant truth but, like a contemporary element in landscape gardening, to evoke a smile of amusement. To ensure that the gently sloping lawn leading down from the house should not be spoiled by the leavings of cows, a small ditch was dug to keep cattle at a distance, its top made level with the slope in order not to interrupt the surface line visually. A person strolling along and coming suddenly upon it would murmur in mild surprise, hence determining its name, the *ha-ha*, and the same response was to be evoked by Pope's 'surprises'. In an era preferring settled, rational thought to the ecstasies and 'enthusiasms' that had so grievously disturbed the previous century, Pope's jolts are mild, and the brief shock, where it occurs, is swiftly resolved by means of a comforting explanation that returns us to the normal, secure world. In the description of Belinda's dressing table, he offers us what appears to be a monstrous image of unseemly coupling:

The Tortoise here and Elephant unite (1:135)

but instead of leading us into some dazzling truth, he reassuringly resolves the phrase in the next line, explaining that he is simply referring to combs composed of tortoiseshell and ivory.

These minor techniques employed by Pope, different though they may seem, have one aspect in common. The periphrasis sounding so impressive but really referring to a mundane pair of 'scissors', the zeugma reducing royal counsel to the level of a tea ritual, or the jolt from some seemingly appalling image to combs resting sedately on the dressing table: all these contribute to the bathos typifying humour, reflecting in such minor details the principle of the mock epic itself. However, there is a variant on the normal puncturing of arrogance or pretentiousness, for it demands repeated reminders of the inflated ideas of the epic which it is lampooning, a need to reinflate after the puncturing. Hence, Lord Petre's failure to notice the symmetry of Arabella's hairdo, the two locks 'which graceful hung behind / In equal Curls' – a failure that was a primary cause of her annoyance – needs first to be puffed up into the magnitude of an act of hubris: 'Ah cease, rash Youth! desist ere 'tis too late, / Fear the just Gods, and think of *Scylla's* Fate!' Only then can the process of deflation occur, as the reader is left to perceive by that vast exaggeration the unwarranted hypersensitivity of the two families in imagining that their dignity had been impugned. By means of comic diminution, Pope's poem creates in us that pleasant satisfaction at our own freedom from the pomposity of Lord Petre and Arabella, their sense of hurt pride that had caused the original dispute.

c) The Vogue of Sentiment

There can be few clearer instances of the pleasure humour takes in mortifying pride than a phenomenon emerging in the eighteenth century, a phenomenon for which we shall need to provide a little background. Jeremy Collier's attack on the libertinism of Restoration drama had proved extraordinarily effective. Unlike earlier opponents of the theatre, such as William Prynne, who had fulminated against every aspect of the Elizabethan and Jacobean stage, Collier, a parson with an excellent knowledge of drama, able to cite specific passages to support his arguments, had in his *A Short View of the Immorality and Profaneness of the English Stage* (1698) attacked Restoration comedy at its most vulnerable point. He argued with considerable justice that its rake hero was a dissolute model, a 'Whoring, Swearing, Smutty, Atheistical Man ... a Man of Breeding and Figure, that burlesques the *Bible*, Swears, and talks Smut to Ladies, speaks ill of his Friend behind his Back, and betrays his Interest: A fine Gentleman that has neither Honesty, nor Honour, Conscience, nor Manners, Good Nature, nor civil hypocrisie: Fine, only in the Insignificancy of Life, the Abuse of Religion, and the Scandals of Conversation.' Collier directed his barbs so effectively, sometimes with wit, that playwrights found it difficult to respond. Congreve, in attempting to defend himself after Collier's attack on his play *The Old Bachelor*, explained somewhat lamely that he had only written it to amuse himself in a slow recovery from a fit of sickness; to which Collier replied pithily: 'What his disease was I am not to inquire: but it must be a very ill one to be worse than the remedy.' The result, rare enough in such disputes, was a silent but fundamental reform of the drama, a reform accepted by the dramatists themselves – although not always to the advantage of the stage.

Authors of the new plays, such as Colley Cibber, inaugurating what came to be known as Sentimental Drama, reversed the policy of their predecessors, now insisting that comedy's purpose be educative, promoting moral principles and evoking sympathy and admiration for the virtuous characters. Although later in the century the term 'sentiment' would come to mean lachrymose sensibility, in this earlier period it denoted (in the other sense of the word) an opinion, phrased as a moral maxim. The 'noble' characters now appearing on the stage repeatedly enunciate such maxims intended to promote ethical conduct, although, as the parodists of that tradition pointed out, they were considerably less adept in exemplifying them.[141] And the crux of the matter lay once again in a prideful element that needed puncturing. For the supposedly admirable characters in such drama are never satisfied with performing noble actions; they invariably follow such acts by congratulating themselves on their high principles, emphasizing the laudability of their conduct, and delivering an axiom intended for the edification of their less perceptive peers. In Cibber's *The Careless Husband* (1705), Lady Eager, having refrained from revealing to her husband her discovery of his infidelity, proceeds to commend herself for her forbearance, concluding with the inevitable apophthegm:

> *Lady Eager*: 'Twas an hard conflict – yet it's a joy to think it over, a secret pride to tell my heart my conduct has been just. How low are vicious minds, that offer injuries: how much superior innocence that bears 'em!

In fact, that new convention, as the dramatists themselves failed to realize, revealed an unbecoming ethical blemish, a deplorable lack of the humility advocated by the religion on which they so often prided themselves. It was an arrogance asking to be deflated, and fully deserving the burlesque with which it came to be treated – a burlesque that provided some of the finest humour of the time.

A question arises whether these plays were indeed comic. With solemn didacticism as his aim, Richard Steele, in the preface to *The Conscious Lovers* (1722), declared unabashedly that, even though his plays were intended to be comedies, he was prepared to sacrifice humour in favour of moral edification.[142] Certain scenes in his play, he claimed, regularly evoked tears from his audiences – 'tears that flowed from reason and good sense'; yet, he maintained, the play remained within the category of comedy on the grounds that it produced '… a joy too exquisite for laughter'. In fact, there is little in the play liable to produce laughter, and when it does occur its source is carefully restricted to the servant class.

Steele and Addison deserve full credit for helping to make morality respectable in their *Tatler* and *Spectator* essays, achieving that purpose with learning, wit and delicacy, but the same cannot be said of Steele's contribution to the stage. Bevil Jr, the hero of his play, is forever informing us of his impeccable probity and the nobility of his behaviour, always of course following that information with an edifying sentiment. When a music master is about to leave the room, he hastens to open the door for him despite the latter's social inferiority, but he cannot refrain from drawing his companion's attention to the example he has offered of *noblesse oblige*, and does so in patently didactic form:

> *Bevil.* You smile, madam, to see me so complaisant to one whom I pay for his visit. Now I own I think it is not enough barely to pay those whose talents are superior to our own. (I mean such talents as would become our condition if we had them.) Methinks we ought to do something more than barely gratify them for what they do at our command only because their fortune is below us (1:2).

He has no doubts about his own merits, either here or elsewhere in the play. When his father asks whether he is willing to marry the lady chosen for him, Bevil replies complacently: 'Did I ever disobey any command of yours, sir? Nay, any inclination that I saw you bent upon?' As Paul E. Parnell has shown, these sentiments are really a form of mask by which the characters conceal from themselves the hypocrisy of their actions.[143] Thus, after promising to marry in accordance with his parents' wishes even though he fully intends to wed another woman, Bevil proceeds to deceive his father with the strange excuse (which Steele seems to regard as clearing him of guilt): 'Then let me resolve upon (what I am not very good at, though it is) an honest dissimulation.'

That form of sentiment intrinsic to the new configuration spilled over to areas outside the drama, forming a central characteristic of Richardson's *Pamela*. The author's declared aim was, of course, '... to cultivate the principles of virtue and Religion in the minds of the youth of both sexes'. The novel is a remarkable psychological study and I am far from minimizing its value as a literary work, but it was vulnerable to attack, not least on the score of Pamela's conviction demonstrated throughout the work that she herself is a model of noble Christian behaviour. Fielding's delightful parody of the novel, *Shamela*, has generally and justifiably been praised for its perception that Pamela, in resisting Mr B.'s sexual advances until a marriage proposal was forthcoming, was really selling herself to the highest bidder, but it has not been noticed that the humour of Fielding's attack focused in large part upon the element we are at present examining, the moral arrogance ineffectively concealed beneath an assumed humility, as expressed in her smug pronouncement of ethical maxims. One of the most effective comic works in this period, therefore, arose from the puncturing of pomposity. Fielding's declaration in the preface to *Joseph Andrews*, that laughter at its best is that aroused by hypocritical affectation, is fully applicable here: '... for to discover any one to be the exact reverse of what he affects is more surprising and consequently more ridiculous than to find him a little deficient in the quality he desires'.

Fielding had believed originally that the novel was by Colley Cibber (*Pamela* was, like *Shamela*, first published anonymously), and he no doubt did so because of the similarity in the proliferation of moral sentiments. Pamela in Richardson's version is, like Lady Eager, constantly praising herself for her virtuous actions even when the self-praise cancels out the supposed virtue, as when she paradoxically prides herself on her humility. Having dressed herself in preparation for leaving Mr B.'s abode, her self-approval is rounded out with the usual axiom:

> When I was quite equipped, I took my straw hat in my hand, with its two blue strings, and looked in the glass, as proud as any thing. To say truth, I never liked myself so well in my life.
> *O the pleasure of descending with ease, innocence, and resignation!* – Indeed there is nothing like it! An humble mind, I plainly see, cannot meet with any very shocking disappointment, let Fortune's wheel turn round as it will (*Letter 24*).[144]

In an epistle to her parents informing them how much she pleases everyone around her except her master (whom she has annoyed by her virtuous rejections of his advances), she provides the usual complacent sentiment: 'How much better it is, by good fame and integrity, to get everyone's good word but *one*, than by *pleasing that one*, to make *every one else* one's enemy, and be an execrable creature besides!' (*Letter 21*)

Fielding declared as his aim in *Shamela* not only to expose 'the notorious falsehoods and misrepresentations' of the book, including its sexual titillation of the reader, but also 'the matchless Arts of that young Politician, set in a true and just Light'; and he perceived very acutely within Pamela's matchless arts the gap between her complacent assurance of her own virtue and her actual behaviour, the claims being expressed for the most part in the 'sentiments' to which we have drawn attention. And Fielding does so in gorgeous comic parody. When Shamela's mother recalls her daughter's previous misdemeanour with Parson Williams, Shamela retorts in kind, not forgetting to add the inevitable apophthegm – the latter always printed in italics to draw attention to the pomposity of Pamela's own axiomatic pronouncements:

> Marry come up, good Madam, the Mother had never looked into the Oven for her Daughter, if she had not been there herself. I shall never have done if you upbraid me with having had a small One by *Arthur Williams*, when you yourself – but I say no more. *O! What fine Times when the Kettle calls the Pot* (Letter IV).

When Shamela replies coyly to Mr Booby's proposal of marriage that she cannot imagine how a man of his fortune could possibly be interested in marrying her, and Booby, mistaking her remark as a rejection, leaves the room in anger, her account of the incident culminates in the usual sentiment, although a sentiment somewhat more honest than those regularly delivered by her virtuous counterpart:

> O Sir, says I, I am sure you can have no such Thoughts, you cannot demean your self so low. Upon my Soul, I am in earnest, says he, – O Pardon me, Sir, says I, you can't persuade me of this. How Mistress, says he, in a violent Rage, do you give me the Lie? … and so he flung from me in a Fury.
> *What a foolish Thing it is for a Woman to dally too long with her Lover's Desires; how many have owed their being old Maids to their holding out too long* (Letter XII).

Time after time Fielding makes fun of Pamela's moral platitudes, undercutting the self-aggrandizement implicit in such sentiments, with much of the humour deriving from his burlesquing of that characteristic:

> why don't you come, says he; what should I come for says I; if you don't come to me, I'll come to you, says he; I shan't come to you I assure you, says I. Upon which he run up, caught me in his Arms, and flung me upon a Chair, and began to offer to touch my Under-Petticoat. Sir, says I, you had better not offer to be rude;

well, says he, no more I won't then; and away he went out of the Room. I was so mad to be sure I could have cry'd.
Oh what a prodigious Vexation it is to a Woman to be made a Fool of (Letter VI).

And when she finally inveigles him into marrying her, her thoughts on her wedding night are occupied with visions of her paramour, Parson Williams, those thoughts again culminating in an advisory sentiment:

Well, at last I went to Bed, and my Husband soon leap'd in after me; where I shall only assure you, I acted my Part in such a manner, that no Bridegroom was ever better satisfied with his Bride's Virginity. And to confess the Truth, I might have been well enough satisfied too, if I had never been acquainted with Parson Williams.
O what regard Men who marry Widows should have to the Qualifications of their former Husbands.

The opposition to such 'educative' sentiments that accounted for most of the humour of *Shamela* was to form a major element animating two of the finest stage comedies of the age. Oliver Goldsmith's essay, *A Comparison between Laughing and Sentimental Comedy* (1773), deplored the style that had come to dominate the theatre, noting the failure of those comedies to produce laughter and their reliance upon sentiment. Instead of attempting to display the virtues of the good characters, they would have been wiser to ridicule the foibles of the foolish:

In these plays almost all the characters are good, and exceedingly generous; they are lavish enough of their 'tin' money on the stage, and, though they want humour, have abundance of sentiment and feeling. If they happen to have faults or foibles, the spectator is taught not only to pardon, but to applaud them, in consideration of the goodness of their hearts; so that folly, instead of being ridiculed, is commended, and the comedy aims at touching our passions without the power of being truly pathetic.

The humour of his own play, *She Stoops to Conquer*, has usually been seen as emanating primarily from an unexplained, eccentric element in Marlow's character, his ability to flirt successfully with any working-class girl contrasted with the paralysing bashfulness that assails him when meeting a young lady of his own class. Having been compelled by his father to pay court to a Miss Hardcastle whom he has never met, and on his way to her home tricked by the practical joker Tony Lumpkin into believing that the house to which he leads Marlow and his friend is really an inn, he and his friend, on arriving there, imperiously order the master of the house to provide for their needs. They cut him short when he begins to regale them with stories of his army experiences, and peremptorily demand service, choosing the menu for their supper, while failing to realize that they are speaking to the father of the proposed bride. All this delightfully presents their swaggering confidence in demanding the best quality food and drink being undercut by the audience's knowledge of their error. But the most amusing moment occurs at the highpoint of the play, when Marlow finally confronts Miss Hardcastle.

At that point, Marlow's supposed bashfulness before women of a higher class turns out to be very different from that normally defined, and indeed is seen to arise not from a failing but from a laudable trait. His success in flirting effectively with housemaids and barmaids while becoming tongue-tied as soon as he meets a lady of his own class has been regarded as reflecting Goldsmith's own speech impediment, a quality that evoked from his friend, David Garrick, the comment that he 'wrote like an angel but talked like poor Poll'. But Marlow's embarrassment before young ladies has, as the text reveals, a different cause: 'Why, George, I can't say fine things to them. They freeze, they petrify me.' The factor that paralyses him is society's requirement that he utter the kind of 'fine things' that the characters in *The Conscious Lovers*, in *Pamela* and in the sentimental tradition at large are able to produce so readily, namely the mouthing of moral platitudes. He has no difficulty in flirting with Miss Hardcastle when he believes her to be a housemaid since domestics do not require such aphorisms, but on meeting her for matrimonial purposes, when he is expected to display his high moral principles in a series of 'sentiments', the effort is beyond him because he is aware of the hypocrisy that usually animates such pronouncements. Unable even to raise his eyes to look at her, and desperately mumbling away as he gazes at the floor, he vainly attempts to provide those well-phrased maxims demanded by society, as his fair companion, amused (as is the audience) at his reluctance to utter them, teasingly fills in the gaps for him, leading him on to offer ever more of what she herself recognizes as mere claptrap:

> *Marlow*: I love to converse only with the more grave and sensible part of the sex. But I'm afraid I grow tiresome.
>
> *Miss Hardcastle*: Not at all, sir; there is nothing I like so much as grave conversation myself; I could hear it for ever. Indeed, I have often been surprised how a man of sentiment could ever admire those light airy pleasures, where nothing reaches the heart.
>
> *Marlow*: It's – a disease – of the mind, madam. In the variety of tastes there must be some who, wanting a relish – for – um – a – um.
>
> *Miss Hardcastle*: I understand you, sir. There must be some, who, wanting a relish for refined pleasures, pretend to despise what they are incapable of tasting.
>
> *Marlow*: My meaning, madam, but infinitely better expressed. And I can't help observing-a –
>
> *Miss Hardcastle*: You were going to observe, sir –
>
> *Marlow*: I was observing, madam – I protest, madam, I forget what I was going to observe.
>
> *Miss Hardcastle*: (*Aside*.) I vow and so do I. (*To him*.) You were observing, sir, that in this age of hypocrisy – something about hypocrisy, sir.
>
> *Marlow*: Yes, madam. In this age of hypocrisy there are few who upon strict inquiry do not – a – a – a –
>
> *Miss Hardcastle*: I understand you perfectly, sir.
>
> *Marlow*: (*Aside*.) Egad! and that's more than I do myself.
>
> *Miss Hardcastle*: You mean that in this hypocritical age there are few that do not condemn in public what they practise in private, and think they pay every debt to virtue when they praise it.
>
> *Marlow*: True, madam; those who have most virtue in their mouths, have least of it in their bosoms. But I'm sure I tire you, madam … (2:1)

That final exchange leaves no doubt that both characters have perceived the hollowness of such sentiments, pronounced by people who think that they pay every debt to virtue when they praise it, whatever they may do in private – comments that prove remarkably apt descriptions of the axioms uttered by Bevil Jr and his peers. A side-aspect of Marlow's disability, no less effective in its contribution to the humour, is his confident bragging – when he imagines he is speaking to a housemaid – of his success as a Rattle at the club, and his crestfallen inability to utter a complete sentence, admirable as the reason for that inability may be.

The same opposition to the vogue of such aphorisms holds true for Sheridan's *The School for Scandal*. One need not list such brilliant episodes in that play as the scene in which Sir Peter, having glimpsed the edge of a petticoat behind the screen, roars with laughter, exulting at discovering that Joseph has a mistress hidden there, but unaware that the lady behind the screen is his wife. It is sufficient here to note how the villain of the piece, Joseph Surface, has achieved his reputation for virtue by his habit of pronouncing such noble axioms as, 'Certainly, Sir Peter, the heart that is conscious of its own integrity is ever slow to credit another's treachery,' or 'When ingratitude barbs the dart of injury, the wound has double danger in it' – sentiments hypocritically addressed to the very man whose wife he is attempting to seduce. Only Sir Oliver sees through him, offering a comment that leaves no doubt of Sheridan's intent: 'Oh, plague of his sentiments! If he salutes me with a scrap of morality in his mouth, I shall be sick directly.'

Once more, these instances involve a change in the concept of wit. In the early eighteenth century, wit had been defined not in the way we tend to regard it today, as a strikingly novel idea, but as an accepted socially approved concept admired for the elegance of its wording. Pope defined that principle in his famed statement: 'True Wit is Nature to advantage drest / What oft was Thought but ne'er so well Exprest.' The purpose of wit was to gratify readers by the 'dress', by the graceful form in which a generally accepted idea was clothed. The fashionable enunciation of 'sentiments' belonged to that same tradition, the supposedly pleasing formulation of moral axioms approved by society. But, by the mid-century, tastes were changing. It is rare indeed that a historian can catch a writer at the moment of responding to cultural change, but such an instance does exist. In the manuscript of Gray's *Elegy in a Country Churchyard* there appear the lines: 'Some mute inglorious Tully here may rest / Some Caesar guiltless of his country's blood'. Gray, on second thoughts, crossed out the Roman names, substituting for them the names of Milton and Cromwell, thereby indicating a shift from classical universalism to a preference for the local and the individualized. In the 1770s when these two plays were written, Romanticism had not yet arrived, but the ridicule directed at the complacency implicit in proclaiming universal moral sentiments for the edification of others and the fun created by mocking the mode of sentiment confirmed that the fashion of universalism was on its way out.

Or was it? It has long been declared that Jane Austen's novels belong essentially to an earlier age than that of 1813 when her most famous novel was published, that the formality of her writing is reminiscent of her preceptor, Dr Johnson. Stylistically, Johnson had marked the acme of this fashion, his opinions being expressed as dogmatic assertions of universal validity, such as his comment: 'Nothing has more retarded the advancement of learning than the disposition of vulgar minds to ridicule and vilify what they cannot comprehend.'[145] Austen has been seen as belonging to that same group, as in such statements as: 'She was a woman of mean under-standing, little information and uncertain temper. When she was discontented, she fancied herself nervous. The business of her life was to get her daughters married; its solace was visiting and news.' Accordingly, as one critic put it:

> To the historian of literary epochs Jane Austen is, or should be, a little inconvenient. She was born a few years later than Wordsworth, Coleridge and Scott. When she died, Byron was famous, and Shelley and Keats had already published. She belongs therefore to the period commonly entitled that of the Romantic Revival, or the Revival of the Imagination. And yet these titles do not suit her in the least … Essentially, it appears to me, her novels belong to the age of Johnson and Cowper.[146]

However, that view of Austen's work misses a major aspect of her wit, for much of her humour was aimed in the opposite direction, and should be seen as in fact parodying the practice of Johnson and of his age. The famed opening of *Pride and Prejudice*, which set the tone for so much that was to follow, sounds indeed as magisterial and incontrovertible as anything written by Dr Johnson:

> It is a truth universally acknowledged, that a single man in possession of a good fortune, must be in want of a wife.[147]

But the sentence is, indeed, the antipole to such pontification. Although possessing the outer form of a traditional 'sentiment', it teasingly inverts the purpose, implying that the supposed truth stated is really an untruth, a principle acknowledged only by such misguided women as Mrs Bennet and Lady Lucas, who regard matrimony as a pass key to property and rank. Its purpose is thus diametrically and wittily opposed to the tradition. Where Bevil and his peers had intended their sentiments to voice the majority opinion sanctioned by society, Austen's purpose, both in that opening comment and throughout her novel, is to persuade the reader to desert the majority view and to join the discriminating minority represented by Elizabeth herself, who despises such notions and who will reject Darcy despite the attractions of his wealth and aristocratic status. When she does accept him towards the end of the novel and asks him what had attracted him to her, she suggests (with his full approval) that she had interested him 'because she was so unlike *them*', so unlike the women who were constantly seeking his approbation.

Much of the humour in the novel derives not only from her difference from other women but also, and more specifically, from her rejection of eighteenth-century 'sentiments'. The influence Elizabeth subtly exerts over Darcy, gradually freeing him from his pomposity, is expressed in large part by her efforts at weaning him away from such pronouncements, and she employs teasing humour to do so. In the earlier part of the novel, when he does deign to speak, it is usually in the form of haughtily dispensed declarations in the style of Johnson, such as: 'Nothing is more deceitful than the appearance of humility. It is often only carelessness of opinion, and sometimes an indirect boast' (pp. 42–3); or, on another occasion, that there is 'in every disposition a tendency to some particular evil – a natural defect, which not even the best education can overcome' (p. 51). Elizabeth repeatedly punctures the self-assurance that those sentiments reveal, bewitching him by her refusal to be impressed by them. At Netherfield Darcy, solemnly concurring with the view that for a woman to be termed accomplished she must have a thorough knowledge of music, singing, drawing, dancing and the modern languages, dogmatically appends the further requirement: 'All this she must possess and to all this she must yet add something more substantial, in the improvement of her mind by extensive reading' – to which Elizabeth archly replies, 'I am no longer surprised at your knowing *only* six accomplished women. I rather wonder now at your knowing *any*.' Her irrepressible humour leads her later to attack him on precisely that point. When, to her surprise, he asks her to dance and while circling the dance floor remains grimly silent, she first makes fun of the conventional conversational gambits which he is too scornful to indulge in – 'It is your turn to say something now, Mr Darcy. I talked about the dance, and you ought to make some sort of remark on the size of the room, or the number of couples.' She then adds a specific barb concerning his tendency to pontificate, remarking that Darcy always desires to say something that will amaze the whole room '… and be handed down to posterity with the éclat of a proverb' (p. 80).[148]

Austen's lampooning of the tradition is not restricted to her characterization of Darcy. Mary too, Elizabeth's younger sister, is gently mocked throughout, presented as a junior aspirant to the Johnsonian model, a girl who, we are informed, '… piqued herself upon the solidity of her reflections'. She amuses us by gravely providing axioms and definitions at the slightest opportunity. On the mere mention of the word 'pride', she informs the company that:

> … human nature is particularly prone to it, and that there are very few of us who do not cherish a feeling of self-complacency on the score of some quality or other, real or imaginary. Vanity and pride are different things, though the words are often used synonymously. A person may be proud without being vain. Pride relates more to our opinion of ourselves, vanity to what we would have others think of us.

Lest that sober pronouncement be taken too seriously, Austen adds the dismissive comment of the young Lucas: 'If I were as rich as Mr Darcy, I should not care how proud I was. I would keep a pack of foxhounds, and drink a bottle of wine a day.' Austen was thus not a follower of Johnson but a witty inverter of his penchant for impressive promulgations.

The attack on the vogue of sentiment in the leading comic works of the period – in works by Fielding, Goldsmith, Sheridan and Austen – evidences once again how rooted literary humour is in the ridiculing of pomposity and affectation, although here in a form specific to the fashions of the time.

d) Sterne, *Tristram Shandy*

After living a penurious and somewhat secluded life as a parson, Lawrence Sterne suddenly found himself both famous and infamous. In the course of a chance visit to London shortly after the publication of the first part of *Tristram Shandy*, he discovered to his delight that the initial edition had sold out and was being greeted with acclaim. Less comforting was the discovery that the positive response was offset by censure from certain quarters, objections to the book's indecency. If indecency had been tolerated for Fielding's novels, it was decried in this instance because of Sterne's religious calling. That latter response does not concern us here, but the extraordinary success of this work does raise certain interests.

The attractive originality of the book is twofold in source. It derives partly from its unconventionally 'sentimental' quality – this time sentiment in its second meaning of lachrymose sensibility which, although popularized by his subsequent *Sentimental Journey Through France and Italy*, was inherent in the earlier work too. The mouthing of solemn moral 'sentiments' was discarded, to be replaced by a warm emotionalism, as in the affectionate relationship between the two Shandy brothers. The bond of love, of mutual regard and of inviolable loyalty evidenced an assumption of human benevolence far removed from the often cruel satire that had dominated literature during the earlier part of the century. When Tristram's father speaks inadvertently of his brother's hobby in a manner that might possibly cause offence, Toby

> ... look'd up into my father's face, with a countenance spread over with so much good-nature; – so placid; – so fraternal; – so inexpressibly tender towards him: – it penetrated my father to his heart: He rose up hastily from his chair, and seizing hold of both my uncle *Toby's* hands as he spoke: – Brother *Toby*, said he: – I beg thy pardon; – forgive, I pray thee, this rash humour which my mother gave me. – My dear, dear brother, answered my uncle *Toby*, rising up by my father's help, say no more about it; – you are heartily welcome, had it been ten times as much, brother (2:12).[149]

The comedy, however, had little to do with sentimentality except in their shared concern with the individual rather than the universal. The book delighted readers primarily by its irreverent *rejection* of 'what oft was thought', its puckish repudiation of socially approved principles and its spurning even of literary conventions. Standard procedure in novels required, on the heroine's first entry, a laudatory description of her ravishing beauty, as in Smollett's description of Narcissa: '... her stature tall, her shape unexceptionable; her hair, that fell down upon her ivory neck in ringlets, black as jet; her arched eyebrows of the same colour; her eyes piercing, yet tender ...'[150] Sterne will have none of this, preferring to offer the surprised reader a blank page, with the droll instruction: '– call for pen and ink – here's paper ready to your hand. – Sit down, Sir, paint her to your own mind – as like your mistress as you can – as unlike your wife as your conscience will let you – 'tis all one to me – please but your own fancy in it' (6:37).

That new interest in individualism ('please but your own fancy'), which was to reach its apogee in the Romantic movement, involved (as Shelley and Byron were to epitomize) a marked scepticism towards authoritative sources, a Promethean desire to overthrow conventions; and much of *Tristram Shandy* consists of a gleeful parody and even inversion of such dictates. Not least in that regard is his relish in ridiculing the eighteenth century's penchant for citing revered sources in order to support their views. For such predecessors, there could be no more effective bulwark for any opinion than a classical precedent that coincided with and hence authorized it. Sterne disdains such subservience. In contrast, his characters are distinguished throughout both by the singularity of their views and the frivolity of their citations. Both Tristram and his father repeatedly quote from obscure academic works, often non-existent sources invented for the purpose, but at all times, even when the sources are valid, the highly selective and idiosyncratic manner in which they are employed undercuts the validity of the process. When Shandy senior does adopt a principle, such as the influence of first names on the lives of their bearers, the principle is invariably odd and unconventional, stubbornly defended by him against all comers: '... he would move both heaven and earth, and twist and torture every thing in nature to support his hypothesis' (1:19). In this, he resembled his gentler and less argumentative brother Toby who, when he held any opinion, 'troubled his head very little with what the world either said or thought about it' (1:24). And the sources they adduce are deliberately idiosyncratic even when the source actually exists. Shandy senior, quoting Henry Swinburne's *Brief Treatise of*

Testaments and Last Wills (1590), reveals the absurdity of reliance upon legal precedent by instancing from it a true case in which, to prevent a son from inheriting his mother's property, the father claimed that a mother was no kin to her son, that strange claim being approved by the learned court.

> – Whereunto not only the temporal lawyers – but the church lawyers – the *juris-consulti* – the *jurisprudentes* – the civilians – the advocates – the commissaries – the judges of the consistory and prerogative courts of *Canterbury* and *York*, with the master of the faculties, were all unanimously of opinion, That the mother was not of (*Mater non numeratur inter consanguineos*, Bald. *in ult.* C. de Verb. *signific.*) kin to her child.

At which point, Yorick muses that the son could have answered the father that, if such was the law, 'You lay'd, Sir, with my mother ... why may I not lay with yours?' (4:29)

The book not only approves the singularity of their opinions but, either implicitly or explicitly, burlesques the Augustan idealization of universal rules and the concomitant demand for conformity, with the injunction of such predecessors that anyone failing to adopt and respect its rationalist principles must be excluded from society as an 'enthusiast' or madman. Such insistence upon precepts, upon the general rather than the particular, was indeed still the dominant mode at the time when Sterne was writing. Only a year before the publication of this work, Imlac, in Johnson's *Rasselas*, provided the oft-quoted principle that the function of a poet is 'to examine, not the individual, but the species; to remark general properties' and not to number the streaks of the tulip, and in 1771, a few years after the publication of *Tristram Shandy*, Sir Joshua Reynolds confirmed in his *Discourses on Art* that painters and sculptors must aim at the universal, criticizing Bernini's *David* for presenting the young warrior as biting his lower lip as he prepared for his fight with Goliath. That expression, Reynolds maintained, was 'far from being general, and still farther from being dignified. He might have seen it in an instance or two; and he mistook accident for generality.'[151]

The time for a change had arrived. Sterne's work presents in an attractive and amusing form characters who refuse to worship at the shrine of the classics or to submit to society's dictates. The novel produces in the reader the same response as we have defined for comedy at large, a pleasant feeling of escape from repressive conformity, together with (as counterweight) an awareness that we are not quite as whimsically crankish and abnormal as his characters and that therefore social dictates will be restored, at least partially, once the laughter is over. As Tristram remarks:

> The deuce of any other rule have I to govern myself by in this affair – and if I had one – as I do all things out of all rule – I would twist it and tear it to pieces, and throw it into the fire when I had done – Am I warm? I am, and the cause demands it – a pretty story! is a man to follow rules – or rules to follow him? (4:10)

That rejection of convention runs throughout, as when he recounts with filial affection the independence of his father who '... would see nothing in the light in which others placed it; – he placed things in his own light; – he would weigh nothing in common scales' (2:19). Hence what Sterne termed the 'hobby-horses' of his characters, especially the one adopted by Toby and his servant Trim who devote their time and money to building the model of a battle long past and forgotten, except in the minds of those two. For them the memory of that battle retains a vital personal importance because it played so memorable a part in their own lives. Everything they hear, even a word resembling the terms relevant to military siege, they interpret in the context of their personal obsessive interest. The mention of bed-curtains sets Toby off on a learned dissertation concerning *curtins*, the technical term for the section of a rampart that lies between the two bastions of a siege-wall (2:12). Such eccentricities on the part of the characters are made loveable through the indulgent manner in which they are received by the others or presented by the narrator, one instance being the squeaking door-hinge that invariably wakes Shandy senior during his afternoon siesta, but which he never gets round to repairing:

> Every day for at least ten years together did my father resolve to have it mended – 'tis not mended yet; – no family but ours would have borne with it an hour – and what is most astonishing, there was not a subject in the world upon which my father was so eloquent, as upon that of door-hinges. – And yet at the same

time, he was certainly one of the greatest bubbles to them, I think, that history can produce: his rhetorick and conduct were at perpetual handy-cuffs. – Never did the parlour-door open – but his philosophy or his principles fell a victim to it; – three drops of oil with a feather, and a smart stroke of a hammer, had saved his honour for ever ... By all that is good and virtuous, if there are three drops of oil to be got, and a hammer to be found within ten miles of *Shandy-Hall* – the parlour door hinge shall be mended this reign (3:21).

Again the humour arises from his confident eloquence on the subject of hinges, his ability to lecture on them, undercut by his failure to take any action. But one notes that there is no hint of adverse criticism on the part of the narrator, only amusement, with the final sentence wrily suggesting that Shandy senior, were it ever repaired, would most probably miss the opportunity of complaining about it. We laugh pleasurably at his abnormalities, not least because they expose the despotic rigidity of normative social principles. Moreover, where 'the man of sentiment' earlier in the century had always assumed, or attempted to ensure others, that his behaviour conformed to the high moral standards approved by society, here Walter is unperturbed that 'his rhetorick and conduct were at perpetual handy-cuffs', that even the principles or philosophies that he accepted theoretically were at variance with his actual behaviour – and Tristram, the narrator, is obviously entertained by the fact.

For most readers the delight of the book lies in its endless digressions, whereby the supposed biography of Tristram doubles back on itself so many times that by the end of Volume II, over 100 pages on, Tristram has not even been born. To argue, as has one critic,[152] that there are really no digressions since the novel has no beginning, no middle and no end is to misconstrue the point, for the narrator repeatedly informs us of a topic he is about to discuss or of an incident he is about to recount, thereby arousing our expectation, and then diverges from it to wander off at a tangent, sometimes returning much later, as in the diagram of these intellectual meanderings that Sterne so aptly provides (6:40):

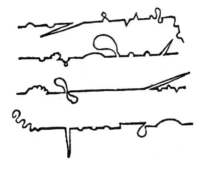

There is indeed an overall structure to the work and a gradual progression in time, but the movements back, forth and sideways are those that charm. The humour thus derives once again from its parodying of the oppressive rules imposed by his predecessors.

There is however, one aspect of the work that would seem to contradict Sterne's rejection of accepted norms and that has generated numerous learned treatises, namely his indebtedness to Locke's influential and widely admired *Essay Concerning Human Understanding* (1700) which had, by his day, become an authoritative work. Wilbur L. Cross set the tone early on, stating that *Tristram Shandy* was simply Locke's essay 'in a novelised form', that Sterne's meanderings reflect the 'association of ideas' that Locke had formulated, that his fictional characters, rather than thinking logically, follow instead any idea that is associated with the thought of the moment. John Traugott too was convinced that Locke's philosophy formed the structural basis of Sterne's work, the adoption of its principles creating the characters and situations in the novel. And more recently Alastair Fowler has, in that tradition, attributed to Locke's influence the fact that 'Sterne needed a digressive method if he was to render the truth of individual experience by following out trains of thought; since these were now believed to work through associations or "chains of ideas"'.[153]

That Sterne was conscious of a relationship cannot be denied, as Locke is quoted by him more frequently than any other author. But a close reading of the work suggests that, so far from following Locke's lead, he was, as a prime source of the humour, teasingly inverting the principles expounded in the *Essay*, treating it with the same cavalier disregard for its authority as he does all other sources. This is not the place to enter into any detailed discussion of Locke's philosophy, but a brief summary is indeed necessary in order to highlight Sterne's divergence from the source, a summary that, I trust, exemplifies without distorting one major impact of that work. Locke had argued that a child, born with a blank mind or *tabula rasa*, gradually learns certain 'ideas', such as gaining the ability to distinguish by touch between a sphere and a cube, to identify texture and to recognize colours. The next stage is the *association* of those disparate ideas, the ability to combine them and deduce from them – to recognize, for example, that in combination a spherical object with a rough surface and a specific colour is an orange, an object that can henceforth be identified as such by its difference from other items. To quote Locke's own statement:

> The acts of the mind, wherein it exerts its power over its simple ideas, are chiefly these three: (1) Combining several simple ideas into one compound one; and thus all complex ideas are made. (2) The second is bringing two ideas, whether simple or complex, together, and setting them by one another, so as to take a view of them at once, without uniting them into one; by which way it gets all its ideas of relations. (3) The third is separating them from all other ideas that accompany them in their real existence (*Essay* 2:12).

The principle depends upon a process of rational deduction, a focusing upon the associated ideas until a recognizable object is finally identified by its difference from others. The opposite to this process – and the very worst scenario in Locke's reckoning – is any irrational or 'wrong connexion', a joining of ideas only loosely or casually related. Such thought process he condemns unequivocally as a form of insanity:

> I shall be pardoned for calling it by so harsh a name as madness, when it is considered that opposition to reason deserves that name, and is really madness; and there is scarce a man so free from it … [It arises] from a wrong connexion of ideas. Some of our ideas have a natural correspondence and connexion one with another: it is the office and excellency of our reason to trace these, and hold them together in that union and correspondence which

is founded in their peculiar beings ... Wrong connexion of ideas [is] a great cause of errors. This wrong connexion in our minds of ideas in themselves loose and independent of one another, has such an influence, and is of so great force to set us awry in our actions (*Essay* 33:1–6).

Sterne, in fact, turns the principle on its head. While he accepts the proposition that the mind proceeds by associating ideas, he inverts the purpose that Locke assigns to that process, adopting the very 'madness' that Locke so sternly condemns. Instead of rationally narrowing down the associated ideas until they focus on an identifiable object or concept, he delights in allowing ideas to wander off haphazardly and irrationally in all directions. Sterne's characters throughout the work reject the dictates of reason that Locke so strongly advocates, preferring to follow the dictates of the emotions. Yorick, for example, remarks regretfully that his sermon had been mis-written, that it came from 'the wrong end of me – it came from my head instead of my heart' (4:26). When a notion sparks off an associated thought, Sterne does not, as Locke requires, search for the unifying connection between the two that will establish their true relationship. Instead he deserts the first idea, rambles off in whatever interesting direction the second notion may lead, continues to branch off whenever further associations are sparked, and often forgets completely the idea from which he originally set out:

> I was just going, for example, to have given you the great outlines of my uncle Toby's most whimsical character; – when my aunt Dinah and the coachman came across us, and led us a vagary some millions of miles into the very heart of the planetary system: (1:22)

To call that an example of Locke's 'association of ideas' is to miss completely its divergence from it. Sterne did follow associations but not in the manner Locke intended, preferring defiantly to follow the path that Locke had termed 'madness'.

Sterne does, as we have said, refer a number of times to Locke, but a close reading of those passages reveals that he is treating the philosopher with the same degree of humorous scepticism as Shandy senior treats all authorities. That cavalier attitude to scholars and philosophers, the humorous displacement of reverence towards magisterial rulings, applies no less to Sterne's attitude to the leading philosophical source of his day. Most often cited by those who take his indebtedness seriously is the passage in which the narrator praises the *Essay* as being 'a history book of what passes in a man's mind' (2:2). But that passage occurs in the midst of Tristram's attempt to answer those critics who argue that the loveable Uncle Toby is merely 'a confused, pudding-headed, muddle-headed fellow', and his use of Locke's theory scarcely redounds to the latter's glory. Tristram begins by correctly comparing the associative process, the principle of the *tabula rasa*, to the impression left when a thimble is pressed upon sealing wax – but he adds what Locke does not mention, that if the wax is too soft or the thimble applied carelessly the resultant impression will be false, hence producing 'the confusion in my Uncle Toby's discourse'. One need scarcely add that our sympathies here, together with those of the narrator, are with Toby and his brother, both of whom fall within that category of 'confused' thinking condemned by Locke. As Tristram says elsewhere, no person could have '… any kind of preconception of how my father would think, speak or act, upon any untried occasion or occurrence of life. – There was that infinitude of oddities in him, and of chances along with it, by which handle he would take a thing, – it baffled, Sir, all calculations. – the truth was, his road lay so very far on one side, from that wherein most men travelled, – that every object before him presented a face and section of itself to his eye, altogether different from the plan and elevation of it seen by the rest of mankind. – In other words, 'twas a different object, and in course was differently considered' (5:24). And we have a similar account of his mother's delightfully confused process of thought, as in the incident that created the trouble concerning Tristram's birth:

> … from an unhappy association of ideas, which have no connection in nature, it so fell out at length, that my poor mother could never hear the said clock wound up, – but the thoughts of some other things unavoidably popped into her head – & *vice versâ*: – Which strange combination of ideas, the sagacious *Locke*, who certainly understood the nature of these things better than most men, affirms to have produced more wry actions than all other sources of prejudice whatsoever (1:4).

The series of ideas 'popping' sporadically into one's head does, as Locke argued, produce 'wry' actions, since it is a *mis*application of the true purpose of logical thinking, that misapplication being presented by Sterne as the most engaging and amusing aspect of human behaviour.

A word recurring throughout Locke's *Essay*, serving as the coordinating element, is the concept in the human mind of 'a train of ideas placed in order, a due comparing of them, and deductions made with attention, before they can be discovered and assented to'. Toby, on hearing in his brother's formulation of the doctrine the word *train*, first characteristically misinterprets it in terms of siege tactics and, when corrected, offers his own very different version of the mental process to which Locke refers. Shandy senior, dogmatically propounding Locke's principle of association, declares:

> Now, whether we observe it or no, continued my father, in every sound man's head, there is a regular succession of ideas of one sort or other, which follow each other in train just like – A train of artillery? said my uncle *Toby* – A train of a fiddle-stick! – quoth my father – which follow and succeed one another in our minds at certain distances, just like the images in the inside of a lanthorn turned round by the heat of a candle. – I declare, quoth my uncle *Toby*, mine are more like a smoak-jack, – Then, brother *Toby*, I have nothing more to say to you upon that subject, said my father (3:18).[154]

The smoke-jack, with its tendency to obscure rather than illumine, is, it turns out, appropriate not only for Toby's haphazard flow of ideas but for Shandy senior's too, despite the latter's claim to the contrary. For we learn a little later that, although he persisted in continuing his exposition of Locke's theory, '... yet he could not get my uncle *Toby's* smoak-jack out of his head, – piqued as he was at first with it; – there was something in the comparison at the bottom, which hit his fancy ... the idea of the smoak-jack soon turned all his ideas upside down' (3:20). Thus, even if at times Shandy senior seems to approve of Locke's principles, Sterne makes it clear that the opposite holds true. And that divergence from the principles proves no less characteristic of Tristram the narrator who, on mentioning some totally irrelevant point, will cheerfully comment: 'But this is neither here nor there – why do I mention it? – ask my pen, – it governs me, – I govern not it' (6:6). Tristam has no desire to govern his pen, to force it to conform to the rational succession of ideas that Locke advocates, and therein lies the comic force of the work.

Elsewhere, the parody of the *Essay* is even more marked, and again humorously. Locke had written at considerable length of wit and judgement as being antipoles. His own stance was unequivocal; for he strongly objected to wit, arguing (no doubt with the metaphysical poets in mind) that want of acuteness, exercise or attention in the understanding leads to illogical and absurd connections, while '... judgment, on the contrary, lies quite on the other side, in separating carefully, one from another, ideas wherein can be found the least difference, thereby to avoid being misled by similitude, and by affinity to take one thing for another' (*Essay* 11:2). Sterne, in the 'Author's Preface' (prankishly inserted in the middle of volume three) takes the contrary view, arguing in the strongest terms that wit, or the linking of ideas by paradox, is an essential and valid part of the human personality. How is it possible, he asks, to argue that wit and judgement are as far apart '... as east is from west. – So says *Locke*, – so are farting and hickuping, say I'. Then, after quixotically comparing wit and judgement to the two knobs affixed to the top of a cane chair whereby the removal of one would destroy the symmetry, he lambasts the injunction to separate the two and thereby prohibit those irrational connections of ideas to which the Shandys are so delightfully addicted, adding that '... the great *Locke*, who was seldom outwitted by false sounds – was nevertheless bubbled here':

> ... did you ever see, in the whole course of your lives, such a ridiculous business as this has made of it? – Why, 'tis as miserable a sight as a sow with one ear; and there is just as much sense and symmetry in the one as in the other: – do – pray, get off your seats only to take a view of it, – Now would any man who valued his character a straw, have turned a piece of work out of his hand in such a condition? – nay, lay your hands upon your hearts, and answer this plain question, Whether this one single knob, which now stands here like a blockhead by itself, can serve any purpose upon earth, but to put one in mind of the want of the other?

In brief, while Sterne admires Locke's concept of the mind as a *tabula rasa* upon which impressions are made, he denies outright the main premise of Locke's argument, the need for distinguishing ideas logically. Sterne prefers the charmingly haphazard connectivity that animates his own work, as he states in patent contradiction to Locke: 'Digressions, incontestably, are the sunshine; – they are the life, the soul of reading! – take them out of this book, for instance, – you might as well take the book along with them; – one cold eternal winter would reign in every page of it; restore them to the writer; – he steps forth like a bridegroom, – bids All-hail; brings in variety, and forbids the appetite to fail' (1:22). Authority is once again comically derided.

In discussion of *Tristram Shandy*, one cannot omit the matter of time. Fluchère proffered the standard view that, 'as a good disciple of Locke', Sterne made a clear distinction between, on the one hand, measurable time designated in hours, days and dates and, on the other, psychological time, a flexible sense of duration based upon the flow of ideas in the mind.[155] But that misses completely the difference between Locke and Sterne; for Locke's purpose was to warn *against* psychological measurement of time and to emphasize the need for reliance upon fixed measurements, such as hours, days and months dependent upon the regular movements of the sun and moon. Puzzled by the mind's ability to think of the future even though it has not experienced it, Locke argued that there exists a process whereby we first obtain an idea of time's movement by watching our own succession of ideas, then '… observing certain lengths or measures of duration, as minutes, hours, days, years, &c.', we grasp the idea of fixed time, and only then are able to conceive of time extended into the future (*Essay* 14:31). One must learn, he argues, to desert dependence upon false psychological impressions based upon the varied speeds of human thought, and learn to rely instead upon ideas derived from scientifically established criteria – 'without some regular periodical returns, we could not measure ourselves, or signify to others, the length of any duration' (*Essay* 14:23).

Sterne accepts the distinction between the two forms of time, psychological and fixed, but to call him a good student of Locke is to overlook not only his preference for the psychological time that Locke sees as misleading, but also his mockery of Locke's insistence upon fixed time. When Shandy senior does quote Locke fairly accurately, acknowledging his source, Toby's comment knocks the point askew, and it is clear with whom Sterne identifies. Thus, Shandy's learned discourse on Locke is interrupted by the narrator's account of the more pragmatic, contrary view of Toby, who (honest man!) generally took every thing as it happened; – and who, of all things in the world, troubled his brain the least with abstruse thinking; – the ideas of time and space – or how we came by those ideas – or of what stuff they were made – or whether they were born with us – or we picked them up after-wards as we went along – or whether we did it in frocks – or not till we had got into breeches – with a thousand other inquiries and disputes about Infinity Prescience, Liberty, Necessity, and so forth, upon whose desperate and unconquerable theories so many fine heads have been turned and cracked.

Shandy senior, however, persists in quoting his learned authority, again to be interrupted by Toby's retort:

To understand what time is aright, without which we never can comprehend *infinity*, insomuch as one is a portion of the other, – we ought seriously to sit down and consider what idea it is we have of *duration*, so as to give a satisfactory account how we came by it. – What is that to any body? quoth my uncle Toby. [footnote: Vide Locke.] *For if you will turn your eyes inwards upon your mind,* continued my father*, and observe attentively* ... You puzzle me to death, cried my uncle Toby (3:18).

In the most famous and most cherished passage in the novel, the concept of time adopted by Tristram proves once again to be a delightful reversal of what Locke would recommend:

I am this month one whole year older than I was this time twelve-month; and having got, as you perceive, almost into the middle of my third volume – and no farther than to my first day's life – 'tis demonstrative that I have three hundred and sixty-four days more life to write just now, than when I first set out; ... It must follow, an' please your worships, that the more I write, the more I shall have to write – and consequently, the more your worships read, the more your worships will have to read (4:13).[156]

Concealed within this statement is a hint of the famed 'Achilles paradox' posed by the philosopher Zeno (alluded to in 2:19) whereby a hare racing against a tortoise that has been given a headstart could, Zeno suggests, never overtake it, since each time the hare covers half of the gap between the two, the tortoise would by then have advanced a little further. Echoing that teasing paradox, Tristram, in describing his descent down a staircase, maintains that he would never reach the bottom of the stairs by the time the chapter ends, and solves the problem by a bright decision:

> Is it not a shame to make two chapters of what passed in going down one pair of stairs? for we are got no farther yet than to the first landing, and there are fifteen more steps down to the bottom; and for aught I know, as my father and my uncle Toby are in a talking humour, there may be as many chapters as steps: – let that be as it will, Sir, I can no more help it than my destiny: – A sudden impulse comes across me – drop the curtain, Shandy – I drop it – Strike a line here across the paper, Tristram – I strike it – and hey for a new chapter (4:10).

Moreover, logic, which would indeed bring Tristram in a few moments to the foot of the stairs, is rejected in favour of the distortions of psychological time whereby '… write as I will, and rush as I may into the middle of things … I shall never overtake myself'. The same Zeno paradox applies to Walter Shandy's plan for Tristram's education on which he works intensively for over three years, the misfortune being, we are told, that Tristram was during all that time totally neglected and growing older, so that, '… by the very delay, the first part of the work, upon which my father had spent the most of his pains, was rendered entirely useless, – every day a page or two became of no consequence' (5:16).

Tristram Shandy, we may conclude, evokes laughter, as does so much successful humour, by burlesquing the dogmatically asserted traditions of its time, especially the solemn citing of authorities that had dominated the earlier part of the century. Moreover a close study of the text reveals, in contrast to the prevailing view of critics, that Locke's association of ideas, so far from being the source of the work, forms a major target of that lampooning. Rejecting the requirement that logical order be imposed on the random flow of thought, Sterne preferred what Locke had termed 'madness', namely the pyrotechnics created as ideas shoot off indiscriminately in all directions, a process that produces the charming idiosyncrasy of his very human characters.

CHAPTER FIVE

THE NINETEENTH CENTURY

a) Austen, *Emma*

Although generally regarded as a satiric observer of society, Jane Austen thought of herself primarily as a writer of comic fiction. Invited on one occasion to pen a historical romance, she refused, remarking: '... if it were indispensable for me to keep it up and never relax into laughing at myself or at other people, I am sure I should be hung before I had finished the first chapter'; and when urged to compose a serious piece about a clergyman, she rejected the suggestion with the comment, 'The comic part of the character I might be equal to' but nothing more.[157] Yet little has been written on the nature of her gift for comedy, almost all studies, while admitting that she saw herself as a humorous writer, concentrating on the structure of the novels and their moral significance. John Wiltshire in the *Cambridge Companion to Jane Austen*, after a brief reference to Emma's 'eager laughing warmth', makes no further allusion to the comic elements, even though they constitute a primary delight of her work.[158] Even feminist writers, such as Audrey Bilger, Deborah Kaplan, Margaret Kirkham and Janet Todd, who could with full justice claim her as a leading humorist, have little to say on that score.[159]

There has, moreover, been a long tradition of applying the term 'irony' to her writing – a term that should be restricted to instances in which the intended meaning is the opposite of that expressed (as in Swift's *Modest Proposal*) but which is often employed, not only in critical accounts of Austen, as a substitute for analytical precision. The opening sentence of *Pride and Prejudice*, quoted earlier, is indeed ironic, but for the most part her comic spirit is not, deriving instead from sheer good humour, a sense of the laughable aspects of human behaviour. As Elizabeth Bennet, her favourite character, remarks, 'Follies and nonsense, whims and inconsistencies, *do* divert me, I own, and I laugh at them whenever I can' (p. 50). The most amusing observations in the novels contain no irony in the strict sense of that term. When Mrs Bennet bewails the fact that Collins will take possession of the estate on her husband's death and leave her destitute, her husband replies: 'My dear, do not give way to such gloomy thoughts. Let us hope for better things. Let us flatter ourselves that *I* may be the survivor' (p. 114). So far from being opposite in meaning to that conveyed by the wording, it drily points out the one possibility that his wife had not bothered to consider, revealing thereby her brash self-concern.

One of the disappointing elements in reading criticism of Austen's novels then is, as in previous works we have examined, the pervasive solemnity, not least in dealing with *Emma*. Lionel Trilling defined the central character as 'a dreadful snob' and Austen Wright sees her as 'vain of her own perceptions, snobbish, domineering, rash, and selfish'.[160] In a fine article, Robert Polhemus did focus on the comedy, praising Austen's love of laughter and her projection of that quality on to her heroines, but he offered no discussion of the ways the laughter is produced. Moreover, he attributed the humour exclusively to the tendency of the heroines to laugh at the eccentricities of others, omitting to note – a major factor in Austen's fiction – their frequent amusement at their own errors and misjudgements.[161]

That point leads us into what forms a central theme of *Emma*, as it does of Austen's other novels, namely marriage. It has been said of her treatment of marriage in this novel that there is 'nothing of the moral fable here'.[162] There is, in fact, a very significant moral element, although we shall need to move back to past traditions in order to perceive Austen's innovation and its effect upon the comedy. In such earlier novels as *Pamela* and *Tom Jones*, the central theme had also been marriage – whether Pamela would eventually catch Mr B. and whether Tom would ever be permitted to wed Sophia – and in both, the criteria for marriage were primarily social and financial. For Pamela, marriage to Mr B. fulfilled her dream of becoming a wealthy lady instead of a penurious servant, and in that pursuit the character of her future husband was totally irrelevant. The moment a proposal is at last forthcoming, the deception and trickery he had employed until that point, his appalling attempts to seduce and subsequently abandon her, are forgotten in the rapture of her success: 'O my exulting heart! how it throbs in my bosom, as if it would reproach me for so lately upbraiding it for giving way to the love of so dear a gentleman.'[163]

Fielding may seem to differ in that regard, for he deplored the pseudo-morality of Richardson's novel, the encouragement it offered serving-girls to sell themselves at the highest price; but his own *Tom Jones* is little better from that angle, again ignoring the character of the proposed bridegroom and relying instead upon the criteria of social and financial status. Squire Western cherishes Tom as a delightful hunting colleague, a lively drinking companion and an excellent young man, but he is transformed into a wrathful enemy at the first hint of Tom's desire to marry Sophia, spurning him as totally unworthy, not because of the young man's character but solely because he is a foundling, financially dependent on Allworthy's charity, and hence entirely unsuited to be the son-in-law of a squire. Since Fielding makes fun of Western's wrath, we may wonder whether the author dissociates himself from that view, but his model figure, the appropriately named Squire Allworthy, is equally opposed to the marriage, castigating Tom for having attempted to win the young lady's heart, an act that he describes as '... a base and barbarous action – an action of which you must have known my abhorrence' (6:11).[164] Yet at the end of the novel, the moment Tom is discovered to be the son of Allworthy's sister, the elevation in social status and his instatement as Allworthy's heir win him the full approval of both squires, who now see him, as does the author/ narrator, as fully worthy of the lovely young lady. And the same holds true of Sophia's response. She knows full well that, if he has remained faithful to her in heart, he has proved abysmally unfaithful in all else, bedding any female who made herself available, including the slut Molly Seagrim, and so casual in his infidelities that he even slept with a woman who might well have been his mother. Yet, with Fielding's approval, everyone, including Sophia, accepts him joyfully once he is raised in rank. Sophia goes through the motions of demanding a trial period to test his supposed reformation but a moment later rescinds the requirement, agreeing to accept him at once and without conditions (18:12). Jane Austen's approach was entirely different. Could one imagine Elizabeth Bennet accepting Wickham's hand once she has learned of his sexual escapades?[165]

Austen's *Pride and Prejudice* thus marked a profound change in the conception of marriage. While social and financial status remain important elements in ensuring compatibility, in her fiction the primary criterion for a prospective husband is character – refinement, moral integrity, intelligence and discrimination. In order to highlight those requirements, Austen designs Elizabeth's situation to be so precarious both socially and financially that she might be expected to welcome any husband who could provide her with security. The estate they live on is entailed to a male heir, the family due to be impoverished upon the father's death, and her marital prospects are further lessened by the impediment of a vulgar mother, her father having unwisely married a woman of inferior intelligence and manners. With those disadvantages, even Collins' proposal ought to have been acceptable to Elizabeth – as it was to her friend Charlotte – but for Elizabeth any consideration of him as a husband is inconceivable on the grounds of his personality. Hence her disgust at her friend's acceptance of his proposal:

> Mr. Collins is a conceited, pompous, narrow-minded, silly man; you know he is, as well as I do; and you must feel, as well as I do, that the woman who marries him, cannot have a proper way of thinking. You shall not defend her, though it is Charlotte Lucas. You shall not, for the sake of one individual, change the meaning of principle and integrity, nor endeavour to persuade yourself or me, that selfishness is prudence, and insensibility of danger, security for happiness (p. 94).

Austen leaves no doubt of her authorial stance on this point, when Mr Bennet, urged by his wife to compel Elizabeth to marry Collins, remarks: 'An unhappy alternative is before you, Elizabeth. From this day you must be a stranger to one of your parents. Your mother will never see you again if you do not marry Mr. Collins, and I will never see you again if you do.' One need not discourse on the significance of Elizabeth's rejection of Darcy, a man of dazzling wealth and high aristocratic background who holds no attraction for her until she can be convinced of his inner qualities. And from the opposite angle, Darcy himself must learn that Elizabeth's refinement, intelligence and moral principles outweigh the social disadvantages of her situation. Character is all.

In *Emma*, there is a change, subtle but fundamental. Definitions of its theme have, as we have mentioned, usually focused upon the 'snobbery' of its central character,[166] as evidenced in her contemptuous dismissal of Harriet's suitor:

'I may have seen him fifty times, but without having any idea of his name. A young farmer, whether on horseback or on foot, is the very last sort of person to raise my curiosity. The yeomanry are precisely the order of people with whom I feel I can have nothing to do. A degree or two lower, and a creditable appearance might interest me; I might hope to be useful to their families in some way or other. But a farmer can need none of my help, and is, therefore, in one sense, as much above my notice as in every other he is below it' (p. 23).[167]

Her haughtiness towards the young farmer does indeed lay her open to the charge of snobbery, although it should be recalled that the remark comes at a time when she is trying to impress Harriet with the need to reject his proposal, and hence is probably exaggerating here the supposed social gap. But to suggest that her snobbery is central to the plot is to miss the point of the novel. For no reader would, in the context of the novel and of the intense class-consciousness prevailing in Jane Austen's time, imagine that young farmer worthy to join her social circle. We are informed in the opening pages that in Highbury the Woodhouses were 'first in consequence', with no one their equal. Even Knightley, who thinks highly of the young man, regards him as a protégé, not as a companion. Hence Emma's fault does not lie in her recognition that a social gap exists between herself and the farmer. It lies in her assumption that a social gap exists between the farmer and Harriet, based on her unwarranted impression that the girl was superior in character to her suitor.

The change here is that Austen has considerable fun in *reversing* the situation of *Pride and Prejudice*. For where Elizabeth Bennet, in her search of a husband, insists from the first upon character and intellectual compatibility as prime criteria, Emma is oblivious to both. It is her disregard for those criteria that amusingly faults her judgement, so that she is constantly mismatching instead of matchmaking. She disqualifies for Harriet a husband of whose character she knows nothing on the false assumption that her friend is socially

superior to him, she attempts to match the vicar to a girl intellectually beneath him merely in order to provide Harriet with improved
security and rank, and she repeatedly errs in imagining possible
pairings and courtships.

Mark Schorer, taking a different view, claimed that Emma does
resemble Elizabeth since both come 'from a society whose morality
and values derive from the economics of class' and both need to
mitigate that propensity in order to achieve self-recognition.[168]
But it is, in fact, there that the two characters differ. In contrast
to Elizabeth, with her financial and social impediments, Emma
is a wealthy heiress, daughter to the leading family of Highbury,
and in no need of marriage as a means to achieving security or
improved status. Moreover, where Elizabeth had been utterly alone
in her principles, inviting the reader to join the minority of one in a
society that regards marriage solely in terms of social and financial
advancement, Emma is, in this novel, alone in her misguided view
of marriage. In that respect, she belongs to the group of women
satirized in the opening line of *Pride and Prejudice*, for she urges
Harriet to marry for material and social advancement irrespective
of the character of the proposed husband, while it is Knightley who
represents chorically the enlightened view to which Austen herself
subscribes. No doubt it was for that reason that Austen was hesitant
about the success of the novel, suspecting that Emma would prove
to be 'a heroine whom no one but myself will much like'.[169] In that
she was wrong, for Emma is indeed very likeable, not least in her
readiness to respect, if not always to follow, her mentor's advice, in
her willingness to admit her errors once they are revealed and, where
necessary, to apologize and make amends. Above all, she is likeable
in her ability to laugh at herself once she discovers her blunders.

The assumption that entertains us and leads her repeatedly to a
fall is thus not snobbery but her unshakeable conviction that her
judgement and perceptions are impeccable, as we watch her step
forward confidently into the potholes and puddles that await her as
each of her matchmaking attempts collapses and she embarks with
undisturbed self-assurance upon the next. When Knightley reproves
her for misjudging character, she airily dismisses his rebuke with the
conviction that he lacked the 'skill of such an observer on such a
question as herself' (p. 58). If one could imagine Miss Bates as the
central character, attempting humbly and out of goodness of heart
to find partners for her single friends, the humour would evaporate.

It is Emma's complacent belief in her astuteness and discrimination that makes her miscalculations so amusing, creating in us a pleasant sense of relief that we have not been guilty of such erroneous judgement.

The importance of that trait, the unwarranted pride one always seeks in comic situations, is highlighted on the opening page even before her misjudgements begin. We are told not only that Emma is a little spoiled, having had rather too much of her own way, but that she also possesses a disposition 'to think a little too well of herself'. A few pages later, evidence of that tendency is forthcoming when she claims full credit for having arranged Miss Taylor's marriage, even though the evidence she cites, the attentions Mr Weston paid to his future bride, suggests the contrary, that he had been inclined that way before the idea occurred to Emma. As she boasts:

> All manner of solemn nonsense was talked on the subject, but I believed none of it. Ever since the day – about four years ago – that Miss Taylor and I met with him in Broadway Lane, when, because it began to drizzle, he darted away with so much gallantry, and borrowed two umbrellas for us from Farmer Mitchell's, I made up my mind on the subject. I planned the match from that hour; and when such success has blessed me in this instance, dear papa, you cannot think that I shall leave off match-making (pp. 7–8).

That remark provides the hint that her future efforts at match-making, while consciously aimed at the good of her protégés, will be prompted to no small degree by a selfish purpose, the desire to bask in the praise of others complimenting her on her success. Her one fear in planning the match between Elton and Harriet was that someone might think of it before she did and thereby gain the credit she so desired for herself: 'She feared it was what every body else must think of and predict. It was not likely, however, that any body should have equaled her in the date of the plan ...' (p. 28) But her criteria are faulty. In embarking on her first attempt, her calculations are based not on the compatibility of her candidates but on two other factors, the financial advantage for Harriet and the malleability of the two prospective lovers, namely how far she would be able to nudge them into wedlock. As she concludes after careful consideration: 'Mr. Elton's situation was most suitable, quite the gentleman himself, and without low connexions; at the same time, not of any family that could fairly object to the doubtful birth of Harriet. He had a comfortable home for her, and Emma imagined a very sufficient income; ... the girl who could be gratified by a Robert Martin's riding about the country to get walnuts for her might very well be conquered by Mr. Elton's admiration' (p. 29). Especially engaging for the reader is her mistaken conviction that Elton will be willing to marry below his social rank, and her horror, once the truth emerges, that he had presumed the same about her. Social distinctions are, in her mind, flexible when applied to her candidates but inviolable when applied to herself. How amazing, she thought, that Elton '... should suppose himself her equal in connexion or mind! – look down upon her friend, so well understanding the gradations of rank below him, and be so blind to what rose above, as to fancy himself shewing no presumption in addressing her! – It was most provoking' (p. 119).

If, as has so often been claimed, her fault were snobbery, we ought in condemning her for it to feel at this point that Elton is indeed a suitable match for Emma, that her sense of superiority to him is unjustified; but our response is very different, the entertaining aspect being, as Austen makes clear, her inability to recognize that the need for compatibility in intelligence, in refinement, and in social standing applies not only to herself but to others too.

In addition to her unsound assessments, we are entertained also by the gap between her resolutions and her failure to carry them through (reminiscent of the lists of books she prepares to read and, as Knightley informs us, then forgets about). Thus, after expressing her determination to allow Harriet to decide for herself concerning Martin's proposal, she so manipulates the simple girl by what she believes to be subtle hints and pressures that eventually she finds herself composing the letter of refusal on the girl's behalf: '... though Emma continued to protest against any assistance being wanted, it was in fact given in the formation of every sentence' (p. 46).

Austen won much of her reputation for her perceptiveness as a narrator, analysing her fictional characters with witty exposure of their foibles in a manner that wins immediate confidence from the reader, as in her description of John Knightley:

> He was not an ill-tempered man, not so often unreasonably cross as to deserve such a reproach; but his temper was not his

great perfection; and, indeed, with such a worshipping wife, it was hardly possible that any natural defects in it should not be increased (p. 81).

In this novel, however, she introduces a technique that should not be missed, the narrator's voice at times shifting, without warning, into Emma's thoughts. When Emma leaves Harriet and Elton alone together, convinced that a proposal will be forthcoming once she herself is out of the way, we read: 'The lovers were standing together at one of the windows. It had a most favourable aspect; and, for half a minute, Emma felt the glory of having schemed successfully. But it would not do; he had not come to the point' (p. 79). The two are, of course, anything but lovers, and in allowing Emma's thoughts to be treated, however momentarily, as if they were facts, Austen highlights the disparity between the reliability of the author's critical assessments and the entertaining deficiencies in Emma's. Where Austen's discrimination is invariably acute, Emma's is unstable. Having assessed Elton as eminently suitable for her friend Harriet, on meeting him after his engagement to Miss Hawkins, she begins 'very much to wonder that she had ever thought him pleasing at all' (p. 158).

The same holds true for the gradual discovery of her major misjudgement. From numerous hints we have long become aware of her incipient love for Knightley, but for her it is a revelation, and the passage achieves its comic effect because of the discrepancy between the slowness of her discovery and her own conviction of the swiftness of her apprehension, as she finally realizes that she is jealous of Knightley's supposed attachment to Harriet:

Emma's eyes were instantly withdrawn: and she sat silently meditating, in a fixed attitude for a few minutes. A few minutes were sufficient in making her acquainted with her own heart. A mind like hers, once opening to suspicion, made rapid progress. She touched – she admitted – she acknowledged the whole truth … It darted through her with the speed of an arrow, that Mr. Knightley must marry no one but herself! (p. 360)

Here too, we slide into Emma's thoughts as she congratulates herself on the extraordinary rapidity of 'a mind like hers', able to reach with the speed of an arrow a truth long obvious to the reader. The passage emerges not as a tribute to her discernment but as confirmation of her lack of perception, her misguided interpretation of the feelings both of others and of herself. We experience, accordingly, a sense of satisfaction at our own sagacity.

The hints of Emma's failings provided by the narrator – never serious failings, since her intentions are always of the best – are at times conveyed obliquely. Mr Woodhouse, Emma's father, is a somewhat tiresome character, and one may wonder why Austen included him. But he has a function to perform, his presence suggesting how far Emma unconsciously resembles him. He is forever advising others to restrict their diet to gruel, to stay indoors lest they catch cold, and to follow at all times his personal predilections: 'His own stomach could bear nothing rich, and he could never believe other people to be different from himself. What was unwholesome to him, he regarded as unfit for any body; and he had therefore, earnestly tried to dissuade them from having any wedding-cake at all.' Emma, as a dutiful and affectionate daughter, while indulging his eccentricities, imagines that she is immune to them, circumventing them, for example by supplying more substantial food to guests when he is not looking. But if she herself is no hypochondriac, she does resemble him only too closely in her constant attempt to impose her own idiosyncratic standards upon those around her, moulding Harriet's character to fit her own ideas, chiding Knightley for supporting Martin, and admonishing Frank Churchill for complaining of the heat. Her father regards the marital tie as a deplorable deprivation of liberty, always referring to the past governess after her marriage as 'poor Miss Taylor', lamenting the destiny of his 'poor Isabella' on her returning to her marital home, even though their home was a model of happiness (p. 123). Here too, Emma may gently reprove him for his gloomy attitude to wedlock, but she herself is no less inimical to marriage, determined to preserve her independence. She casually brushes aside with the blind self-assurance of youth the threat of becoming an old maid like Miss Bates:

> I am sure I should be a fool to change such a situation as mine. Fortune I do not want; employment I do not want; consequence I do not want: I believe few married women are half as much mistress of their husband's house as I am of Hartfield; and never, never could I expect to be so truly beloved and important; so

always first and always right in any man's eyes as I am in my father's (p. 74).

True, she will always be right in her father's eyes, but, as she suspects, she will not always be right in the eyes of Mr Knightley. He is there to remind us of the true situation, providing her with warnings that she blithely disregards as she assures him, while proceeding on her perilous path, that seniority in years is no guarantee of impeccable judgement. Again, we see the potholes ahead, and watch her move resolutely towards them, with the comforting thought that we are free from such erroneous judgements. Admonitions from others are dismissed with equal scorn. When Knightley's brother warns her that Elton is in love not with Harriet but with her, Emma remains happily convinced of her superior assessment, '... amusing herself in the consideration of the blunders which often arise from a partial knowledge of circumstances, of the mistakes which people of high pretensions to judgment are for ever falling into' (p. 98) – a comment applying so accurately to her own blunders and pretensions rather than to those of her adviser.

Her progress, wrong as it may be, is softened by delightful touches on the way, including her recognition, however momentary, of her own foibles. Austen is at her best when Emma, having finally learned how seriously she has erred in one of her matchmaking attempts, determines to cease such interference for ever:

> It was foolish, it was wrong, to take so active a part in bringing any two people together. It was adventuring too far, assuming too much, making light of what ought to be serious, a trick of what ought to be simple. She was quite concerned and ashamed, and resolved to do such things no more.

only to find herself a moment later planning a new match for Harriet: 'She stopt to blush and laugh at her own relapse ...' (pp. 120–1) In this, there is indeed one engaging similarity between Elizabeth Bennet and Emma, the quality we noted earlier, that both are capable of laughing at themselves and hence of encouraging us to laugh with them.

One need not detail the events that follow as she analyses, with unshakeable confidence in her judgement, the various pairings that she imagines are developing around her – concluding that Jane is conducting an affair with a married man, that Harriet is in love with Frank Churchill and that Knightley is about to propose to Harriet. That she believes Frank to be in love with her is not her fault, as he has deliberately misled her, but in all other instances, including her inability to recognize that she herself is in love with Knightley, the errors are hers, and we enjoy perceiving her inability to acknowledge failings so obvious to us. In brief, where we had laughed with Elizabeth Bennet as she exposed the foibles of others, here it is Emma herself at whom we laugh with genial sympathy, as we watch her learning, always a little too late, from each of her mistakes – most of all, as we perceive her unshakeable confidence in her personal sapience, a self-assurance repeatedly leading her into amusing misjudgements.

It is, however, gratifying to know at the end that she has not lost her sense of fun. When Knightley comments that Mrs Weston will, no doubt, spoil her own daughter as much as she had indulged Emma when serving as her governess, Emma replies gaily:

> I was very often influenced rightly by you – oftener than I would own at the time. I am very sure you did me good. And if poor little Anna Weston is to be spoiled, it will be the greatest humanity in you to do as much for her as you have done for me, except falling in love with her when she is thirteen (p. 407).

b) Dickens, *The Pickwick Papers*

Dickens' first major venture into fiction produced his only comic novel. There were to be numerous amusing characters in his future fiction, but the novels were not themselves comic. While the account of Pickwick's travels does include depictions of human suffering – the debtors' prison, the defects of the lawcourts and the pettifogging of the lawyers themselves – condemnation of social abuse never thrusts itself into the foreground as it does in *Oliver Twist* and *Bleak House*. The scenes one carries away from *The Pickwick Papers* are not of the fogs, grime, workhouses and poverty, nor of murders and mysteries in the dank depths of the city, but of the joyful picnic at Dingley Dell, of celebrants kissing under the mistletoe in Mr Wardle's home, of Pickwick awakening in the village animal pound, and the lament of the elder Weller at the conclusion of the trial, 'Oh, Sammy, Sammy, vy worn't there a alleybi!' John Gross justly remarked, 'Perhaps one ought to applaud Dickens when one finds him funny and leave it at that, but taking his humour for granted comes after a time to suggest a failure of response'; yet, in the collection of essays he co-edited that aspect is absent, as it is from most other critical studies. John Killham's discussion of *The Pickwick Papers* in that collection treats the novel with marked seriousness, making not the slightest mention of its humour.[170] The title of James R. Kincaid's study *Dickens and the Rhetoric of Laughter* sounds promising; its interest, however, is not in the nature of the comedy but in the sombre effects he believed that the rhetoric produced.[171] Sam's account of how the elder Weller pitched some electors out of his coach Kincaid selects as a prime instance of the 'grim reality' that affects Pickwick's vision of the world, creating in him 'a resiliency in the face of death':

'You wouldn't believe, sir,' continued Sam, with a look of inexpressible impudence at his master, 'that on the wery day as he came down with them woters, his coach *was* upset on that 'ere wery spot, and ev'ry man on 'em was turned into the canal.'
'And got out again?' inquired Mr. Pickwick hastily.
'Why,' replied Sam very slowly, 'I rather think one old gen'l'm'n was missin'; I know his hat was found, but I ain't quite certain whether his head was in it or not' (p. 175) [172]

The 'look of inexpressible impudence' with which Sam relates the story scarcely accords with his supposed instructing of Pickwick in the grim reality of the human condition; and the comment concerning the hat is clearly one of those jocose inventions characterizing Sam's humour throughout – in the same category as: 'Avay vith melincholly, as the little boy said ven his schoolmissus died' or 'If you walley my precious life don't upset me, as the gen'l'm'n said to the driver when they was a-carryin' him to Tyburn.' The aspect that won the novel its immediate popularity was not any sombre lesson learned by Pickwick but the sheer fun and liveliness of its variegated scenes, the laughter evoked by Bob Sawyer's altercation with his landlady, the boisterous account of the electors at Eatanswill, and the vision of Pickwick joining his friends on the ice, where he moves '… slowly and gravely down the slide, with his feet about a yard and a quarter apart, amidst the gratified shouts of all the spectators' (p. 397).

As G. K. Chesterton noted long ago, and as Dickens himself admitted in the preface to the 1847 edition, the publication of

the early chapters before the author had worked out the continuation resulted in Pickwick's transformation during the course of
the novel from the less attractive figure in the opening sections to
the benevolent and loveable gentleman at the end.[173] Yet the initial
presentation in fact functions as an essential preparation for the
continuation. W. H. Auden claimed that Pickwick's situation as we
first meet him is Edenic. Comfortably ensconced in his sitting room,
his needs provided by a comely woman with a natural genius for
cooking, he is untroubled by children, and fully at ease in a house
where his word is law.[174] But Auden misses the real purpose of the
early chapters. The opening scene does not present him seated in his
comfortable sitting room but participating in a meeting at the Club
held to honour his name, where the eloquent Pickwick discourses
with an assumed modesty on his personal achievements:

> He had felt some pride – he acknowledged it freely, and let his
> enemies make the most of it – he had felt some pride when
> he presented his Tittlebatian Theory to the world; it might be
> celebrated or it might not. (A cry of 'It is,' and great cheering.) He
> would take the assertion of that honourable Pickwickian whose
> voice he had just heard – it was celebrated; but if the fame of
> that treatise were to extend to the farthest confines of the known
> world, the pride with which he should reflect on the authorship of
> that production would be a nothing compared with the pride with
> which he looked around him ...

That is no minor point, since his conviction that the dilettante
treatise on Tittlebats has won him an honoured place in science and
hence that he is, indeed, a gifted analytical observer serves as the
basis for much of the fun that is to follow. For the travels on which
he is about to embark with his friends, the travels that will occupy
the rest of the novel, are not undertaken for relaxation or pleasure
but, as was gravely recorded in those minutes, are to be extensions
of Pickwick's research, aimed at '... enlarging his sphere of obser-
vation; to the advancement of knowledge, and the diffusion of
learning'. It is the exposure of that claim to scholarly erudition and
the revelation of Pickwick's gullibility that evoke laughter, notably in
a charming scene in the opening instalment when, in the interests of
scientific enquiry, he solemnly records details concerning the life and
labours of the equine species, totally unaware that he is being joshed:

'How old is that horse, my friend?' inquired Mr. Pickwick ...

'Forty-two,' replied the driver, eyeing him askant.

'What!' ejaculated Mr. Pickwick, laying his hand upon his note-book. The driver reiterated his former statement. Mr. Pickwick looked very hard at the man's face, but his features were immovable, so he noted down the fact forthwith.

'And how long do you keep him out at a time?' inquired Mr. Pickwick, searching for further information.

'Two or three veeks,' replied the man.

'Weeks!' said Mr. Pickwick in astonishment, and out came the note-book again.

'He lives at Pentonwil when he's at home,' observed the driver coolly, 'but we seldom takes him home, on account of his weakness.'

'On account of his weakness!' reiterated the perplexed Mr. Pickwick.

'He always falls down when he's took out o' the cab,' continued the driver, 'but when he's in it, we bears him up werry tight, and takes him in werry short, so as he can't werry well fall down; and we've got a pair o' precious large wheels on, so ven he does move, they run after him, and he must go on – he can't help it.' Mr. Pickwick entered every word of this statement in his notebook, with the view of communicating it to the club, as a singular instance of the tenacity of life in horses under trying circumstances (p. 21).

Subsequent chapters, when the element of scientific pursuit has receded into the background, continue to base the humour on Pickwick's sense of personal dignity and pride, as recorded in the opening scene. His comfortable existence in his sitting room where his word was law included a complacent contentment with his bachelorhood, a conviction that will lend especial force to later scenes – Mrs Bardell's belief that he has proposed marriage, his being locked into a closet as a potential rapist by the headmistress of a ladies' seminary, and his being vilified, however unintentional the act, as the invader of a lady's bedroom.

Whenever that sense of personal dignity is about to be punctured, Dickens carefully reminds us of it. The arrival of the letter from Dodson and Fogg informing Pickwick that he will be charged with breach of promise could have stood alone as an item necessary for furthering the plot; but Dickens is too consummate a humorist to let the opportunity slip by. Accordingly, he inserts a scene immediately prior to the document's arrival. There, Pickwick, the confirmed bachelor, reprimands in the sternest terms both Tupman and Winkle for their involvement in amorous escapades, his anger being directed especially at the fact that they are 'my followers' and hence damaging *his* reputation. His brow darkens and he strikes the table emphatically with his clenched fist:

> 'Does it not, I ask, bespeak the indiscretion, or, worse than that, the blackness of heart – that I should say so! – of my followers, that, beneath whatever roof they locate, they disturb the peace of mind and happiness of some confiding female? Is it not, I say – '
> Mr. Pickwick would in all probability have gone on for some time, had not the entrance of Sam with a letter, caused him to break off his eloquent discourse.

Lest we miss the relevance, on the disclosure of the contents of the legal document a few moments later, we are offered a thoughtfully sardonic echo of his earlier stricture:

> 'Peace of mind and happiness of confiding females,' murmured Mr.Winkle with an air of abstraction (pp. 242–3).

That principle of pride due to be deflated holds true for the initial introduction of Pickwick's companions. In that early speech recorded in the Club's minutes, Pickwick had praised his friends for the quality for which each was distinguished, for traits that he regarded as admirable but that, as we shall learn, are forms of unjustified *amour propre* due to be exposed in the subsequent misadventures: 'Poetic fame,' Pickwick declared, 'was dear to the heart of his friend Snodgrass; the fame of conquest was equally dear to his friend Tupman; and the desire of earning fame in the sports of the field, the air, and the water was uppermost in the breast of his friend Winkle.' To follow are Tupman's discomfiture in the affair with Rachael Wardle, and Winkle's repeated ignominy as he fails to live up to the reputation he has cultivated – the horse that stubbornly moves sideways despite his efforts to control it, and his terrified handling of the gun that his clumsiness sets off to the horror of those around him. Were it not for the reputation for expertise in sport that Winkle had cultivated among his friends, resulting in the belief that he is about to perform elegant figure-eights on the ice, there would be little humour in his desperately holding on to Sam for support as, before their eyes, he slithers helplessly in all directions. Snodgrass's poetic aspirations seem to have been forgotten in the course of the novel, but the reference had obviously been inserted in that opening scene with the intention that some fun should be directed later at his poetic effusions. The opportunity was not ignored completely, being transferred to the person of Mrs Leo Hunter, incorrigibly proud of having composed an 'Ode to an Expiring Frog' which, we learn, had appeared in a lady's magazine modestly signed with an 'L' followed by eight stars (p. 199). We are spared the entirety of the poem, but the opening is sufficiently instructive:

> Can I view thee panting, lying
> On thy stomach, without sighing;
> Can I unmoved see thee dying
> On a log
> Expiring frog!

Even the character of Jingle belongs within this process of deflated pretensions. His extravagant claims to membership in high society and to personal wealth – 'Brown paper parcel here, that's all – other luggage gone by water – packing-cases, nailed up – big as houses – heavy, heavy, damned heavy' – are belied by the shabby green coat he wears, a coat that had once adorned a much shorter man and whose soiled and faded sleeves scarcely reach to his wrists. If Pickwick and his friends are deceived initially, the reader is, from the first, amusedly aware of the gap between his accounts of his romantic or military successes and the reality of his condition, as when, on being told of Snodgrass's poetic ability, he professes himself to have composed a ten-thousand-line epic while on the battlefield: 'fired a musket – fired with an idea – rushed into wine shop – wrote it down – back again – whiz, bang – another idea – wine shop again – pen and ink – back again – cut and slash – noble time, Sir.' His distinctive style of speech is itself a parody of the stenography at which Dickens himself had laboured so hard in order to earn money as a recorder of parliamentary debates. Thomas Burney's *Brachygraphy*, from which he learned shorthand, like the Pitman system that appeared just after Dickens completed this novel, was designed to record each word phonetically. But, at the remarkable speed Dickens attained, he no doubt adopted the practice of omitting unimportant connectives from the parliamentary orations and inserting them in the final versions, so that his actual notes must have resembled Jingle's spasmodic form of speech.

Sam Weller, from the moment of his entrance into the novel, takes over as a major source of humour, not least by the kind of characteristic comment cited above, his far-fetched comparisons to outrageously exaggerated incidents supposedly illustrative of the matter being discussed: 'Business first, pleasure arterwards, as King Richard the Third said when he stabbed t'other king in the Tower, afore he smothered the babbies.' Their total irrelevance to the matter under discussion leaves his interlocutors, who usually address him in the condescending tone suited to a servant or inferior, momentarily dumbfounded, the above sally in the magistrate's court plunging the prosecuting clerk, Mr Jinks, into awed silence (p. 329). The comic aspect arises not so much from the fecundity of Sam's imagination as from the discomfiture produced in the person he is addressing, a technique he employs at the moment of his greatest triumph when he is in the witness stand, imperturbably demolishing the pretensions of the law and the arrogance of its representatives. Serjeant Buzfuz, attempting to undercut Sam's testimony and at the same time to impress the jury with his own sense of humour, remarks jocularly of Sam's service with Pickwick: 'Little to do, and plenty to get, I suppose?' to which Sam replies brightly: 'Oh, quite enough to get, Sir, as the soldier said ven they ordered him three hundred and fifty lashes.' The court titters, the judge reprimands him and the solemnity of the trial is successfully interrupted. The climax of his triumph occurs a few moments later:

> 'Do you mean to tell me, Mr. Weller,' said Serjeant Buzfuz, folding his arms emphatically, and turning half-round to the jury, as if in mute assurance that he would bother the witness yet – 'Do you mean to tell me, Mr. Weller, that you saw nothing of this fainting on the part of the plaintiff in the arms of the defendant, which you have heard described by the witnesses? ... You were in the passage, and yet saw nothing of what was going forward. Have you a pair of eyes, Mr. Weller?'
>
> 'Yes, I have a pair of eyes,' replied Sam, 'and that's just it. If they wos a pair o' patent double million magnifyin' gas microscopes of hextra power, p'raps I might be able to see through a flight o'

stairs and a deal door; but bein' only eyes, you see, my wision's limited' (p. 464).

Had the question simply been whether Sam had witnessed the scene, the humour in his reply would have been significantly reduced. Its effect derives from his blithe resistance to the supposedly intimidating cross-examination, his refusal to be impressed by the Serjeant's stern, 'Do you mean to tell me … ? Have you a pair of eyes?' accompanied by pregnant pauses – elements intended to awe the witness into submission. The result is the barrister's precipitous descent from bloated self-importance to chagrin, together with the lawcourt's plunge from authoritative dignity to exposure of its perverse browbeating of witnesses. And of course Sam does the same soon afterwards, when, citing Mrs Bardell's admiration of the honourable conduct of Dodson and Fogg (who smirk with pleasure at the praise), he swiftly demolishes their self-esteem by revealing, as though through a compliment, the damaging fact that they have taken the case illegally on speculation. He thus carefully puffs up their pride before puncturing it, a process especially effective here as it involves a public degradation, while of course assisting his employer's cause.

Sam's refusal to be impressed by any form of authority was a projection of Dickens' own delight in debunking the pompous, a trait emerging even at minor moments in the story. The supposedly majestic sign hanging in front of the inn at Muggleton, a heraldic device intended to imply the existence of an aristocratic patron, he delineates as representing '… an object very common in art, but rarely met with in nature – to wit, a blue lion, with three bow legs in the air, balancing himself on the extreme point of the centre claw of his fourth foot' (p. 99). And a Valentine card, whose mythological symbolism has been designed to inspire young lovers, is disrespect-fully described as '… a highly coloured representation of a couple of human hearts skewered together with an arrow, cooking before a cheerful fire, while a male and female cannibal in modern attire, the gentleman being clad in a blue coat and white trousers, and the lady in a deep red pelisse with a parasol of the same, were approaching the meal with hungry eyes, up a serpentine gravel path leading thereunto. A decidedly indelicate young gentleman, in a pair of wings and nothing else, was depicted as superintending the cooking' (p. 431).

Everything intended to inculcate veneration is available for ridicule, including those scenes of duels that proliferated in the contemporary novel, with each participant pronouncing the formal phrases testifying to the honour, courage and defiance of the participants. Dickens' version burlesques the tradition:

> 'I request that you'll favour me with your card, Sir,' said Mr. Noddy.
> 'I'll do nothing of the kind, Sir,' replied Mr. Gunter.
> 'Why not, Sir?' inquired Mr. Noddy.
> 'Because you'll stick it up over your chimney-piece, and delude your visitors into the false belief that a gentleman has been to see you, Sir,' replied Mr. Gunter.
> 'Sir, a friend of mine shall wait on you in the morning,' said Mr. Noddy.
> 'Sir, I'm very much obliged to you for the caution, and I'll leave particular directions with the servant to lock up the spoons,' replied Mr. Gunter (p. 426).

The humour functions at every turn to disparage the inflated notions both of individuals and of society at large, producing the kind of 'spoofing' that Dickens so greatly enjoyed and his readers found so entertaining. It is that which accounts for the famous scene at Bob Sawyer's lodging. Our initial introduction to the pair of 'sawbones' highlights their extraordinary brashness and self-confidence, Sam describing how he had seen them disporting themselves in the public room of the inn:

> One on 'em's got his legs on the table, and is a-drinking brandy neat, vile the t'other one – him in the barnacles – has got a barrel o' oysters atween his knees, which he's a-openin' like steam, and as fast as he eats 'em, he takes a aim vith the shells at young dropsy, who's a-sittin' down fast asleep, in the chimbley corner (p. 391).

That brashness is severely undercut when Pickwick is invited to visit them in their lodging, Bob Sawyer, in attempting to impress his visitors, being dismally discomfited by a landlady whose bill he has failed to meet. Just when a convivial atmosphere has been created, hosts and guests singing joyfully if somewhat discordantly as each applies to the words of a song the tune he knows best, a voice is heard from the two-pair landing, to which Bob replies meekly, asking what she wants:

'What do you mean by this, Mr. Sawyer?' replied the voice, with great shrillness and rapidity of utterance. 'Ain't it enough to be swindled out of one's rent, and money lent out of pocket besides, and abused and insulted by your friends that dares to call themselves men, without having the house turned out of the window, and noise enough made to bring the fire-engines here, at two o'clock in the morning? – Turn them wretches away' (p. 427).

Bob assures her miserably that they are leaving, and the guests skulk off, Mrs Raddle reserving her parting shot for Pickwick himself: 'You old wretch. Old enough to be his grandfather, you villin! You're worse than any of 'em.'

This novel reflects a contemporary change, for in contrast to the tradition of earlier fiction, it contains no aristocrats, no concern with upward class mobility, nor with the attainment of wealth and status through marriage such as had motivated the writings of Fielding, Smollet and Austen. Sam Weller does not prove to be the long-lost son of Pickwick, nor does Arabella's marriage to Winkle involve any social advancement. Only Jingle and Bob Sawyer regard marriage as a financial tool, and they are both placed outside the pale of settled society. Instead, in a period when the middle class was becoming acknowledged as valid in its own right, the characters not only belong solidly within their social level, but are content to be there. Pickwick and his friends are sufficiently affluent to be untroubled by financial pressures, as well as undesirous of enlarging their assets, while the liveried servants, housemaids and coachmen seem not only satisfied with their occupations but proud of them. And that sense of pride is again targeted. The 'soirée' of the Bath footmen is as formal, dignified and absurd as the meeting of the Pickwick Club, both marked by the members' exaggerated sense of their personal importance and their use of a form of rhetoric more appropriate to a parliamentary debate:

After a short silence, a gentleman in an embroidered coat reaching down to his heels, and a waistcoat of the same which kept one half of his legs warm, stirred his gin-and-water with great energy, and putting himself upon his feet, all at once by a violent effort, said he was desirous of offering a few remarks to the company, whereupon the person in the cocked hat had no doubt that the company would be very happy to hear any remarks that the man in the long coat might wish to offer (p. 501).

The senior Weller declares it to be self-evident that a coachman is 'a privileged indiwidual', to which comment he adds that, had Mr Pickwick been a coachman, no jury would ever have convicted him (p. 694). Indeed, the general warmth and benevolence pervading the novel, represented by Wardle's unstinting hospitality, Pickwick's generosity to the needy and Sam's refusal to leave Pickwick even to wed his beloved Mary until their marriage can be made to suit his master's needs, all confirm the settled form of society within this novel. The law is, indeed, an ass, and its representatives are, at their worst, devious and avaricious, but even that criticism is offset by the presence of Pickwick's friendly and honest lawyer, Perker.

The general absence of social concern is to no small extent responsible for the uniqueness of this work as the only comic novel Dickens produced. Once he began his crusade against the social abuses of his time and introduced murky scenes of crime and mystery, a grimness entered his writing precluding the good-humoured geniality characterizing this novel, such humour, as has been noted, being relegated henceforth to minor characters and incidents. Dickens had no desire to diminish, even by tangential ridicule, the solemnity of his crusade against the cruelty of orphanages or the heartlessness of the Murdstones. Humour is accordingly absent from the chilling descriptions of Squeer and Uriah Heep, and where there is comedy in these later novels it is confined to Swiveller in *The Old Curiosity Shop* or Mantalini in *Nicholas Nickleby*. But in *The Pickwick Papers* the humour functions throughout as the animating force, teasingly undercutting the pomposity, posturing or assumed dignity of its vastly entertaining characters.

c) Poking Fun at the Establishment

The use of humour as a means of correcting society's norms was to reach its acme some decades later. But before examining that phenomenon, a word about Lewis Carroll. *Alice's Adventures in Wonderland* and *Through the Looking Glass* are among the most charming of books, evoking pleasure, surprise and admiration for their inversions of logic and of actuality – with a rabbit wearing kid gloves, flamingoes employed as croquet mallets and a baby gradually turning into a piglet. They are enchanting, but they belong to fantasy, not comedy, eliciting appreciative smiles rather than laughter for their dreamlike contradiction of reality, with objects shrinking, expanding or disappearing in incidents lacking any deep implications. Puns can be genuinely amusing, but the puns offered here are for the most part deliberately juvenile, designed to appeal to the children for whom they were originally created rather than to adults. We are informed that the Tortoise 'taught us' and that the lessons 'lessened' from day to day, while the Gnat, remarking to Alice that if her governess called her 'Miss' she would miss her lessons, adds feebly 'That's a joke', to which Alice replies that it is a very bad one.

On the few occasions when there are implications beyond mere inversion of actuality, the implications carry lugubrious undertones militating against laughter that a nineteenth-century reader would not have missed. Isaac Watts' hymn from the *Divine Songs for Children* – 'How doth the little busy bee / Improve each shining hour ...' with its assumption that God's in his heaven and all's right with the world, begins as light-hearted parody in Carroll's version, but it concludes chillingly:

> How doth the little crocodile
>   Improve his shining tail
> And pour the waters of the Nile
>   On every golden scale!
>
> How cheerfully he seems to grin,
>   How neatly spreads his claws,
> And welcome little fishes in
>   With gently smiling jaws!

It reflects the Victorians' growing sense of Nature 'red in tooth and claw', the poem only lightly camouflaging the dread that haunted the author himself. Throughout his verse, the 'nonsense' is an attempt to hide, however momentarily, the fears shrouded in his subconscious. His *Hunting of the Snark*, again seemingly frivolous in tone, was in fact composed during circumstances far removed from hilarity, after a night spent nursing his dying godchild, in a mood when he was deeply disturbed and spiritually exhausted. In that poem, the flippancy of serving the Snark with greens and using it to strike a light leads to the throb of trepidation experienced in the dark, the Victorians' growing suspicion that death may, after all, be a disappearance into nothingness:

> I engage with the Snark – every night after dark –
>   In a dreamy delirious fight:
> I serve it with greens in those shadowy scenes,
>   And I use it for striking a light.
>
> But if ever I meet with a Boojuin, that day,
>   In a moment (of this I am sure),
> I shall softly and suddenly vanish away –
>   And the notion I cannot endure!

It echoed those many deathbed scenes in the novels of the time in which friends gather around the dying person, anxiously waiting for some sign that the moribund patient has, at the moment of death, experienced a vision of heaven and thereby proved the existence of an afterlife:

> They watched her breathing become more and more difficult, until evening deepened into night, and until midnight was past. About half-past twelve she seemed to be trying to speak, and they leaned to catch her words.
> 'Music – music – didn't you hear it?'[175]

In matters of Christian faith, Carroll was one of the most extraordinarily solemn and unbending dogmatists of his age. He would not suffer the slightest hint of religious irreverence in his presence, on one occasion sternly reprimanding a friend for having repeated to him some amusingly ingenuous remarks of children concerning the deity. While such remarks might be forgivable in the young, Carroll austerely insisted, they could never be so when quoted by an adult. On another occasion, he rebuked a bishop for having included a mildly humorous comment in a sermon, on the grounds that it '... went far to undo, in the minds of many of your hearers, and especially among the young men, much of the good effect of the rest of the sermon'. Nor would he willingly enter into any discussion on matters of Christian belief, admitting: 'I have a deep dread of argument on religious topics; it has many risks and little chance of doing good.'[176] It requires little knowledge of psychology to recognize that behind that dread of participating in religious argument was a fear of exposing his own religious doubts.

For those reasons I do not include the Alice books in this study of the comic, but there is an interesting exception, namely 'Jabberwocky'. It has become for linguists the classic illustration of 'portmanteau' wordplay, suggesting entertainingly, yet with serious implications, the speed with which the mind grasps allusions to the meaning of words:

> Twas brillig, and the slithy toves
>   Did gyre and gimble in the wabe:
> All mimsy were the borogoves,
>   And the mome raths outgrabe ...
> And, as in uffish thought he stood,
>   The Jabberwock, with eyes of flame,
> Came whiffling through the tulgey wood,
>   And burbled as it came! ...

As Humpty Dumpty obligingly explains to Alice, each of the puzzling words is a verbal amalgam, *slithy* combining *lithe* and *slimy*. With that hint, it becomes apparent that *toves* merges *toads* with *elves*, and *burble* is a blend of *babble* with *warble*, the neologisms proving so attractive that *uffish* and *burble* came into general usage. All this is well known, but does not explain the humour of the poem, which resides in the fact that, even after the source of the mergers has been perceived and we know that the word *whiffle* combines *whiff* with *whistle*, the words still fail to make any sense in the context. We have no final idea what the Jabberwock was actually doing when he 'whiffled', nor does the description of his thoughts as *uffish* indicate their nature. Most important, as Carroll later admitted, some of the words convey no meaning at all. The result is that it takes the principle of wordplay, the challenging of the authority of language, a stage further, evidencing to our amusement not only that words can be ambiguous but that they can at times give the impression of conveying meaning while failing to do so.

To return for a moment to the Victorian obsession with death, it did indeed produce works of humour, and the fact is instructive.

For if one major aspect of the comic is its temporary rebuffing of oppressive authority, the target here was one of the most disturbing for that era, the ominous threat of death in an age constantly emphasizing the hell that awaited the unrepentant yet at the same time doubtful, during the current spread of atheism and agnosticism, whether in fact any existence awaited them beyond the grave. Confronting death with jocularity provided a welcome relief, however brief, from that nagging doubt. The events in Thomas Hood's 'Faithless Nelly Gray' are indeed gruesome, but by means of a series of outrageous puns, attention is distracted from the potential horror of dismemberment and death:[177]

> Ben Battle was a soldier bold,
>   And used to war's alarms:
> But a cannon-ball took off his legs,
>   So he laid down his arms!
>
> Now, as they bore him off the field,
>   Said he, 'Let others shoot,
> For here I leave my second leg,
>   And the Forty-second Foot!' ...

That deflection of potential horror occurs even at the moment of his suicide, with the play on *steak*:

> And there he hung till he was dead
>   As any nail in town, –
> For though distress had cut him up,
>   It could not cut him down!
>
> A dozen men sat on his corpse,
>   To find out why he died –
> And they buried Ben in four cross-roads,
>   With a *stake* in his inside!

What emerges as of primary interest here is the tendency to use death, often in its most ghoulish forms, as a source of humour. Harry Graham's *Ruthless Rhymes* and Hilaire Belloc's series on such topics as *Henry King, Who Chewed Bits of String and Was Early Cut Off in Dreadful Agonies*, or *Matilda, Who Told Lies and Was Burned to Death,* were poems pretending to be instructive for the young, but their popularity among adults reveals the reprieve they offered, however brief, from the nagging concern with mortality. Although they entertained the Victorians, I have never found them amusing, so let us focus upon a different and more truly comic aspect of the Victorian age.

Difficult though it may be to define national forms of humour, there is, I believe, one element that may be termed essentially British and that may have had a more profound impact on its history than is generally thought. Almost all countries have, during recent centuries, experienced major revolutions or internecine warfare, among them France, America, Italy and Russia, but Britain, once the Puritan era was behind it (a period to which we shall return in a moment), experienced no such strife.[178] Nor were the motives for rebellion absent. In the early nineteenth century, the country seemed to be on the verge of an insurrection paralleling the revolution in France, and conditions were indeed ripe for such an event. The appalling poverty created by a series of failed harvests, by the enclosure of common land and by the unemployment attendant upon mechanization had incited the masses to widespread acts of vandalism. 'The country,' Arthur Hallam recorded in 1830, 'is in a more awful state than you can well conceive. While I write, Maddingley or some adjoining village, is in a state of conflagration and the sky above is coloured flame-red ... The laws are almost suspended; the money of foreign factions is at work with a population exasperated into reckless fury.'[179] Yet no rebellion materialized. Pitt's suppression of a protest meeting at 'Peterloo', in which a number of protesters were killed, provided the perfect occasion for a nationwide uprising, but instead, tempers subsided and further bloodshed was avoided. In 1848, there arose a further crisis when Chartists organized a huge demonstration in London to support the presentation of a petition to Parliament. London braced itself for a massive siege, Wellington calling out thousands of police in preparation, but after the protesters were permitted to hand in the petition, the Chartists quietly withdrew and peace was restored.

One reason for Britain's freedom from the horrors experienced by so many other countries was, one suspects, its tendency not to take its leaders too seriously, its readiness to poke fun at its generals, to regard the Law as an ass and its agents, the constabulary, as amusing incompetents. The Russians, it is true, did under the Soviet regime win a reputation for witty comments aimed against the authorities, but those were almost invariably tinged with bitterness, attacks on the government by a people knowingly impotent to effect any real change, such as the barb concerning Adam and Eve's nationality – that only Russians would run about barefoot, without a roof over their heads, sharing one apple between two, and yet be required to declare that they are in paradise. Britain, in contrast, has a tradition of amiable humour, a gentle lampooning of politicians and law enforcers, such laughter diverting or mitigating potential violence. The one serious revolution Britain did suffer was, significantly, instigated by a sect notorious for its lack of humour, Puritans such as William Prynne, who fulminated against the authorities with a religious fervour devoid of any hint of jocularity. In contrast, Jeremy Collier's attack on the theatre in 1698 was permeated by wit, as in his response to Congreve cited above, and as a result, his criticism resulted in a quiet revolution on the stage, free from animosity or bloodshed. Indeed, unlike the Puritans, Collier, a clergyman, had no objection to comedy as such, asking only that it be more moral in its aims, that the '... exposing of Knavery and making *Lewdness* ridiculous, is a much better occasion for laughter'.[180]

There were hints of the gentle ribbing of the authorities in earlier eras before the Puritans took over, as in the depiction of the doddering Justice Shallow, more concerned with phraseology than the duties of a magistrate:

> 'It is well said, in faith, sir; and it is well said indeed too. "Better accommodated!" It is good; yea, indeed, is it. Good phrases are surely, and ever were, very commendable. "Accommodated!" It comes of *accommodo*. Very good; a good phrase.' (*Henry IV Pt.2*, 3:2:68–72)

And such bumbling keepers of the peace as the watchman Dogberry and his crew were to serve as prototypes for later depictions of the constabulary:

> *Dogberry*: You are thought here to be the most senseless and fit men for the constable of the watch. Therefore bear you the lanthorn. This is your charge: you shall comprehend all vagrom men; you are to bid any man stand, in the Prince's name.
> *Second Watchman*: How if 'a will not stand?

Dogberry: Why then, take no note of him, but let him go, and presently call the rest of the watch together and thank God you are rid of a knave (*Much Ado* 3:3:22–30).

But it was in the nineteenth century that the refusal of the British public to take its parliamentary, military or judicial leaders too seriously reached its finest level, providing a healthy outlet for potential hostility, a safety valve that prevented anger from boiling over into rebellion. The mid-century was to see bitter attacks by Dickens and Mrs Gaskell on the horrendous workhouses, orphanages and housing of the poor, attacks that produced valuable legislation to alleviate the situation. But those novels offered no hint of incitement to violence, the chilling scenes of rioting in *Barnaby Rudge* providing a solemn warning against such action.

The tendency gently to lampoon the authorities was to reach its fullest expression soon after, as audiences rocked with laughter at the indulgent fun aimed at the judiciary, at the House of Lords, at the Admiralty and at that comparatively new body enforcing the law, the Metropolitan Police. The librettos provided by W. S. Gilbert and set to music by Arthur Sullivan are as entertaining today as when first performed in the 1870s and they rely for their humour on that same amiable ridiculing of supposedly magisterial authority that we have seen functioning in all comedy. Himself a lawyer, Gilbert could see the comic aspects even of the most solemn of legal functions, burlesquing in *Iolanthe* the Lord Chancellor's responsibility for wards in Chancery, for orphans needing guardianship:

The Law is the true embodiment
Of everything that's excellent.
It has no kind of fault or flaw,
And I, my Lords, embody the Law.
The constitutional guardian I
Of pretty young Wards in Chancery ...
And in my court I sit all day,
Giving agreeable girls away,
With one for him – and one for he –
And one for you – and one for ye –
And one for thou – and one for thee –

> But never, oh, never a one for me!
>   Which is exasperating for
>   A highly susceptible Chancellor!

Gilbert paraded members of the House of Lords on stage in their gorgeous robes of office (robes ordered from the official outfitters of the House), where they boast of their blue-blooded ancestry. With a glance at the new 1870 law requiring competitive examinations for acceptance into the civil service, Gilbert has them (since they admit their lack of the requisite intelligence to pass such exams) decide eventually to abscond into fairyland with the charming sprites, renaming their House of Peers the House of Peris.

The Pirates of Penzance provided what is probably the earliest and finest parody of the new constabulary. Established by Sir Robert Peel to impose law and order, they are amusingly presented as hopelessly incompetent, incapable of catching malefactors, and mournfully complaining, in what was to become a catchphrase, that 'A policeman's lot is not a happy one.' The conclusion of that operetta, in which the police are defeated, is especially interesting for its revelation of the patriotism underlying the humour, the indication that, for all the fun directed at the authorities, loyalty to Crown and the legislature remained paramount. If the police are bumblingly incapable of defeating the pirates, they have one final recourse when they lose the battle:

> *Sergeant*: On your allegiance we've a stronger claim –
> We charge you yield, in Queen Victoria's name!
> *Pirate King (baffled)*: You do!
> *Police*: We do!
> We charge you yield, in Queen Victoria's name!
> *(Pirates kneel, Police stand over them triumphantly.)*
> *Pirate King*: We yield at once, with humbled mien,
> Because, with all our faults, we love our Queen.[181]

The Keystone Kops, who emerged in Hollywood movies in 1912, were acknowledgedly modelled by Mack Sennett on the Gilbert and Sullivan version; but across the Atlantic that approach failed to survive, being replaced in subsequent Hollywood depictions by a predominant reverence for the police as efficient officers of the law, relentlessly pursuing and apprehending criminal elements. In

Britain, however, the comic tradition continued as intrinsic to the national disposition, the constable in detective stories and on the stage being almost invariably presented as a stolid, dim, but amiable incompetent, while an intelligent individual outside the force – Sherlock Holmes, Lord Peter Wimsey, the elderly Miss Marple or the French inspector Hercule Poirot visiting from the continent – uncovers the truth.[182]

Gilbert parodied not only the judiciary, the police and the military (the model Major General in *The Pirates of Penzance* and the First Lord of the Admiralty in *H.M.S.Pinafore*) but also the fashionable affectations of the day. Japonisme had recently come into vogue. Whistler, after introducing oriental items into such paintings as *La Princesse du Pays de Porcelaine*, had in 1876 designed the famous Peacock Room in London (later removed to the Freer Museum in Washington), and the fashion became widespread. It did so not, as most history books record, because of a rise in the importation of Japanese goods – goods were being imported from countries throughout the world. The specific appeal of Japanese painting and woodcuts was its answer to a new need, the contemporary search for a highly stylized model. The concept of the benevolence of Nature that had inspired the Romantics had now been discredited by Darwinism, with its recognition of the cruelty of the various species savagely fighting each other for survival. In Art Nouveau, therefore, Nature was now replaced as a model by the artefact, regarded as superior to Nature because of its unchanging, eternal form. Where Keats had chosen the song of the nightingale as his symbol of poetry, Yeats adopted instead a bird of hammered gold, reminiscent of the jewelled animal forms being produced by Fabergé. The stylization in Japanese art suited that need perfectly, and became the model for highbrows, *Punch* publishing in 1880 George du Maurier's cartoon of a newly married couple gazing reverently at the oriental teapot they had received as a gift, the bride proclaiming in the caption, 'Oh, Algernon, let us live up to it!' The time was ripe for *The Mikado* to debunk the claims of the aesthetes:

> If you want to know who we are,
>   We are gentlemen of Japan:
> On many a vase and jar –
>   On many a screen and fan,
>   We figure in lively paint:
>   Our attitude's queer and quaint …

The operetta offered a view of the Far East considerably less flattering than that in Art Nouveau, with an Emperor, unhampered by the laws pertaining in Britain, chopping off citizens' heads at will. Once again, the Victorian obsession with death is treated here with a jocularity eschewing gloomy thoughts. The Lord High Executioner is less concerned with ridding the country of criminals than with ridding it of annoying individuals, his 'little list' including people who have flabby hands or irritating laughs, who eat peppermint and puff it in your face, added to that list being the perpetrators of the Japanese vogue itself – 'The idiot who praises, with enthusiastic tone, / All centuries but this, and every country but his own.' Moreover, the foreign setting of the operetta provided useful camouflage for comments tangentially spoofing the British scene, as in the sly dig at the prudery as well as the complacency of the Victorian era in one of the laws instituted by the Mikado, who had

> Resolved to try
> A plan whereby
> Young men might best be steadied.
> So he decreed in words succinct,
> That all who flirted, leered or winked
> (Unless connubially linked),
> Should forthwith be beheaded.
> And I expect you'll all agree
> That he was right to so decree.
> And I am right.
> And you are right,
> And all is right as right can be!

Whatever the tangential references, the placing of the spoof in a Japan employing casual impositions of the death penalty created the congenial feeling in British audiences of a superiority to the Far East, and hence a comforting accord with and affection for their own legal system. But most relevant to our present study, one should note how the humour was, once again, based upon a deflating of claims to superiority, a burlesque of a vogue taken so seriously by the artists and intellectuals of the time constantly prating of their elitist sensibilities.

That process achieved one of its most successful parodies by focusing upon the leading advocates of Aestheticism, Rossetti and

Swinburne, at a time when Oscar Wilde was gradually taking over the lead from them, the target then being transferred to Wilde himself. There was, however, a peculiar twist to the situation. For where most individuals resent being parodied, Wilde basked in publicity, particularly when it was adverse, being never happier than when arousing the scorn of his detractors. The D'Oyly Carte company, having decided to send its production of *Patience* to America but doubtful whether it would succeed on a continent less familiar with the aesthetes' affectations, invited Wilde to undertake a lecture tour there before the production opened, an offer he readily accepted. The fact that he enjoyed being parodied did not alter the function of the humour in holding him up to ridicule, since ultimately such parody highlighted the gap between his pretensions and reality, with its suggestion that Wilde's aestheticism was a fake, a pose aimed at winning the admiration of those foolish enough to believe it. Thus, Wilde's counterpart within the operetta, the aesthetic poet Bunthorne, after checking that he cannot be overheard, admits the hollowness of his artistic pretensions:

Am I alone,
And unobserved? I am!
Then let me own
I'm an aesthetic sham! ...
A languid love for Lilies does not blight me!
Lank limbs and haggard cheeks do not delight me!
I do not care for dirty greens
By any means.
I do not long for all one sees
That's Japanese.
I am not fond of uttering platitudes
In stained-glass attitudes.
In short, my mediaevalism's affectation,
Born of a morbid love of admiration!
If you're anxious for to shine in the high aesthetic line as a man of culture rare,
You must get up all the germs of the transcendental terms, and plant them ev'rywhere.
You must lie upon the daisies and discourse in novel phrases of your complicated state of mind,

The meaning doesn't matter if it's only idle chatter of a transcen-
dental kind.
  And ev'ry one will say,
  As you walk your mystic way,
'If this young man expresses himself in terms too deep for me,
Why, what a very singularly deep young man this deep young man
must be!' ...

One can imagine the delight of audiences, in Britain as well as
America, irritated by and resentful of the pretensions of the Aesthetic
Movement, especially of Wilde himself, on hearing him described in
such terms as 'uttering platitudes / In stained-glass attitudes.' At the
conclusion of the operetta, deprived of his lady-love, Bunthorne
comforts himself with the alternative:

In that case unprecedented,
  Single I must live and die –
I shall have to be contented
  With a tulip or lily!
(He takes a lily from his buttonhole and gazes affectionately at it.)

Debunking of pretentiousness could scarcely be more effective than
this.

d) Wilde, *The Importance of Being Earnest*

If Wilde could be tiresome in cultivating eccentricity, as a writer he
could be brilliant, as is evidenced when we turn from Wilde as the
object of humour to Wilde as its creator. The leading humorists
of that time, Wilde himself, G. K. Chesterton and Bernard Shaw
– all of whom presented serious themes in entertaining form –
shared one characteristic, a penchant for the inverted cliché. Wilde
cynically reversed the axiom 'Marriages are made in heaven' to read
'Divorces are made in heaven', Shaw entitled a play, *Too True to be
Good*, and Chesterton's wit as a debater lay largely in his ability to
refute his opponents' arguments by reversing the wording. Where
Shaw the socialist solemnly urged, 'Abolish private property which
has produced this ghastly poverty,' Chesterton replied pithily but
very seriously, 'Abolish this ghastly poverty by restoring private
property.'[183] Indeed, a major attraction of the many public debates

between these two was the ability of each to invert the other's remarks and turn them to advantage, the humour always on an amicable note since they respected and admired each other as individuals however contrasting their political and religious views were. Chesterton was, of course, of enormous girth, a lover of good food and wine, while Shaw was thin, a vegetarian and something of an ascetic. On one occasion, Chesterton remarked good-humouredly in his opening speech that to look at his friend, Shaw, one would think there was a famine in the land, to which Shaw replied at once that to look at Chesterton one would think he had caused it. Again the general principle is confirmed since our laughter is directed at that moment at Chesterton, confident that he has made an effective thrust at his fellow debater only to find himself reduced to the victim instead of the creator of the wit.

Seen in a larger perspective, this shared tendency to invert axioms was the ideal tool for challenging the solidity of Victorian assumptions, of beliefs generally regarded as so unassailable that they could be treated as proverbial. Their witty inversion was a perfect instance of the puncturing of established authority. Such reversed aphorisms startled readers and audiences into reassessing their most cherished assumptions, while the humour implicit in the unexpected inversion softened potential annoyance. Wilde's comment concerning divorces might amuse initially as merely a clever quip but it carried serious implications, casting doubt on the Victorians' cherished concept of a benevolent deity arranging everything for the good of mankind. Wilde had, in fact, adopted very early in his career this technique of startling his hearers by sarcastic challenges to normal assumptions. An outstanding classics student at Oxford, in his final oral examination he was asked to translate from the Greek text of the New Testament the account of Jesus' arrest. He did so with such fluency that his examiners, more than satisfied, informed him that he could stop, but Wilde imperturbably continued translating. Eventually they succeeded in halting him, at which point Wilde cried, 'Oh, do let me go on – I want to see how it ends.'[184]

A valuable key to appreciating the success of *The Importance of Being Earnest* is the fact that *Salomé*, the play he wrote in the 'Decadent' or *fin de siècle* tradition, he composed in French, no doubt recognizing that the scene of Salome depravedly kissing the gory lips of the beheaded John the Baptist would never be allowed on the English stage (Lord Douglas' translation of the play into English was, as expected, refused a licence somewhat later). That need to satisfy the censors has implications for this comedy, since it reveals how necessary it was for Wilde to ensure that any parody of Victorian ideas be discreetly veiled if it was ever to be allowed stage performance. Accordingly, the action of the play conforms closely to the moral requirements of the age, carefully avoiding impropriety. Jack takes his responsibilities as a guardian with the utmost seriousness, not only caring for his ward Cecily's upbringing but also ensuring that he himself should at all times serve for her as an impeccable model of propriety. Hence his recourse to a counterpart, a fictitious brother whose iniquitous behaviour could serve as an educative warning to Cecily and, since fraternal responsibilities would require his frequent monitory presence, the arrangement would allow him to relax a little outside his home while yet preserving the gravity of his role as her mentor. Ostensibly, therefore, all is as it should be, while the sly digs at the Victorian world, such as the dreariness of conforming to propriety, are tucked away inconspicuously, as in his explanation to Algernon of the system he has adopted:

> *Jack:* When one is placed in the position of guardian, one has to adopt a very high moral tone on all subjects. It's one's duty to do so. And as a high moral tone can hardly be said to conduce very much to either one's health or one's happiness, in order to get up to town I have always pretended to have a younger brother of the name of Ernest, who lives in the Albany, and gets into the most dreadful scrapes.[185]

There is, one should note, no hint of misconduct on the part of the four lovers, each eager for a formal engagement to be duly followed by a formal marriage. Moreover, the 'Bunburying' of both leading males is presented as entirely innocuous – for Jack an opportunity to be temporarily freed from the boredom of the country, for Algernon an excuse for absenting himself from tiresome family gatherings. Yet beneath that surface conventionality lurks a patent allusion to the murkier side of Victorian practice, the hypocrisy of so many supposedly respectable heads of households keeping a mistress in town while strictly preserving the pose of moral uprightness in the family setting.

That discrepancy both animates the play and explains its effectiveness. Where Restoration dramatists, voicing the libertine concepts prevalent among the aristocracy, had aimed their barbs at the exceptions within their society, at the False Wits conceitedly imagining themselves to personify those ideas yet failing woefully to live up to them, here the situation is closer to the general pattern of humour as we have defined it. For the target is the mainstream, namely society at large, whose authority needed to be challenged in a manner that would subtly win over audiences without shocking them too far. The result is a play providing relief from the oppressive dictates of social norms, yet without causing its Victorian audiences to feel that their moral principles were being too seriously undermined. If, on leaving the theatre, they might ponder whether the challenges were, after all, more seriously based, during the performance itself, the humour mitigated any potential acerbity.

The title of the play exemplifies this approach, with its seemingly casual reference to the young ladies' determination to find a husband named Ernest. Allan Rodway has assumed, with others, that the search for a husband of that name is the real purpose of the play, and that if there was any mockery of Victorian seriousness 'we are not particularly encouraged to see it'.[186] The opposite is true, for by presenting the demand for earnestness as if it were merely a matter of nomenclature, an idle preference on the part of the ladies, Wilde was providing a palliative to his audience while attacking one of the pillars of Victorian society. In 1835, the word 'earnest' had first come into fashion as a moral principle, Samuel Butler recalling in his semi-autobiographical novel, *The Way of All Flesh*, the emergence of that term as a criterion of respectability during the period of his youth. John Newman, at the height of the Oxford Movement, subtitled one of his influential *Parochial Sermons*: 'The Test of Religious Earnestness'; Carlyle, the revered sage of the era, made 'earnestness' of character a criterion for inclusion in his *Heroes and Hero-worship* of 1841, and the *Edinburgh Review* noted that to Matthew Arnold and his admirers, '… we owe the substitution of the word *earnest* for its predecessor *serious*'. By 1862 it had become an accepted precept, Charles Kingsley commenting with approval on the 'increased earnestness and high-mindedness' of his generation.[187]

Instead of challenging the principle outright, then, Wilde presented it as a mere laughable idiosyncrasy, the young ladies' absurd assumption that the name Ernest would produce the desired gravity of demeanour. What was really being burlesqued, however, was the ladies' conviction that earnestness was an essential characteristic for any future husband:

Gwendolen: For me you have always had an irresistible fasci-
nation. Even before I met you I was far from indifferent to you.
[*Jack looks at her in amazement*.] We live, as I hope you know, Mr.
Worthing, in an age of ideals. The fact is constantly mentioned
in the more expensive monthly magazines, and has reached the
provincial pulpits, I am told; and my ideal has always been to
love some one of the name of Ernest. There is something in that
name that inspires absolute confidence. The moment Algernon
first mentioned to me that he had a friend called Ernest, I knew I
was destined to love you.

Wilde's subtitle for the play – 'A Trivial Comedy for Serious People'
– reminded audiences that the theme should not be dismissed as
a mere frolic, that there was potent criticism within the humorous
presentation.

His treatment of the formidable Lady Bracknell exemplifies his
approach. On the one hand, she represents the solemn inflexibility
of Victorian morality; yet on the other hand, tucked away in parentheses are Wilde's gibes at the truths behind the facade, suggesting
that she too (and hence Victorian society itself) was aware of the
gap between its pretensions and actuality, between the ideals to
which it ostensibly subscribed and its flouting of them in practice. A
photograph frequently displayed in Victorian homes depicted Queen
Victoria gazing up subserviently to her husband, Prince Albert,
thereby proclaiming the principle that the husband was at all times
to be revered as the head of the household and his word regarded
as law, even where the wife was the rightful queen and the husband
only her consort. Patriarchal authority within the family was a basic
creed, dining-room furniture of the time consisting not, as today,
of a set of identical chairs but varied – one imposing chair with
armrests being assigned to the father, a slightly smaller armrested
version for the mother, and straight-back chairs devoid of armrests
for the remainder – and heaven help any child who dared to sit in
the father's chair during his absence. Hence the tale of 'The Three
Bears'. Against that background, a somewhat different picture
emerges of that hierarchical principle in practice, the play drolly
presenting a heavy matriarchal dominance. In the proposal scene,
Gwendolen takes command of the situation in a manner clearly
indicating who will be master (or mistress) of their house after
marriage:

Jack. Well … may I propose to you now?

Gwendolen. I think it would be an admirable opportunity. And to spare you any possible disappointment, Mr. Worthing, I think it only fair to tell you quite frankly beforehand that I am fully determined to accept you.

Jack. Gwendolen!

Gwendolen. Yes, Mr. Worthing, what have you got to say to me?

Jack. You know what I have got to say to you.

Gwendolen. Yes, but you don't say it.

Jack. Gwendolen, will you marry me? [*Goes on his knees.*]

Gwendolen. Of course I will, darling. How long you have been about it! I am afraid you have had very little experience in how to propose.

Lady Bracknell, who enters a few moments later, leaves no doubt who commands the Bracknell residence:

Gwendolen: I am engaged to Mr. Worthing, mamma. [*They rise together.*]

Lady Bracknell: Pardon me, you are not engaged to anyone. When you do become engaged to someone, I, or your father should his health permit him, will inform you of the fact.

As Lady Bracknell had remarked a little earlier, if the number of guests at her dinner party should prove uneven, her husband would, as usual, be banished from the scene, condemned to dine upstairs on the same pretext of his ill-health. Patriarchal hegemony emerges as valid only in theory.

Again with delicacy, Wilde exposes the gap between, on the one hand, the assumption in Victorian fiction that all must be sacrificed to love and, on the other, the fact that marriage in that period was most often a mercenary arrangement dependent upon property. Despite Coventry Patmore's poem *The Angel in the House*, whose title was widely adopted as defining the Victorian conception of the marital relationship permeated by the purest love, G. R. Drysdale wrote more soberly in 1854 that, 'A great proportion of the marriages we see around us did not take place from love at all, but from some interested motive, such as wealth, social position or other advantages; and in fact it is *rare* to see a marriage in which true love has been the predominating feeling on both sides.'[188] In *Daniel Deronda*,

George Eliot, whose sympathies lay, as was usual in the fiction of the period, with marriages based on love, assigned to a minister of the church the standard Victorian viewpoint, as he solemnly advises the wealthy Gwendolen Harleth of her duty to marry appropriately: 'You hold your fortune in your own hands, – a fortune such as rarely happens to a girl in your circumstances, – a fortune in fact which almost takes the question out of the range of mere personal feeling, and makes your acceptance of it a duty. If Providence offers you power and position, – especially when unclogged by any conditions that are repugnant to you, – your course is one of responsibility, into which caprice must not enter.' Outside the realm of fiction, insistence on love as a prerequisite for marriage was thus generally regarded as a mere caprice, personal feelings (as the word 'especially' denotes) to be suppressed even when the proposed spouse or the attendant conditions were indeed 'repugnant'. Wilde again avoids confronting outright the hypocrisy involved in this gap between Victorian ideal and Victorian practice by assigning such materialistic purposes to the awesome Lady Bracknell and hence aligning the audience's sympathies with the young couples, but as Lady Bracknell represents the authoritative code of the time, the Victorians' preference for property over love is made patent. Hence her sudden change on learning that Cecily is possessed of a sizeable dowry, with the delightful play on the term 'attractive':

> *Lady Bracknell (sitting down again).* A moment, Mr. Worthing. A hundred and thirty thousand pounds! And in the Funds! Miss Cardew seems to me a most attractive young lady, now that I look at her. Few girls of the present day have any really solid qualities, any of the qualities that last, and improve with time.

Money, or what Carlyle called 'the god Mammon', is for her, together with social status, a primary criterion. Hence, on learning that, according to the will, Cecily will not come of age until she is 35, and that Jack has threatened to prevent his ward marrying until then, her resourceful response is the gratifying thought that by that time 'there will be a large accumulation of property'. She does add, however, in vindication of her stance, that in principle she disapproves of mercenary marriages, although the reason for her disapproval is again in the form of a witty inversion, the principle being applied by her only when advantageous: 'When I married Lord Bracknell, I had no fortune of any kind. But I never dreamed for a moment of allowing that to stand in my way.' Consistent with Wilde's wry attack upon the loveless marriages so common in that era is the remark concerning Lady Harbury that, after her husband's death, her hair turned quite gold with grief, as well as Lady Bracknell's comment in the final scene that Jack's father, the General, 'was essentially a man of peace, except in his domestic life'.

Barbs aimed at Victorianism occur even in the most minor scenes. The opening of the play may seem mere badinage as Algernon at the piano asks grandly if Lane had heard what he was playing, and the butler replies, 'I did not think it polite to listen, sir.' The primary humour here is, of course, the implication that the playing was too bad to be commented on, but the remark has further rever-berations. One of the basic concerns of Victorian society was to preserve the privacy of the upper class, to ensure that no marital disputes, no discussion of scandals ever take place in the presence of the domestics. In wealthy country homes, an intricate system of hidden passageways was devised enabling the servants to move from kitchen to dining hall, from laundry to bedrooms without ever being seen by or seeing their employers. At Welbeck Abbey, the Duke of Portland dismissed instantly any housemaid who had the misfortune to meet him in a corridor and in other houses maids had to flatten themselves with their faces to the wall, making themselves as incon-spicuous as possible as soon as they saw anyone approaching.[189] In middle-class homes with their more compact space, such preser-vation of privacy was little more than a farce, the well-trained Lane adopting the accepted practice of pretending neither to hear nor see anything that could be thought discreditable.

The subsequent exchange parodies a further norm. Victorians, with their insistence on moral earnestness, were, of course, extra-ordinarily strict concerning their servants' morals. Not only were the sleeping quarters of male and female domestics kept entirely separate in the newly built country houses, but frequently different staircases were installed for each gender so that the servants should never pass the opposite sex on the way to bed.[190] In all such homes, including those of the middle class, the servants' activities were rigorously supervised even on their days off, lest they become involved with undesirable companions – all this when the employers themselves were so often considerably less upright in their own pursuits, when in many country houses weekend guests were discreetly assigned to rooms offering easy access to their extra-marital companions. Hence Algernon's irreverent inversion: 'Really, if the lower orders don't set us a good example, what on earth is the use of them?'

Not all the humour arises from taunts at the rules imposed by contemporary society, some instances conforming to a more general pattern of deflation. While Algernon is essentially mischievous in character, cheerfully admitting to his misdemeanours, Jack, although sharing his dislike of formalities, is just that little bit pompous – as Algernon remarks, he is 'the most earnest-looking person I ever saw in my life' – and we delight in watching him trapped, striving ineffectually to preserve his dignity when Algernon queries him concerning the cigarette case:

> *Algernon.* But this isn't your cigarette case. This cigarette case is a present from some one of the name of Cecily, and you said you didn't know any one of that name.
> *Jack.* Well, if you want to know, Cecily happens to be my aunt.
> *Algernon.* Your aunt!
> *Jack.* Yes. Charming old lady she is, too. Lives at Tunbridge Wells. Just give it back to me, Algy.
> *Algernon.* [*Retreating to back of sofa.*] But why does she call herself little Cecily if she is your aunt and lives at Tunbridge Wells? [*Reading.*] 'From little Cecily with her fondest love.'

It is a scene beautifully paralleled later, when Jack, determined at last to kill off his fictitious counterpart, appears in the full mourning regalia requisite at the time, only to be confronted to his dismay by the individual whom he is supposed to be mourning.

Indeed, the principle of deflation functions throughout, as in the repartee between the two men, where Algernon repeatedly invalidates Jack's imperious statements by inverting Jack's words:

> *Jack.* As for your conduct towards Miss Cardew, I must say that your taking in a sweet, simple, innocent girl like that is quite inexcusable. To say nothing of the fact that she is my ward.
> *Algernon.* I can see no possible defence at all for your deceiving a brilliant, clever, thoroughly experienced young lady like Miss Fairfax. To say nothing of the fact that she is my cousin.
> *Jack.* I wanted to be engaged to Gwendolen, that is all. I love her.
> *Algernon.* Well, I simply wanted to be engaged to Cecily. I adore her.

Jack. There is certainly no chance of your marrying Miss Cardew. *Algernon.* I don't think there is much likelihood, Jack, of you and Miss Fairfax being united.

The plot itself is perfectly devised, as in the scene when confusion over the two supposed 'Ernests' leads the young ladies to imagine that they are engaged to the same man and hence to indulge in a politely vituperous exchange in the garden. Well-bred young ladies must at all times conform to the dictates of etiquette, so that their mutual insults, especially in the presence of the butler, are presented under a veneer of courtesy. Cecily, attempting to end their meeting, in which Gwendolen has claimed to be engaged to her own Ernest, comments icily: 'It seems to me, Miss Fairfax, that I am trespassing on your valuable time. No doubt you have many other calls of a similar character to make in the neighbourhood.' Each in turn stands on her dignity, only to be trounced by the opponent's next remark. Cecily, accusing her supposed rival of prevaricating, announces that she herself insists on calling a spade a spade, to which Gwendolen replies haughtily: 'I am glad to say that I have never seen a spade. It is obvious that our social spheres have been widely different.' We are presented with the gap between a pretence to dignified courtesy and the reality of mutual insults in the cut-throat competition for husbands.

Such pricking of pomposity affects even the most minor scenes, as in Canon Chasuble's unfortunate attempt to display his literary sophistication:

Chasuble: Were I fortunate enough to be Miss Prism's pupil, I would hang upon her lips. [*Miss Prism glares.*] I spoke metaphorically. – My metaphor was drawn from bees.

But the main source of the humour is, of course, Wilde's sly targeting of social convention, his teasing discrediting of Victorian complacency and, above all, his exposure of the discrepancies between the contemporary claim to moral earnestness and the actualities of Victorian social behaviour.

e) Jerome K. Jerome, *Three Men in a Boat*

The book had not been planned as a humorous work. It had been intended as a topographical account of the River Thames, recording interesting events in history that had occurred at various places on its banks and describing the buildings and other monuments located nearby, all this in the framework of a boating trip conducted along its upper reaches. From the first, however, the author's sense of humour intruded, and the editors of the journal *Home Chimes*, in which it was appearing in serial form, noting that their readers relished the humour more than the topography, wisely began excising or minimizing the more solemn historical sections. Its reception as a comic book came as a surprise to the author, as did its enormous success, with sales of over a million copies in Britain, a further million in the United States (for which he received no payment, as there was at that time no copyright law to prevent piracy), and the numerous editions that followed. The sequel to the work, *Three Men on a Bummel*, proved less successful, consisting for the most part of an acerbic attack on the pedantry of the German people; but the earlier work has deservedly retained its popularity.

Jerome insisted in his preface to the first edition that all incidents in the story had really occurred, that 'Harris' and 'George' were not fictitious characters but based on his friends Carl Hentschel and George Wingrave who had accompanied him on the trip, adding that Montmorency was his own dog. Yet his modest attribution of the tale to actuality overlooked the true source of its entertainment, the method he developed for relating or embellishing the incidents that had occurred. For, from the opening of the book, he adopted a technique subtly different from the norm but recalling, with variations, the technique adopted by both Chaucer and Marvell. By means of a first-person narration, he created a pseudo-self, a projection of himself seemingly unaware of the foibles, misapprehensions and illusions for which the story lampoons him, a fictitious being supremely confident of his own impeccable standards and therefore to be laughed at whenever the gap between his illusions and the reality of his situation is perceived. At the same time, the reader is encouraged to perceive behind that account the shadowy presence of the author, an author fully aware of those elements of which his other self is supposedly ignorant. The result is to produce in the reader a conspiratorial feeling of identification with Jerome for, in effect, so readily laughing at himself while functioning simultaneously as both the humorist and the object of the humour.

The opening incident establishes the pattern, the scene in which the narrator, on chancing to consult a medical book, discovers to his horror that he is suffering from every illness listed there, with the possible exception of housemaid's knee: 'I came to typhoid fever, read the symptoms, discovered that I had typhoid fever, must have had it for months without knowing it, wondered what else I had got; turned up St. Vitus's Dance found, as I expected, that I had that too, began to get interested in my case, and determined to sift it to the bottom, and so started alphabetically, read up ague ... I tried to look at my tongue. I stuck it out as far as ever it would go, and I shut one eye, and tried to examine it with the other. I could only see the tip, and the only thing that I could gain from that was to feel more certain than before that I had scarlet fever. I had walked into that reading-room a happy, healthy man. I crawled out a decrepit wreck.' The only debility the speaker suffers from is, of course, hypochondria; and if we laugh at him for the firm conviction of his multiple maladies, we are aware at the same moment of the author laughing at his self-projection.

The separation of author from narrator provides Jerome with the opportunity of endowing his other self with the kind of boastfulness that he would no doubt have avoided in real life, an unwarranted confidence that lends particular force to the fall that follows, as in the following passage:

> I rather pride myself on my packing. Packing is one of those many things that I feel I know more about than any other person living. (It surprises me myself, sometimes, how many of these subjects there are.) I impressed the fact upon George and Harris, and told them that they had better leave the whole matter entirely to me. They fell into the suggestion with a readiness that had something uncanny about it. George put on a pipe and spread himself over the easy-chair, and Harris cocked his legs on the table and lit a cigar[191] (p. 33).

One need not describe in any detail the disastrous results of the packing as he discovers, after finally strapping down the case, that he has forgotten to put in his boots; and, once they have been with great difficulty inserted, that he has inadvertently packed his tobacco pouch which he must now struggle to retrieve.

That technique has an added advantage. Since Jerome, while preserving a protective distance from his fictitious self, can make unlimited fun of the latter's absurdities, the corollary of this regard is the realization that we ourselves, however hesitant we may be to admit the fact, are as subject to those delusions and weaknesses as the fictional character. Even when recounting some general tendency, he increases the effect greatly by the first-person account, as in his admission that for him early morning dips in the sea are not quite as pleasurable as had been imagined when planned the night before. After oversleeping on a number of mornings subsequent to his decision, he finally wakes early enough one day, seizes a towel, and running out to the beach, finds to his dismay that the sea has moved two miles out. Hopping painfully over sharp stones and then wading, shivering with cold, through water only six inches deep, when he does reach the sea, a huge wave casts him

> ... as hard as ever it can, down on to a rock which has been put there for me. And, before I've said 'Oh! Ugh!' and found out what has gone, the wave comes back and carries me out to mid-ocean. I begin to strike out frantically for the shore, and wonder if I shall ever see home and friends again, and wish I'd been kinder to my little sister when a boy (when *I* was a boy, I mean). Just when I have given up all hope, a wave retires and leaves me sprawling like a star-fish on the sand, and I get up and look back and find that I've been swimming for my life in two feet of water (p. 25).

Each of these incidents is preceded by some hint of personal vanity to ensure the humour of the 'fall', in this instance the parenthetical comment as he begins the tale that he always buys red swimsuits as he rather fancies himself in them.

It is instructive to note how these touches of vanity – the self-satisfaction so central to humour – create the effectiveness of the tales, as in the story of the practical jokers who, relying on their peers' ignorance of German, mislead the company into believing that a song about to be rendered in that language by a German professor is hilariously funny, when it is in fact a deeply tragic tale of a young girl who dies to save her lover. The incident could have been related quite amusingly with the narrator functioning as the successful perpetrator of the joke, triumphing over his peers. However, with far greater effect, Jerome presents himself as one of the victims, laughing uproariously at the song in order to hide his lack of German and regarding with pride the 'particularly artful' method he has devised for concealing his linguistic deficiency: 'I did not want the people there to guess my ignorance; so I hit upon what I thought to be rather a good idea. I kept my eye on the two young students, and followed them. When they tittered, I tittered; when they roared, I roared; and I also threw in a little snigger all by myself now and then, as if I had seen a bit of humour that had escaped the others. I considered this particularly artful on my part. I noticed, as the song progressed, that a good many other people seemed to have their eye fixed on the two young men, as well as myself. These other people also tittered when the young men tittered, and roared when the young men roared; and, as the two young men tittered and roared and exploded with laughter pretty continuously all through the song, it went exceedingly well. And yet that German Professor did not seem happy ...' (p. 71)

Not all the humour is directed at his pseudo-self, a classic instance being the moment when the latter accidentally drops his shirt into the water – to his annoyance and to the immense amusement of George, until the moment when George suddenly realizes that the shirt is his own:

'What!' he yelled, springing up. 'You silly cuckoo! Why can't you be more careful what you're doing? Why the deuce don't you go and dress on the bank? You're not fit to be in a boat, you're not. Gimme the hitcher.' I tried to make him see the fun of the thing, but he could not. George is very dense at seeing a joke sometimes (p. 100).

That final comment returns the target to himself, typifying the pattern at large, reminding us of the speaker's own inability to see the joke earlier when he himself had been the target of the laughter.

The humour is often achieved in a manner reminiscent of the mock epic, which first inflates in order to produce the subsequent bathetic plunge, but it succeeds here in a special way, by employing the more serious passages on the charm and historical interest of the Thames area that had formed the original purpose of the book. Those passages not excised by the editors are generally meditations on the beauty of the river or romantic musings on past events, as in the evocation of the scene at the signing of the Magna Carta: '... little banners are fluttering lazily in the warm breeze, and every now and then there is a deeper stir as the ranks make way on either side, and some great baron on his war-horse, with his guard of squires around him, passes along to take his station at the head of his serfs and vassals ...' Accordingly, when a passage of that type occurs elsewhere, the reader assumes it to be serious. Thus the narrator, as he steers the boat along the river, is deeply moved by the red sunset that provides a mystic background to the scene of three men quietly fishing from their punt, the language verging on the poetic: 'It was an hour of deep enchantment, of ecstatic hope and longing. The little sail stood out against the purple sky, the gloaming lay around us, wrapping the world in rainbow shadows; and, behind us, crept the night. We seemed like knights of some old legend, sailing across some mystic lake into the unknown realm of twilight, unto the great land of the sunset. We did not go into the realm of twilight; we went slap into that punt, where those three old men were fishing.' As the men pick themselves up from the bottom of the punt, '... they cursed us – not with a common cursory curse, but with long, carefully-thought-out, comprehensive curses, that embraced the whole of our career, and went away into the distant future, and included all our relations, and covered everything connected with us ...' (pp. 114–15). Our amusement is not only with the unexpected break in poetic mood but also, and perhaps primarily, with the narrator's discomfiture as his evident pride in his romantic sensibility leads him to be oblivious of the realities of his situation. Moreover, we laugh at ourselves for having taken seriously the account of the mystic sunset.

Because of the rich variety of incidents, the relaxed setting and the masterly raconteurship, each incident retains its freshness, as in the description of a young couple immersed in conversation as they walk along the path pulling the tow rope behind them, only to discover to their consternation that its other end is unattached, that the boat with their aunt in it has been left floating steerlessly far behind. That last instance belongs to those scenes extraneous to the actual trip, incidents that are inserted as though recalled by events in the story. Such is the account of Uncle Podger's attempt to hang a picture on the wall – an individual supremely sure of his proficiency as a handyman:

'Now you go and get me my hammer, Will,' he would shout; 'and you bring me the rule, Tom; and I shall want the step-ladder, and I had better have a kitchen-chair, too; and, Jim! you run round to Mr. Goggles, and tell him, "Pa's kind regards, and hopes his leg's better; and will he lend him his spirit-level?" And don't you go, Maria, because I shall want somebody to hold me the light; and when the girl comes back, she must go out again for a bit of picture-cord; and Tom! where's Tom? Tom, you come here; I shall want you to hand me up the picture.' And then he would lift up the picture, and drop it, and it would come out of the frame, and he would try to save the glass, and cut himself; and then he would spring round the room, looking for his handkerchief. He could not find his handkerchief, because it was in the pocket of the coat he had taken off, and he did not know where he had put the coat, and all the house had to leave off looking for his tools, and start looking for his coat; while he would dance round and hinder them ... (pp. 19–20)

Uncle Podger in that account may be thought to bear an affinity to the three characters participating in the boat trip, all of whom are presented as subject to self-delusion and folly. But there exists a substantial difference, for where the uncle is, as in so many examples of humour outside this story, the unknowing target of ridicule remaining as impervious to his failings at the end of the tale as he was at its beginning, here the bifurcation of author and pseudo-self, with the author fully aware of what his counterpart seems unable to perceive, produces by extension a recognition that ultimately all three participants share in the amusement, that, although they may seem the objects of ridicule, they are in fact fully capable of laughing at themselves, a feature responsible in no small part for the book's perennial appeal. And perhaps most important of all, it creates in us an amused recognition of our own susceptibilities and self-delusions at which we can now laugh more readily with the knowledge that they are shared by others.

CHAPTER SIX

THE TWENTIETH CENTURY

a) George Bernard Shaw

No less critical of Victorian tradition than Wilde – in his writings if not in his personal behaviour – Shaw comes so obviously into the category of a humorist deflating accepted assumptions that it would appear superfluous to analyse the nature of his comedy or to attempt to show how neatly he fits into the pattern we have been investigating. He was forever wittily puncturing the pompous and the self-satisfied, undermining the pillars of society and challenging the complacency of religionists. Yet he deserves investigation as he introduced varia- tions into the pattern that not only freshened the approach but also served as major delights in his plays. His purpose was to effect change but he managed to avoid iconoclastic fervour by a willingness to laugh at his own notions, as in his 'unsocialist' depiction of the bibulous and appropriately named dustman, Doolittle.

A theatre critic as well as music critic by profession, he had learned to despise the shallowness of the contemporary stage. Indeed, it is easy to forget how close the professional stage of that time was to the facile melodramas attended by the boisterous, unruly members of the working class. For the teeming masses that had found their way to London, new theatres had been opened, such as the Britannia in Hoxton whose 3,000 seats offered prices from threepence upwards, with the possibility of paying half-price if entering after eight-thirty. As Dickens noted in 1860 on paying a visit to such a performance, the audience consisted of dock labourers, costermongers, petty tradesmen, small clerks, milliners, stay-makers, shoe-binders, slop- workers, poor workers in a hundred highways and byways, most of them not at all clean, and not at all choice in their lives or conversation[192] – and the situation in those theatres had not changed radically in Shaw's time, the melodramas that were offered catering to the unsophisticated interests of that class.

For such an audience, subtleties of plot or character were superfluous. Even before he had uttered a word, the villain, marked out by his dark clothing and swarthy complexion, would be greeted on his first entrance with a hearty chorus of boos and hisses, and the sweet heroine with lively applause. The plot was minimal, again with virtue and vice vividly polarized to save the audience any intellectual effort. Such stock figures were easily transferred to the screen when the early movies appeared, the evil cowboy in the ever-popular Westerns being marked out by his black stetson and drooping mustachios, and the hero by the white stallion on which he gallops to the heroine's rescue. As with the staged melodrama, accompanying music, provided in the silent movies by a pianist, ensured the appropriate emotional response to the virtuous and the vicious characters.[193]

Those elements may seem absurd to us today, but night after night Shaw as a critic was compelled to witness scenes in the major theatres that were scarcely less absurd. T. W. Robertson's *Caste*, performed with great success at the Prince of Wales Theatre in 1867 and remaining in the popular repertory well into Shaw's own time, was praised in its day as having introduced greater realism to the stage and as representing the better type of play, yet it differed very little from others in its use of stock characters and melodramatic highpoints. An excerpt from Act II of *Caste*, when the hero is about to depart for battle, may indicate the reasons for Shaw's castigation of contemporary drama and his determination to change theatrical practice.

> *George* [*to the Marchioness*]. Don't go in anger. You may not see me again.
> [*Esther rises in nervous excitement, clutches George's hand*].
> *Esther* [*with arm round his neck*]. Oh, George! must you go?
> *George*. Yes.
> *Esther*. I can't leave you! I'll go with you!
> *George*. Impossible! The country is too unsettled.
> *Esther*. May I come after you?
> *George*. Yes.
> *Esther* [*with her head on his shoulder*]. I may.

Marchioness. It is his duty to go. His honour calls him. The honour of his family – our honour!
Esther. But I love him so! Pray don't be angry with me!
Hawtree [*looking at watch*]. George!
George. I must go, love!
Marchioness [*advancing*]. Let me arm you, George – let your mother, as in the days of old. There is blood – and blood, my son. See, your wife cries when she should be proud of you!
George. My Esther is all that is good and noble. No lady born to a coronet could be gentler or more true. Esther, my wife, fetch me my sword, and buckle my belt around me.
Esther [*clinging to him*]. No, no; I cant!
George. Try. [*Whispers to Esther.*] To please my mother. [*To Marchioness.*] You shall see.
[*Esther totters up-stage, Polly assisting her, brings down his sword, and tries to buckle his belt*] ... [194]

As Shaw remarked, 'George and Esther have nothing but a milkcan to differentiate them from the heroes and heroines of a thousand sentimental dramas ... [the Marchioness] is not an original study from life but simply a ladyfication of the conventional haughty mother.'[195]

In the large bulk of commentary on Shaw published over the years, most critics and historians have concentrated upon his socialist ideas, his attacks upon conventional religion and his dramatic innovations, with (here too) very little on the quality of his humour. Fred Mayne's *The Wit and Satire of Bernard Shaw* bears a promising title but the author confesses in the opening pages that he will develop no theory of comedy, nor of wit, nor will he show those aspects in action – instead, the book focuses disappointingly upon such technical elements as Shaw's use of alliteration, consonance and monosyl-lables. In the collection of essays on Shaw edited by R. J. Kaufmann, only one essay, by Bruce R. Park, claims to deal with comedy and there too the title proves misleading, the essay only discussing Shaw's desire to be known as a 'poet' and his attitude to tragedy.[196] Shaw surely deserves more than this.

Arms and the Man is dated for many reasons – for its parody of theatrical traditions that have long disappeared from the stage, for its evocation of the Crimean War and for its placing of the events in the context of the long-forgotten Serbian–Bulgarian battles.

But Shakespeare's plays too are dated by such elements as their assumption of the divine right of kings, yet we forget those differences as the ambience of the scenes imposes itself upon us. Shaw's play is still a joy to watch, as a viewing of the fine BBC version of 1989, with Helena Bonham-Carter as Raina, will confirm.[197] Because of its anti-military stance at a time when such views were anathema, the play failed on its initial run, lasting only 11 weeks, but it won considerable popularity towards the end of the First World War when its views no longer seemed unpatriotic and the humour could be appreciated for its own sake.

The fact that Shaw's main purpose was to challenge the prevailing concepts both of warfare and of theatrical practice places him firmly within the generic pattern of humour as the lampooning of socially imposed notions, but there were two differences. The first, and most obvious, is that in this instance the parodying was intended not as a temporary derogation. Shaw's purposes were very serious, a rejection in principle of the practice of warfare and, as well, the hope of replacing the melodramatic aspects of the theatre by a new realism closer to that recently introduced by Ibsen. But he added an innovative aspect contributing significantly to the comic effectiveness of the play. Martin Meisel did note correctly that Shaw's purpose was 'the disillusioning of a central figure with current ideals',[198] but that sombre statement misses the humour whereby Shaw achieved that aim.

Shaw's representation of current concepts of romantic love would not, for contemporary audiences, have been regarded as exaggerated, accustomed as they were to the kind of scene cited above:

> Raina [placing her hands on his shoulder as she looks up at him with admiration and worship]: My hero! My king.
> Sergius: My queen! [He kisses her on the forehead with holy awe.]
> Raina: How I have envied you, Sergius! You have been out in the world, on the field of battle, able to prove yourself there worthy of any woman in the world; whilst I have had to sit at home inactive, – dreaming – useless – doing nothing that could give me the right to call myself worthy of any man.
> Sergius: Dearest, all my deeds have been yours. You inspired me. I have gone through the war like a knight in a tournament with his lady looking on at him!
> Raina: And you have never been absent from my thoughts for a moment. [Very solemnly] Sergius, I think we two have found the

higher love. When I think of you, I feel that I could never do a base deed, or think an ignoble thought.
Sergius: My lady, and my saint! [*Clasping her reverently.*]
Raina [*returning his embrace*]: My Lord and my –

Now would be the time for the kind of debunking we, and contemporary audiences, would expect from an iconoclast, the cynical remark of some more enlightened character on the stage mocking at these supposedly noble sentiments. That is provided to some extent, and a little later, by the pragmatic Bluntschli, who sees through the histrionics of the other characters. However, the innovation largely responsible for the comedy occurs when the deflation of the melodrama comes not from any choric figure representing the author's views but, surprisingly, from Sergius himself, the practitioner of this higher love. A moment after the above scene, as Raina leaves and the attractive housemaid Louka enters, it is the leading apostle of such elevated courtship who provides the anti-climactic bump:

Sergius: Louka: do you know what the higher love is?
Louka (astonished): No, sir.
Sergius: Very fatiguing thing to keep up for any length of time, Louka. One feels the need of some relief after it ... (*Coming clear of the table and drawing her with him*) I am surprised at myself, Louka. What would Sergius, the hero of Slivnitza, say if he saw me now? What would Sergius, the apostle of the higher love, say if he saw me now? What would the half dozen Sergiuses who keep popping in and out of this handsome figure of mine say if they caught us here? (*Letting go her hand and slipping his arm dexterously round her waist.*)

That reversal is not merely an effective comic device, amusing us by its unexpectedness. It conveys also a more damaging criticism of contemporary modes by the suggestion that even those most committed to the noble concepts advocated by society and so faithfully reproduced on the stage are, at some level, themselves aware of the hollowness of the pretence and of its inapplicability to real life. Sergius' confession provides a hint of the moral hypocrisy pervading Victorian sentiments that was to tarnish its image for the following generation. Moreover, the self-revelation performed a further function of considerable importance. Were Sergius simply to begin flirting with Louka on Raina's departure, he would have appeared as no more than an unscrupulous philanderer, thereby slipping inevitably into the role of the unfaithful lover, automatically classed as the villain in the contemporary theatre. But Shaw cleverly softens the implications of his behaviour by presenting him as genuinely guilt-stricken, uncomfortably aware of the gap between the lofty standards to which he aspires and the reality of his natural impulses. As a result, while Shaw's attack on such Victorian delusions retains its full force, the exposure is made more acceptable to his contemporary audiences by the sympathy that Sergius' puzzlement elicits.

Nor is this confession of double standards an isolated phenomenon. It holds true for the other leading characters, there too ameliorating the attack on socially accepted principles by evoking laughter. At the moment of one of the play's highlights, Raina's fury at Bluntschli's refusal to take her melodramatics seriously suddenly collapses when she charmingly – and again unexpectedly – admits laughingly that he is right. In both instances, therefore, it is the characters themselves who deflate their own pretensions:

> *Bluntschli*: When you strike that noble attitude and speak in that thrilling voice, I admire you; but I find it impossible to believe a single word you say.
> *Raina* [*superbly*]: Captain Bluntschli!
> *Bluntschli* [*unmoved*]: Yes?
> *Raina* (*coming a little towards him, as if she could not believe her senses*); Do you mean what you said just now? Do you know what you said just now?
> *Bluntschli*: I do.
> *Raina* (*gasping*): I! I!!! [*She points to herself incredulously, meaning 'I, Raina Petkoff, tell lies!' He meets her gaze unflinchingly. She suddenly sits down beside him, and adds, with a complete change of manner from the heroic to the familiar*] How did you find me out?
> *Bluntschli* (*promptly*): Instinct, dear young lady. Instinct, and experience of the world.
> *Raina* (*wonderingly*): Do you know, you are the first man I ever met who did not take me seriously?
> *Bluntschli*: You mean, dont you, that I am the first man that has ever taken you quite seriously?
> *Raina*: Yes, I suppose I do mean that. (*Cosily, quite at her ease*

with him.) How strange it is to be talked to in such a way! You know, I've always gone on like that – I mean the noble attitude and the thrilling voice. I did it when I was a tiny child to my nurse. She believed in it. I do it before my parents. They believe in it. I do it before Sergius. He believes in it.

Shaw's exposure of the Victorians' subliminal doubts concerning the noble principles to which they consciously subscribed applies not only to their idealization of love but also to their jingoistic celebration of warfare, the two aspects being slily combined in the title he assigned to the play. Referring most obviously to the opening line of Vergil's martial epic and therefore preparing us for a hero who will represent the glories of war, it hints at the same time at the second theme, the Victorian males' notorious readiness to use their arms in another sense, to embrace housemaids while formally betrothed to a member of their own class.

As regards the martial aspect, Sergius' magnificent cavalry charge, patently evocative of the Charge of the Light Brigade immortalized for that generation by Tennyson's poem, turns out, like its original, to have been totally unjustified in military terms (an element generally suppressed in that era's idealization of the incident). The original charge had in fact resulted from the misunderstanding of a garbled order from the military command and accordingly had, while achieving almost nothing militarily, been responsible for the deaths of 40 per cent of the cavalrymen; yet it was exalted as heroic. The debunking of Sergius' exploit as utterly foolish (having succeeded, we learn, only because the enemy ran out of ammunition at that moment) once again comes not from some cynical outsider but from Sergius himself. Retrospectively, he admits his error, casting doubt on the very authority that he was thought to represent. As he declares sarcastically: 'I won the battle the wrong way when our worthy Russian generals were losing it the right way. That upset their plans, and wounded their self-esteem. Two of their colonels got their regiments driven back on the correct principles of scientific warfare. Two major-generals got killed strictly according to military etiquette. Those two colonels are now major-generals; and I am still a simple major.' He therefore resigns from the army with a withering attack upon soldiering, thereby echoing Shaw's own pacifist principles. Rejecting the concepts of gallantry currently attributed to fighting, Sergius, the hero of Slivnitza, concludes bitterly that it is, 'the coward's art of attacking mercilessly when you are strong, and keeping out of harm's way when you are weak, the whole secret of successful fighting being to get your enemy at a disadvantage and never, on any account, fight him on equal terms'. The definition was, of course, quite unjustified, for while it is true that, from the larger viewpoint, a general chooses a plan likely to give superiority to his own forces, that principle does not apply to the individual soldier who has no say in determining the strategy. He must risk his life in the process of the attack however vulnerable he may be. Shaw is thus providing one of those witty inversions beloved by Chesterton and Wilde. By seeming to transform the soldier into a bully rather than a hero, he compels the audience at the very least to reassess their normal assumptions, the wit of the inversion again acting as a palliative.

Even the seemingly pragmatic Bluntschli, prosaically demolishing the illusions of those around him, is made to admit to latent predilections that contradict his overt pragmatism. In the earlier part of the play, his entertaining depiction as a 'chocolate-cream soldier', storing his holster with candy instead of ammunition, furthers the depiction of the absurdity of warfare. But there is also a social purpose. Modelled in part upon the dramatist's friend and fellow Fabian, Sidney Webb, whose forebears had been innkeepers and petty tradesmen,[199] Bluntschli spearheads the attack upon the class-system, as this bourgeois son of an innkeeper proves infinitely more efficient than the aristocrats in command who, we learn, are incapable of mastering the logistics involved in moving a regiment from one point to another without his assistance. He is thus portrayed as an admirably pragmatic individual. In the final scene, however, he too undergoes self-exposure as we learn that, while seeming to embody hard-headed materialism, he is, in fact, an incorrigible romantic at heart. How, he asks, could he possibly regard himself as an aspirant for Raina's hand?

> *Bluntschli*: I, a common-place Swiss soldier who hardly knows what a decent life is after fifteen years of barracks and battles – a vagabond – a man who has spoiled all his chances in life through an incurably romantic disposition – a man –
> *Sergius (starting as if a needle had pricked him and interrupting Bluntschli in incredulous amazement)*: Excuse me, Bluntschli: what did you say had spoiled your chances in life?

Bluntschli (*promptly*): An incurably romantic disposition. I ran away from home twice when I was a boy. I went into the army instead of into my father's business. I climbed the balcony of this house when a man of sense would have dived into the nearest cellar. I came sneaking back here to have another look at the young lady when any other man of my age would have sent the coat back –

That revelation was, of course, needed to end the play effectively, especially when her father's objection on the grounds of his supposed poverty is countered by Bluntschli reading the list of items he has just inherited from his hotelier father – 4,000 tablecloths, 600 sets of sheets and blankets, and far more horses and carriages than Sergius could have afforded – not the kind of dowry of which a Bulgarian aristocrat would normally approve, but very attractive in monetary terms. Yet that inconsistency between Bluntchli's pragmatism and his latent romanticism was somewhat more than a dramatic device, being closer to the dramatist's own condition than Shaw may have realized, Chesterton having shrewdly remarked that the seemingly secular iconoclast liberated from all restrictions was, as his ascetic way of life indicated, really a Puritan at heart – just as Bluntschli was really a romantic.

Important as these confessions of inconsistency are, both as sources of the comedy and as innovative devices, with the characters here deflating their own confident poses, it would be unfair to place the full weight of the play's success upon them. Shaw, while serving as a dramatic critic, had learned the tricks of the trade, adopting certain standard devices that could be relied upon to elicit laughter. There is the diverting disappearance and reappearance of Major Petkoff's coat with the compromising photo in its pocket, a scene that amuses because of his unshakeable confidence in himelf, his conviction that his eyes have not deceived him and his readiness to wager a huge sum that the coat is missing, to be followed by his crest-fallen discovery a moment later when the coat is produced. There is the dramatist's scoffing at the Bulgarians' conviction of their sophis-tication after having installed an electric bell in the library, and their pride in their new habit of washing their hands once a day, all with a side-glance at England's assumption of cultural advancement. These are concomitants to the main innovation, creating together a comedy of perennial delight.

Pygmalion has, in the course of time, been replaced in popularity by the charming musical version. But although *My Fair Lady*, with its songs and Ascot ladies, is more aurally and visually colourful, most of the humour in that later version remains indebted to the source. There was, as usual with Shaw, a serious social purpose behind the play. Where dialects in other countries are generally regional, bearing no social implications – distinguishing the Bostonian from the New Yorker – in Britain the Cockney accent is a social identifier, immediately placing the speaker as belonging to London's working class. Shaw believed that the removal of such speech distinctions could contribute to the levelling of society that he, as a Fabian, so earnestly desired. He knew, as he remarked in the preface to the play, that the subject, being 'intensely and deliberately didactic', was liable to be extremely dry, but the wit he employed transformed the play into a remarkably light-hearted and entertaining drama without obscuring its message.

Shaw loved to shock his audiences. In contrast to the noble males peopling the contemporary stage, with their invariable chivalry towards the ladies, Professor Higgins fascinates from the first by his boorishness. The character was in fact based on the phonetician Henry Sweet, with whom Shaw was acquainted, a learned but cantankerous individual, intolerant of anyone not sharing his own philological and linguistic fervour. Shaw, of course, vastly exaggerated that trait, making Higgins contemptuous of all social restraints, supremely confident of his right to abuse others, castigating Eliza on their first meeting (and without the slightest provocation) as 'a squashed cabbage leaf, a disgrace to the noble architecture of Covent Garden' and, a little later, as 'a draggletailed guttersnipe'. He is rude to society ladies, if not quite so abusive, his mother needing to apologize for her celebrated son's lack of manners. All this would seem to make him into a mere vulgarian, but Shaw introduces a dimension that makes Higgins into a figure both attractive and entertaining, for there exists in him a charming gap between his outrageously insulting attitude to others and his own benign and unshakeable belief that he is the mildest and most indulgent of men. After his housekeeper has pleaded with him to be a little more temperate, he remarks wonderingly to his friend:

You know, Pickering, that woman has the most extraordinary ideas about me. Here I am, a shy, diffident sort of man. I've never been able to feel really grown-up and tremendous, like other chaps. And yet she's firmly persuaded that I'm an arbitrary overbearing bossing kind of person. I cant account for it.

Passionately devoted to linguistic research, he lives, like Aristophanes' Socrates, in an academic cloud, despising the terra firma so clearly visible to the audience. He is only occasionally made aware of it by his mother's strictures and those of his housekeeper, those two representing the prosaic, factual world. Treating him, deservedly, as an overgrown schoolboy, his mother forbids him to attend her receptions because of the offence he causes to her guests, and points out to him, often in vain, such practical matters as the need to plan for Eliza's future once the experiment is over. Again, as in the comedy that lampooned Socrates, the attack is light-hearted, since the obsession that prevents Higgins from respecting others is, like Socrates' pursuit of philosophy, a lofty concern ultimately worthy of regard – and especially so, as that constitutes here the serious message of the play. Shaw, we may add, was himself fired by linguistic fervour, insisting that in the printed editions of his plays words such as *don't* and *can't* be printed without the apostrophe on the grounds that the current usage was obsolete.

One high point of the comedy is the wonderful scene in which Eliza's progress is first subjected to test, her introduction to a small group of upper-class visitors at an afternoon tea at Mrs Higgins' home. Eliza, immensely proud of her newly acquired pronunciation, has, we discover, been totally untutored concerning the themes to be discussed, the difference between standard gossip among workers in the Covent Garden market and the refined small-talk at an aristocratic tea session. Higgins, who was himself insensitive to such distinctions, had briefly informed her to limit her remarks to the two subjects demanded by English convention, the weather and people's health. The result is indeed incongruity, but a specific type of incongruity, the discrepancy between Eliza's unshakeable self-assurance as she chats happily away, convinced she is managing superbly, and the consternation of her listeners at the extraordinary subject-matter of her discourse. After the requisite comment on the weather, Eliza moves on confidently to the second recommended theme, people's health, if not in quite the way Higgins had intended:

Liza [*darkly*]: My aunt died of influenza: so they said.

[*Mrs. Eynsford Hill clicks her tongue sympathetically*]

Liza [*in the same tragic tone*]: But it's my belief they done the old woman in.

Mrs. Higgins [*puzzled*]: Done her in?

Liza: Y-e-e-e-es, Lord love you! Why should she die of influenza? She come through diphtheria right enough the year before. I saw her with my own eyes. Fairly blue with it, she was. They all thought she was dead; but my father he kept ladling gin down her throat till she came to so sudden that she bit the bowl off the spoon.

Mrs. Eynsford Hill [*startled*]: Dear me!

Liza [*piling up the indictment*]: What call would a woman with that strength in her have to die of influenza? What become of her new straw hat that should have come to me? Somebody pinched it; and what I say is, them as pinched it done her in …

Freddy, convulsed with laughter, evokes Eliza's understandable query: 'If I was doing it proper, what was you laughing at?'

The conclusion of that scene seems incredibly mild today, but the forbidden word was so shocking at the time that Shaw was repeatedly warned before opening night that it must be removed. He remained adamant, and proved to be fully justified.

Freddy [*opening the door for her*]: Are you walking across the Park, Miss Doolittle? If so –

Liza: Walk! Not bloody likely. [*Sensation*]. I am going in a taxi.

As the word came off Mrs Campbell's lips, we are told, '… there was a great gasp, followed in a few moments by an extraordinary roar of laughter'.[200] Social conformity had been challenged.

One of Shaw's finest qualities as a dramatist is his ability to surprise, often paradoxically by frustrating expectations of iconoclasm. One might have expected from a leading member of the Fabian society, a socialist defending the rights of the poor, that he would make Eliza's dustman father an admirable figure, heroically resisting the oppression suffered by his class. But he makes him a comic personality, cheerfully committed to idleness and drink, and unabashedly undercutting accepted ethical principles. On his being asked somewhat sternly why he does not make an honest woman of the female he lives with, his reply inverts the basic assumption of the questioner, casting doubt on the entire system of wedlock and thereby making the questioner look foolish:

> *Pickering*: Why dont you marry that missus of yours? I rather draw the line at encouraging that sort of immorality.
> *Doolittle*: Tell her so, Governor: tell her so. I'm willing. It's me that suffers by it. Ive no hold on her. I got to be agreeable to her. I got to give her presents. I got to buy her clothes something sinful. I'm a slave to that woman, Governor, just because I'm not her lawful husband. And she knows it too. Catch her marrying me! Take my advice, Governor: marry Eliza while she's young and dont know no better. If you dont youll be sorry for it after.

Ostensibly, the reply points to the unmarried woman's hold over her lover but, by inversion, it hints more forcefully at the woman's loss of that power once she submits to a husband's authority.

In one respect, Shaw did not succeed. Objecting to the conventional endings of melodramas where the hero and heroine are happily united, and attempting, like Ibsen, to be more realistic, he refused to let Eliza marry Higgins. Instead, he had her marry Freddy and set up a flower shop. Audiences were so obviously disappointed that Shaw, in an attempt to justify his decision, found it necessary to append to the published version an account of Eliza's life after the events delineated in the play. His arguments failed to persuade. Interestingly, the producers of *My Fair Lady* many years after his death and conscious of the public's disappointment, while not actually depicting her as marrying Professor Higgins, added the scene of her returning to his home and bringing him his slippers, thereby suggesting, without actually reversing Shaw's decision, the happy ending that audiences desired. But that failure on Shaw's part to counter melodramatic endings was a minor defect in a remarkable series of plays with social messages in which with consummate skill he, like Wilde, employed comedy to subvert traditional assumptions, the laughter he aroused softening potential hostility.

b) Stella Gibbons, *Cold Comfort Farm*

This novel has an unusual aspect to it. Parody can only function effectively when the object of the lampooning is familiar to the reader – the parody of *Hiawatha* cited in the introductory chapter would mean little to anyone who had not read the original. Yet in this instance the principle seems contradicted. Published in 1932, its humour targeted a literary vogue current at that time, the 'earthy rustic' genre represented by the novels of Mary E. Mann, Sheila Kaye-Smith and Mary Webb, with their portrayal of gloomy characters located in the depths of the countryside and subject to mysterious obsessions.[201] But public interest in those novels faded and, although they experienced a limited revival in the 1970s when republished, they were insufficiently known to serve as objects of burlesque. Yet Stella Gibbons' parody not only retained its popularity throughout the years but was awarded the accolade of becoming a Penguin Classic. The reason for the apparent anomaly lies in the indebtedness of the 'earthy rustic' genre to the long-established tradition of the 'Gothic' novel, whose main exemplars could serve as effective substitutes when the original targets had been forgotten.

The 'Gothic' tradition had not taken itself very seriously at the time of its emergence in the eighteenth century. The pseudo-medieval buildings placed in the landscape gardens of William Kent and Launcelot Brown were dubbed 'follies' even by their creators, decorative elements intended, together with obelisks and Doric temples, to add variety to the planned walks. Horace Walpole, affixing battlements to the roof of his *Strawberry Hill* and installing imitation fan-vaulting to its interior, transformed it into a fanciful extravaganza, a curiosity visited by many.[202] His novel *The Castle of Otranto* won similar popularity, absurd as it may seem today. As Manfred is about to rape a terrified Isabella,

> ... at that instant, the portrait of her grandfather, which hung over the bench where they had been sitting, uttered a deep sigh, and heaved its breast ... He saw it quit its panel and descend on the floor with a grave and melancholy air ...

This fashion of fictional horror, with ghosts, hidden staircases in medieval castles and mysterious manuscripts, did not escape unscathed, Jane Austen's *Northanger Abbey* providing a well-known parody. Catherine Morland, visiting an ancient mansion, fearfully opens at night the door of a bedroom closet:

> ... her quick eyes directly fell on a roll of paper pushed back into the further part of the cavity, apparently for concealment, and her

feelings at that moment were indescribable. Her heart fluttered, her knees trembled, and her cheeks grew pale. She seized, with an unsteady hand, the precious manuscript, for half a glance sufficed to ascertain written characters.

As a gust of wind blows out her candle, she leaps terrified into bed, hiding beneath the covers, only to reveal in the morning light that it is a discarded laundry list.

Austen wrote that parody in 1798, when Matthew Lewis' *The Monk*, with its grisly account of carnal lust and murder, and Mrs Radcliffe's *The Mysteries of Udolpho*, in which a worm-infested corpse is discovered within the dark recesses of a monastery, had marked the climax of that somewhat ludicrous tradition. But in the following years, the genre underwent a profound change, producing such major works as *Wuthering Heights* and *Jane Eyre*. The latter were indeed familiar to the twentieth-century reader, and could be relied upon as substitutes for the 'earthy rural' novels that had disappeared from the scene. If it might be thought sacrilege to lampoon such distinguished works of literature, we should recall that parody, although making fun of an object, does not disqualify it, Pope's *The Rape of the Lock* implying no disrespect for Milton's epic.

Had *Cold Comfort Farm* followed Austen's precedent, offering a seemingly serious Gothic scene of horror before duly puncturing it, it would have been merely imitative, but it employed a remarkably effective innovation, more suited to the modern era. Where Austen's Catherine had been a credulous, easily terrified girl, Gibbons – an early feminist – created as her central figure a very different personage, a clear-headed, imperturbable young lady, confidently entering the world of the Gothic rustics, amusedly relieving them of their obsessions, and steering them towards a more rational and, for them, an ultimately more satisfying way of life. In the process, the cult of Gothic horror and mystery becomes transformed, at least during the reading of her book, from a fearsome fantasy to an amusing, rather foolish aberration.

Flora Poste, choosing to reside with distant relatives whom she has never met and who are entrenched in a farm named 'Howling' in Sussex, finds them to be an assortment of crazed individuals living out their dreary, savage and frustrated lives under the domination of Aunt Ada Doom (the madwoman in the attic) who had in her youth 'seen something nasty in the woodshed'. The bathetic technique functions entertainingly in the book, as Flora breezes in, unimpressed by the lugubrious atmosphere. Her meeting with Reuben, a brooding figure committed to misogyny and to tilling the soil, is typical:

> ***His thoughts swirled like a beck in spate behind the sodden grey furrows of his face. A woman ... Blast! Blast! Come to wrest away from him the land whose love fermented in his veins like slow yeast. She-woman. Young, soft-coloured, insolent. His gaze was suddenly edged by a fleshy taint. Break her. Break. Keep and hold and hold fast the land. The land, the iron furrows of frosted earth under the rain-lust, the fecund spears of rain, the swelling, slow burst of seed-sheaths, the slow smell of cows and cry of cows, the trampling bride-path of the bull in his hour. All his, his ...
> 'Will you have some bread and butter?' asked Flora, handing him a cup of tea (p. 82).[203]

The three asterisks prefixed to the paragraph are facetiously inserted for readers who might otherwise fail to recognize it as a 'purple passage', intended, as so often in novels, to display the stylistic prowess of the author.

Joseph, the religious fanatic in Emily Brontë's novel, is paralleled here by Amos, fervently calling down divine punishment on the heads of all sinners, and preaching fire and brimstone to his sect of 'Quivering Brethren'. Solemnly he informs Flora, '... 'tes my mission. Aye, I mun tell the Brethren to prepare in time for torment, when the roarin' red flames will lick round their feet like the dogs lickin' Jezebel's blood in the Good Book' (p. 95). Flora fails to be affected. Employing modern psychological insights, she perceives that he thoroughly enjoys his fulminations, that 'he got no end of a kick out of his job'. With a side-glance at Sinclair Lewis' recently published *Elmer Gantry*, she slily suggests that he would obtain a wider audience for his preaching if he travelled around the country in a Ford van as a popular evangelist. The idea, of course, appeals to him, and by the end of the book he is off happily indulging his favourite pursuit while, as Flora had planned, leaving the running of the farm to Reuben, the next heir in line, who can now devote himself undisturbed to his agricultural fixation.

Requisite for such a setting, but with echoes also of Thomas Hardy, is a woodland female, flitting from scene to scene as she attempts to lure into marriage the handsome heir to the local estate. An appropriately named Elfine fulfils that role, if in a somewhat exaggerated form, arousing the unwanted ardour of a resident yokel:

> ... suddenly, something like a kingfisher streaked across the kitchen, in a glimmer of green skirts and flying gold hair and the chime of a laugh was followed a second later by the slam of the gate leading through the starveling garden out on to the Downs. Adam flung round violently on hearing the sound, dropping his thorn twig and breaking two plates. 'Elfine ... my little bird,' he whispered, starting towards the open door (p. 45).

Elfine's woodland qualities, Flora realizes, need to be modernized and significantly toned down if she is ever to win the hand of the aristocratic hero. No more dancing in the woods with the wildflowers and birds like some dryad; '... her artiness must be rooted out. Her mind must match the properly groomed head in which it was housed. Her movements must be made less frequent, and her conversation less artless. She must write no more poetry nor go for any long walks ...' (p. 137) Sure enough, with a new hairstyle, attractively chic clothes, and instructions on the best tactics for attracting a male, Elfine succeeds in her matrimonial ambitions.

Heathcliff's dark, 'erect and handsome figure' with its panther-like grace had served in Brontë's novel to transport the reader into the haunting world of fantasy, arousing in Catherine a passion reaching across the barrier of death. But Seth is, through Flora, diverted into a more prosaic destiny. He stands

> ... in the warm light of the declining sun, his bare throat and boldly moulded features looking as though they were bathed in gold. His pose was easy and graceful. A superb self-confidence radiated from him, as it does from any healthy animal (p. 195).

Noting how vain he is of his manly appearance, she introduces him to a movie producer, through whom he is destined to become a second Clark Gable, swooned over by millions of women.

D. H. Lawrence, too, is targeted, when a visitor, Myburg, with a side-glance at *Lady Chatterley's Lover*, recommends a return au naturel, fondly recalling how once: '... little Harriet Belmont sat naked in the grass and played to us on her flute. It was delicious; so gay and simple and natural (p. 129).[204] In the 1930s, the word 'gay' did not, of course, have its present connotation.

By the end of the novel, all members of this disoriented family have been straightened out, including Judith who, like Lawrence's Mrs Morel, was subject to a sexual fixation on her son. Flora adopts the simple expedient of taking her to a psychiatrist for appropriate treatment. The Gothic horrors have disappeared, the gloom has lifted, and sanity has been restored. More important is the implication that, impressive as those fictional mysteries and idyllic scenes may be, they needed to be placed in due perspective and the fantasy entertainingly transferred to a mundane setting. Under Flora's guidance, even Aunt Ada Doom is reformed, led to admit what a nasty time she has had for the past 20 years through cultivating her supposed madness. At the end of the novel, dressed in the height of fashion, she leaves in excellent spirits for the Hotel Miramar in Paris, determined henceforth to enjoy life to the full. We are never informed what it was she saw in the woodshed.

c) Beckett, *Waiting for Godot*

Despite Shaw's efforts to raise the level of the theatre, the British stage continued for many years to ignore his innovations, resorting for its comedy to light, frothy plays such as Noël Coward's *Hay Fever* (1925) and Terence Rattigan's *French Without Tears* (1936). An excerpt from the former may indicate the general reliance of such plays upon pointless persiflage:

> *Sorel*: Clara says Amy's got toothache.
> *Judith*: Poor dear! There's some oil of cloves in my medicine cupboard. Who is Amy?
> *Sorel*: The scullery-maid, I think.
> *Judith*: How extraordinary! She doesn't look Amy a bit, does she? Much more Flossie.

That tendency to flippancy ended, of course, in the 1950s, with the introduction of an essentially new form of drama, intensely serious, even morose, yet including scenes of genuine humour that evoked laughter in the midst of the gloom. Those scenes were not comic relief intended to highlight by contrast the graver matter, but intrinsic to the main mood and purpose. For the new genre, the Theatre of the Absurd, with its sense of the vacuity of human existence, saw the pointlessness of life as itself a grim comedy. With the growing realization that Darwinian theory and Freudian psychology seemed to have reduced the individual to an automaton responding to preconditioned reflexes in an unending struggle for survival merely in order to reproduce, the purpose of comic scenes had changed. They no longer functioned to induce a temporary relaxation of social pressures or moral precepts but as a permanent negation of all positive standards, with the human condition itself as the target. The conventional – including the ethical concepts to which we imagine we subscribe – had become the object of ridicule but, instead of being comfortably reinstated or gently mocked, such principles were now left entirely negated. The result is, in a real sense, tragicomedy; not comic scenes inserted into a tragic play but a merger of the two modes wherein the comedy becomes tragic as an exposure of the absurdity of life itself.

The pathetic, clownish figures of Estragon and Vladimir, the audience realizes, are not, as in most comedy, persons at whom we can laugh because of our immunity to their foibles, but are projections of ourselves, representing the purposeless suffering of humankind at large. A typical instance occurs when Pozzo, now totally blind, is fearful lest he has fallen among enemies:

Pozzo: … are you friends?
Estragon: (*laughing noisily*) He wants to know if we are friends!
Vladimir: No, he means friends of his.
Estragon: Well?
Vladimir: We've proved we are, by helping him.
Estragon: Exactly. Would we have helped him if we weren't his friends?
Vladimir: Possibly.
Estragon: Don't let's quibble about that now.

Estragon's initial misunderstanding of Pozzo's question is a standard music-hall joke. We laugh, grasping a little late (as in all wordplay) the ambiguity implicit in Pozzo's question; but we are abruptly returned to seriousness by the unexpected 'Possibly', with its implication, reiterated throughout the play, of the frailty of human relationships, an unreliability echoed a moment later as Pozzo pleads desperately for their help:

Pozzo: Don't leave me!
Vladimir: No question of it.
Estragon: For the moment.

Estragon's unanticipated modification provides that sudden change of direction that humour so often requires. In this instance, however, the standard process of comedy is profoundly changed. He hints that Vladimir's prompt assurance may conform to the ideal of loving one's neighbour as oneself, but it does not conform to reality. As Beckett claimed elsewhere, human friendship is a pretence, a camouflage of human selfishness, a function of man's cowardice, '… the attempt to communicate where no communication is possible is merely a simian vulgarity, or horribly comic, like madness that holds a conversation with furniture'.[205] The oxymoron in his term 'horribly comic' defines with remarkable aptness the effect of the clowning in his own plays, comic in so far as it momentarily arouses laughter yet leading ultimately to a dreadful vision of vacuity and despair. The underlying comic principle remains, as Vladimir's confident statement is suddenly undercut by Estragon's modification.

At times, the tragicomedy is more compressed, becoming instrinsic to the despair, as in the scene in which the two characters contemplate suicide:

Estragon: Let's hang ourselves immediately!
Vladimir: From a bough? (*They go towards the tree.*) I wouldn't trust it.
Estragon: We can always try.
Vladimir: Go ahead.
Estragon: After you.
Vladimir: No no, you first.
Estragon: Why me?
Vladimir: You're lighter than I am.
Estragon: Just so!
Vladimir: I don't understand.
Estragon: Use your intelligence, can't you?
   [*Vladimir uses his intelligence.*]
Vladimir: (*finally*) I remain in the dark.
Estragon: This is how it is. (*He reflects.*) The bough … the bough … (*Angrily*)
   Use your head, can't you?

Vladimir: You're my only hope.
Estragon: (*with effort*) Gogo light – bough not break – Gogo dead. Didi heavy – bough break – Didi alone. Whereas –
Vladimir: I hadn't thought of that.
Estragon: If it hangs you it'll hang anything.
Vladimir: But am I heavier than you?
Estragon: So you tell me. I don't know. There's an even chance. Or nearly.
Vladimir: Well? What do we do?
Estragon: Don't let's do anything. It's safer.

The humour in this grim scene relies on the slowness of the stage presentation, the lengthy pauses and protracted silences that Beckett insisted upon at the rehearsals he attended, and that here punctuate the dialogue. The courteous exchange, 'After you … No no, you first', with each character politely gesturing in turn towards the tree, amuses by our recognition that the politeness is really a pretext masking the reluctance of each to be the first to test the bough, with the far-fetched reasoning that follows being a device to conceal that reluctance. Estragon here takes the lead, his annoyance at Vladimir's incomprehension providing the excessive confidence that is about to be punctured, as his claim of being lighter in weight, on which the argument is based, turns out to be unfounded. And again illustrative of the tragicomedy is the fact, never to be forgotten, that the humorous exchange has as its topic the contemplation of suicide.

Beckett loved vaudeville[206] and adopted certain of its techniques into the play, such as the routine with the hats for which he inserted a lengthy stage direction, beginning: *Estragon takes Vladimir's hat. Vladimir adjusts Lucky's hat on his head. Estragon puts on Vladimir's hat in place of his own which he hands to Vladimir. Vladimir takes Estragon's hat. Estragon adjusts Vladimir's hat on his head* … In the music hall, such a scene is amusing in itself – we relax knowing it is a mere frolic for our entertainment. But in this setting its effect is of a desperate attempt on the part of the two to pass the time in a world not only devoid of humour but racked with pain, a pain that even comedy cannot alleviate. As they end the hat-routine and Estragon seems about to leave, Vladimir asks sadly, 'Will you not play?' only to have Estragon gaze at him in stupefaction for even suggesting that they continue.

The main point to be deduced from the extraordinarily effective use of comedy in this play is its difference from the norm, Beckett's refusal, after the laughter, to re-validate the social or moral concepts being targeted, so that, although such scenes are indeed humorous, either the overall gloom of the setting or the melancholy comments following immediately upon the comic exchange ensures that the laughter is muted, never countering the gloom as it usually does elsewhere. How powerfully Beckett employs that technique is never more clearly evidenced than in the final exchange:

> *Vladimir*: Well? Shall we go?
> *Estragon*: Yes, let's go.
> *They do not move.*

There is a momentary pause as the audience gradually grasps the anomaly, a ripple of laughter in acknowledgement, but ultimately a mood of sadness as the reason behind their immobility is grasped – the utter pointlessness of moving anywhere in the dismal world of human agony that forms the setting of the play. The result is, as we have noted, not comedy but tragicomedy in the fullest sense of the term.

d) Kingsley Amis, *Lucky Jim*

The appearance, in close proximity, of John Wain's *Hurry on Down* (1953), Kingsley Amis' *Lucky Jim* (1954), and John Osborne's *Look Back in Anger* (1956) won the group the misnomer of 'The Angry Young Men'. That term did apply to Osborne. His central character was indeed angry at the modern world, especially at post-war Britain, as he looked back longingly to what he imagined was the peace and security of the Victorian era, but it was inapplicable to the other two. Wain's novel was a light-hearted account, in the picaresque tradition, of a feckless young man from a middle-class background trying to earn a living as a window-cleaner, then as a truck-driver and finally as a drug-trafficker. Charles Lumley did, in the process, express annoyance, often amusingly, at elements around him, but his barbs were aimed not at social problems nor with especial anger. They were aimed only at minor irritants, such as a nagging landlady or the foul-smelling smoke from an old man's pipe, and the initial popularity of the novel did not last long. *Lucky Jim*, too, was no vehicle for social anger, providing as it did an entertaining anecdote of a young lecturer attempting to obtain tenure at university while, at the same time, trying to extricate himself from an entanglement with a neurotic female. Amis himself insisted that his only aim had been to write an amusing novel, but it won immediate and lasting acclaim for two reasons, the first of which is obvious enough, although the second was to prove of greater importance.

On the obvious side was the fact that it lampooned what had been regarded until then as a primary achievement of the post-war era. The sweeping from power of Churchill's party immediately peace was declared and its replacement by a socialist government had led to major reforms, among them the opening of universities to all social groups. Oxford and Cambridge had until then preserved in their admissions policy a long-established preference for sons of the wealthier classes, especially where the family had generational bonds with or had made impressive donations to a particular college. Even when scholarship winners from a lower class were admitted, the lifestyle encouraged by the authorities paralleled closely that of the well-to-do – a situation admirably recalled in the opening chapters of Evelyn Waugh's *Brideshead Revisited*. On the new socialist principles, Britain now provided generous governmental scholarships covering living expenses as well as tuition fees, whereby members drawn from the working class were enabled to obtain university degrees. Part of that process involved the establishment of new universities to cope with the increased numbers, often by elevating teachers' colleges and technical institutes to that status. It was a situation of which the public felt justifiably proud.

Pride, however, is liable to head for a fall, especially when targeted by humour, and Amis, a graduate of Oxford coming from a working-class home and himself a lecturer at a provincial university, amused his readers by providing an unabashed spoof of one such institution, fictional but not unduly exaggerated. The surprise and pleasure for the reading public was the reversal of expectation involved – that the first beneficiaries of the Welfare State, generously granted free university tuition, instead of expressing gratitude for the opportunities offered them were responding with laughter, burlesquing the small-mindedness and pretentiousness of the new academic communities as well as providing some well-deserved criticism of academia in general. With the consequent increase in the number of doctoral students, the search for thesis topics on subjects that had not yet been worked to death had become intense, and in a passage that was to become proverbial, Jim acknowledges the utter futility of the dissertation he has been assigned by the history department, a study of *The Economic Influence of the Developments in Shipbuilding Techniques, 1450 to 1485*:

> It was a perfect title, in that it crystallised the article's niggling mindlessness, its funereal parade of yawn-enforcing facts, the pseudo-light it threw upon non-problems. Dixon had read or begun to read, dozens like it, but his own seemed worse than most in its air of being convinced of its own usefulness and significance. 'In considering this strangely neglected topic,' it began. This what neglected topic? This strangely neglected what? ...[207]

Not least was the derision poured upon the attempt in the provincial universities to ape the traditions of the more established institutions without paralleling their academic distinction. Welch, a professor of history, attempting to impress Jim with the breadth of his cultural interests, discourses on his prowess as an amateur musician. Jim, while trying to look reverently attentive, finds his thoughts moving elsewhere, wondering how on earth Welch had become a professor '... even at a place like this? By published work? No. By extra good teaching? No in italics. Then how? As usual, Dixon shelved this question, telling himself that what mattered was that this man had decisive power over his future, at any rate until the next four or five weeks were up' (p. 8). The humour, as usual, derives from poking fun at established institutions solemnly priding themselves on their achievements.

There was, however, a more fundamental reason for the book's success, its inauguration of the comic anti-hero as a counterpart to the serious anti-hero then emerging in fiction. The collapse of traditional values in the early twentieth century had made it almost impossible by the 1950s to create in the novel the kind of admirable central character that had characterized earlier versions. The heroes and heroines of nineteenth-century novels had appealed to readers because they embodied the ideals to which society subscribed – for the males, courage, moral uprightness and loyalty in both love and war; for females chastity, sweetness and compassion. This is not the place to discuss in any detail the causes that led to the undermining of those ideals, but it may suffice to note the more salient features of that change as Freudian psychology claimed (with evidence that could not easily be refuted, at least when such theories were regarded as authoritative) that courage in battle may derive from a suppressed suicidal complex, thereby downgrading it to a form of neurosis, and that marital fidelity was a relic of primitive tribal taboos, thereby derogating that principle too. Even the seemingly unassailable virtue of respect for one's parents – a quality invariably possessed by the nineteenth-century hero or heroine – was now tainted by, at the very least, a suspicion that it derived from an oedipal complex, critics arguing precisely that of Paul Morel's affection for his mother when D. H. Lawrence's *Sons and Lovers* first appeared, and charging that, so far from being a study of a maturing individual, it merely described a psychological disorder.

With the heroic tradition severely damaged, it became well-nigh impossible to create a central character on the basis of principles now outmoded. As a result, and as a means of circumventing the difficulty, there emerged in the mid-century the anti-hero – not the opposite of a hero (for that, one still had the villain), nor simply a ragbag of social failures as Ihab Hassan defined the group – '... the fool, the clown, the hipster, the criminal, the poor sod, the freak, the outsider, the scapegoat, the scrubby opportunist, the rebel without a cause ...'[208] Instead, the modern anti-hero was more subtly delineated, a figure appearing initially to lack the qualities previously distinguishing the hero (thereby disarming any suspicion of the author's ignorance of the change), yet gradually winning the reader's admiration in the course of the novel. Holden Caulfield in Salinger's *Catcher in the Rye* seems at first a total failure – dismissed from one school after another to the despair of his parents, depressed by his ineffectiveness as a lover, unable to settle to any serious task, he succumbs to a nervous breakdown and flees from Prencey Prep. But as the reasons for his failures gradually come to light, the fault, we discover, lies not with him but with society. His dislike of the schools to which he is sent arises, it transpires, from justified disgust at their cheap commercialism and false standards; his lack of female conquests derives, as we only ascertain later, from respect for his girlfriends – while Stradlater cannot even remember the names of the girls he seduces, Holden regards his as individuals, not sex objects, refusing to take advantage of them as they begin to succumb to his embraces. And his headlong flight is not through weakness but through an admirable sensitivity to the faults of society, as he searches desperately for an answer to the nagging question, where the ducks go when the lake is frozen over, namely, where can one find refuge in a world that has turned into a spiritual wasteland. Such was the anti-hero as he appeared, in such mid-century novels as Graham Greene's *The Power and the Glory*, Saul Bellow's *Herzog* and Philip Roth's *Eli the Fanatic*.

Amis offered an essentially new type of anti-hero, a comic version, an individual who frankly burlesqued the heroic tradition itself. Jim Dixon is not transformed in the course of the novel from apparent failure to dignity and respect but wins the reader's sympathy from the first despite his unheroic qualities because he so readily and amusingly contradicts the expected role. He acknowledges his total unsuitability for it and to some extent revels in that unsuitability because he perceives the faults in the society to which he is supposed to offer subservience. He thus embodies in himself and hence conveys to the reader the gap between the lofty notion of the fictional hero and the twentieth-century reality. Short in stature, clumsy (as a weekend guest in Professor Welch's home, he falls asleep with his cigarette still alight, finding in the morning to his horror huge holes burned in the bedding), and aware of the pseudo-intellectualism and false values of the institution to which he belongs, he recognizes that he is unable to effect any change, expressing his frustration by pulling derisive faces when no one is looking: 'Dixon rolled his eyes together like marbles and sucked in his cheeks to give a consumptive or wasted appearance to his face, moaning loudly as he crossed the sunlit street to his front door' (p. 30) – and occasionally being caught in the act. Forced to participate in some four-part singing at Welch's home, yet unable to read music, he attempts to conceal his shortcoming by silently mouthing the words, leaving the others to provide the singing, only to discover to his consternation that an approaching section requires a solo on his part. Although he is the clown at whose antics and misfortunes we laugh, the humour is really directed at these gatherings, at the pseudo-intellectualism at the new red-brick universities and at Welch himself, for using his seniority to compel his minions to participate in musical sessions intended to flatter his ego.

Jim, hating the profession in which he finds himself, treats it with a cavalier disregard for scholarly responsibility, planning a seminar he has been assigned for the next term in a way calculated to attract two or three charming female students while excluding a too-keen male liable to expose Jim's ignorance of the subject. Needless to say, the sole student eventually enrolled in the seminar is the intimidating male. Desperate to publish in order to improve his chances of tenure, he submits to an academic journal an article based on his thesis topic, only to find a few weeks later that its contents have been appropriated by the editor and published under the latter's name.

The burlesque is, however, not aimed exclusively at university life. Amis seizes the opportunity of lampooning too the pseudo-artistry of the world outside the campus, when Welch's son deigns to pay a visit to the campus. To a polite enquiry concerning the nature of his work, Bertrand replies in a braying voice with an arrogance arousing Jim's instant detestation: 'I am a painter. Not, alas, a painter of houses, or I should have been able to make my pile and retire by now. No no; I paint pictures. Not, alas again, pictures of trade unionists or town halls or naked women, or I should now be squatting on an even larger pile. No no; just pictures, mere pictures, pictures *tout court*, or, as our American cousins would say, pictures period.' Jim's purpose is to deflate such bragging.

Paralleling Jim's academic worries is his entanglement with a neurotic female – the latter marvellously depicted – who has embroiled him in an affair from which he strives ineffectually to escape, only to become further enmeshed through fear of hurting her feelings. The antithesis of the traditional hero, who in novels is ever loyal to his beloved, Jim squirms at her advances but (redeemingly), through a compassion he scarcely understands, finds it impossible to break away:

> At his side, Margaret heaved the sigh which invariably preluded the worst avowals. She waited until he had to look at her and said: 'How close we seem to be tonight, James' ... Finding this unanswerable, Dixon gazed at her, slowly nodding his head, half expecting a round of applause from some invisible auditorium. What wouldn't he give for a fierce purging draught of fury or contempt, a really efficient worming from the sense of responsibility? (p. 25)

One notes the subtlety in the phrase 'half expecting a round of applause from some invisible auditorium', an allusion to the silent self-congratulation of the conventional hero in fulfilling his noble role.

The climax of the novel is reached in the scene of Jim's lecture, where his exasperation at the pomposities and hypocrisies of academia – not least the attempt to impress distinguished visitors with academic standards that are far from distinguished – makes him incapable of joining the process. Compelled to deliver a public talk on *Merrie England*, a lecture upon which his future career will depend, he indulges in a few drinks beforehand to fortify his courage. The drinks in fact force his subdued rebelliousness to surface, so that he finds himself, to the delight of the students and the consternation of the university authorities, unconsciously imitating Welch's well-known nasal intonations and characteristic phrases. Then gradually,

> ... but not as gradually as it seemed to some parts of his brain, he began to infuse his tones with a sarcastic, wounding bitterness. Nobody outside a madhouse, he tried to imply, could take seriously a single phrase of this conjectural, nugatory, deluded, tedious rubbish. Within quite a short time he was contriving to sound like an unusually fanatical Nazi trooper in charge of a book-burning, reading out to the crowd excerpts from a pamphlet written by a pacifist, Jewish, literate Communist. A growing mutter, half-amused, half-indignant, arose about him, but he closed his ears to it and read on. Almost unconsciously, he began to adopt an unnameable foreign accent and to read faster and faster, his head spinning ... (p. 226)

A few moments later, he collapses in a drunken stupor. Underscoring the comic scene is our sense of the justice of his rebellion against the falseness both of his position and of academia at large, including the traditional idealization of the Middle Ages to which he is expected to subscribe. At last, through his drunken stupor, he reveals the truth not only of that era but even more so of his own:

> Listen and I'll tell you. The point about Merrie England is that it was about the most un-Merrie period in our history. It's only the home-made pottery crowd, organic husbandry crowd, recorder-playing crowd, the Esperanto ...

Like Holden Caulfield, the comic anti-hero emerges as more honest and more ethical than the hypocritical society around him.

All ends well. The discovery, related to him by her previous victim, that Margaret's suicide attempt had been carefully staged in order to arouse his compassion and inveigle him into taking the place of the lost suitor, at last frees him from any sense of guilt. The appearance early in the novel of a beautiful young lady had created a sub-theme culminating, after various fiascoes, in her desertion of Bertrand in favour of Dixon himself, while the offer of a well-paying position in the outside world frees him for ever from the oppressive halls of academe. Those successes, it should be noted, are not achieved by any effort or ability on his part but, in a sense, result from his supposed deficiencies, Jim's most attractive quality both for the young lady and for his future employer being precisely the maladroit, bumbling traits marking his unsuitability to the heroic tradition. As his new patron, Gore-Urquhart remarks: 'It's not that you've got the qualifications, for this or any other work ... You haven't got the disqualifications, though, and that's much rarer.'

Some of the older generation were horrified at the behavioural standards of Lucky Jim and his compeers within the new genre, Somerset Maugham charging them (with remarkable lack of humour) as being reprehensible characters: 'They do not go to university to acquire culture, but to get a job, and when they have got one, scamp it. They have no manners, and are woefully unable to deal with any social predicament. Their idea of a celebration is to go to a public house and drink six beers ... They will write anonymous letters to harass a fellow undergraduate and listen to a telephone conversation that is no business of theirs. Charity, kindliness, generosity are qualities which they hold in contempt.'[209]

For the public at large, however, the humour justified the seeming lack of morals. It made fun of the public's most treasured concepts, including their provision of higher learning for the working class, and, not least, created an amusing replacement for the invalidated heroic tradition of past novels, those two elements providing a refreshingly new direction for comic fiction.

e) Malcolm Bradbury, *The History Man*

Amis' novel not only marked the arrival of the comic anti-hero; it also inaugurated in Britain the genre of the campus novel, leading to David Lodge's *Changing Places* and *Small World*, both making fun of academia.[210] Lodge's novels humorously suggested (with considerable justice) that, while ostensibly organized in order to further research, sabbatical exchanges as well as scholarly conferences now being held in such exotic places as Hawaii were really opportunities for free vacations combined with sexual adventures, the latter made conveniently possible by the wife's absence. The success of Lodge's novels encouraged his friend, Bradbury, to embark on the same path with *Stepping Westward* and *Rates of Exchange*, although his finest novel, still addressing the academic scene, adopted a different approach.

The central character, unlike Amis' Lucky Jim, is no anti-hero. On the contrary, Howard Kirk is presented from the first as a man succeeding at everything he undertakes, an academic with two scholarly books to his credit and a third on the way, a tenured lecturer at Watermouth University, and already a television personality frequently called upon to comment on contemporary social affairs. He has a beautiful wife, two bright children, and a comfortable renovated Georgian home, and both he and his wife are committed welfare volunteers, busily engaged in local affairs. Barbara moves in 'constant indignation' through playgroups, schools, surgeries and parks, demanding free abortion and obtaining signatures for endless ecological petitions, while Howard is involved in race issues, class struggle, alienated sectors, the Claimants' Union, and is a thorn in the side of the municipal council. They are in many ways admirable, and it is not Howard, therefore, who is being burlesqued – at least ostensibly – Bradbury treating him with a degree of respect, almost of awe.

The humour, it transpires, is aimed in a different direction. In contrast to Amis' parody of the somewhat pathetic attempts by provincial universities to ape their more distinguished sister institutions, Bradbury turns his attention to a new and formidable type of university whose aim was not to imitate but to break away from the traditions of Oxford and Cambridge and to forge centres of higher learning more suited to the fast-changing world. The University of Sussex, for example, founded in 1960 and attracting to its faculty such eminent scholars as Asa Briggs, had chosen to jettison the traditional single major for students, adopting an interdisciplinary approach that would broaden studies. It fostered provocatively new teaching methods calculated to stimulate independence of mind rather than learning by rote. Small seminars replaced large lecture halls, tutors were urged to introduce the latest technology into their classrooms, to exhort students to challenge accepted ideas and to venture experimentally into uncharted areas. In the humanities, the study of history took on a new vitality by the adoption both of

Marxist principles and of a radical liberalism, those elements not forming an official part of university policy but resulting from the institution's openness to new ideas, an openness that tended to attract to its faculty lecturers eager to innovate. Moreover, the principle of encouraging independence among students meant granting them greater freedom of political action, as well as (in contrast to the proctor-system still operating at Oxford and Cambridge) placing their sexual activities outside the jurisdiction of the authorities.

Bradbury, who taught for most of his academic career at the University of East Anglia, which was founded at the same time as the Sussex campus and shared many of its aims, clearly respected the desire for educational innovation at these new institutions. He was himself a distinguished academic, producing respected scholarly works, but he was aware also of the negative aspects of these institutions, teasingly exposing the weaknesses of the new system and the absurdities into which, at times, the weaknesses were liable to lead. In brief, his novel was aimed at suggesting that the pride of these campuses in their originality, as well as their self-congratulation concerning the splendid innovations they had introduced into their academic processes, were not quite as justified as they had imagined.

Thoroughly familiar with the new trends and extraordinarily acute in his observations, Bradbury possessed a knack for burlesquing precisely those elements that these ultra-modern universities regarded as their major achievements. On the multifunctional architectural environment aimed at replacing the pseudo-Gothicism of the older campuses and the dull red-brick of the provincial schools by creating forms and spaces reflecting new styles of human relationship, he writes:

There is a dining-hall with a roof of perspex domes, looking like sun umbrellas, by the man-made lake; there is an Auditorium in the shape of a whale, its hinder parts hung out on an elegant device of metal ropes over the lake; the buildings poke and prod and shine in a landscape itself reconstituted, as hills are moved here and valleys there. Some eclecticism and tolerance prevails; at the Auditorium they perform that week a Marxist adaptation of *King Lear*, this week a capitalist adaptation of *The Good Woman of Setzuan*. But a zealous equality prevails in the air, and the place has become a little modern state, with the appropriate services, in all their inconsistency: a post office and a pub and a Mace super-market and a newsagent stand side by side with the psychiatric service, the creche, the telephone life-line for the drug addicts, the offices of the Securicor patrol (p. 65).[211]

The slick, swift-moving style of writing echoes the new mode, making Bradbury appear part of this modern era. But there are barbs in the description, suggesting that both the building and the performances that take place within it are motivated not by a desire for aesthetic or theatrical excellence but, like the building itself, by a determination to innovate at all costs. The performances, it is clear, exploit art in the cause of political propaganda, distorting the original aims of the dramatists. And if the description of the Auditorium sounds exaggerated, the alert reader of the time would have immediately recognized the reference to the Hockey Rink shaped like a whale, recently erected at Yale to the design of Eero Saarinen, his name, of course, echoed in Kaakinen, the fictional architect of Watermouth.

Bradbury is especially amusing in noting how the innovations can produce precisely the opposite of their intended purpose, again contrasting the high-minded ideological aim of the designers with the resulting effect. The cafeteria, we learn, was designed with the aim of obliterating at one stroke the traditional, hierarchical separation of dining facilities in the Halls of the older universities, where members of faculty sit at a 'high table' overlooking the under-graduates. The new idea was to create a democratic setting ensuring social integration under one roof. The cafeteria consists, accordingly, of variegated areas available to all, some more expensively furnished where, surrounded by exotic plants, diners could eat in some degree of grandeur, while other areas are simpler and cheaper, providing ready-packed food to be consumed with the aid of plastic cutlery ('forks that look like spoons and knives that look like forks'). But, as Bradbury comments, in such sociological matters the unexpected may occur; for the students eat in the expensive section in order to express their proletarian indignation, while the faculty eat in the cheaper area to demonstrate their egalitarianism, that reversal preserving the very separation that the architect had hoped to end. Similarly, as part of the university's insistence upon tolerance, pluralism and lack of discrimination, it has opened a multi-denominational chapel, '... named, to avoid offence, the Contemplation Centre, with rabbis and gurus, ethical secularists and macrobiotic organicists presiding at what was carefully not called its consecration'. That last phrase slyly reveals the negation of the sanctity supposedly intrinsic to a chapel, now available to the profane. Moreover, the new freedom accorded to student activities has produced a change in the course of time. Where, during the period of the university's foundation, students had appeared on the glossy pages of magazines photographed as engaged in earnest and companionable study, they now appear instead in the news columns, usually hanging upside-down between two policemen.

And now to Howard Kirk himself. Although Bradbury acknowledges Kirk's success as a sociologist, even in the opening pages there are minor barbs aimed at the inflated jargon of the new science, his use of extravagant Marxist-oriented vocabulary for comparatively simple concepts. Marriage, as Howard Kirk defines it, is 'society's technique for permanentizing the inherent contingency of relationships in the interests of political stability', while human nature is 'a relationship to the temporal and historical process, culturally conditioned and afforded a particular performance within the available role-sets but with the capacity to innovate through manipulating options'. Bradbury himself often employs such phraseology tongue-in-cheek as if acknowledging its validity, but at other times wrily inverts an accepted sociological term, as in his comment on the couple's dress habits. They of course wear the requisite jeans and kaftans in order to display their egalitarianism, their membership in the proletariat, but, as Howard's two published books have brought them a welcome side-income, those items of clothing are in their case rather more expensive than those of their peers – a factor that Bradbury mischievously terms, with echoes of Veblen, 'inconspicuous unconsumption'.

But there are more serious faults to which at first Bradbury only alludes, leaving readers to draw their own conclusions. Howard, in inviting friends to a party at his home, does more than act as a convivial host; he ponders how to provide 'relevant forms of inter-action' and to establish 'the parameters of the encounter'. In order to produce a creative mixture, he invites a potpourri of '... heteros with homos, painters with advanced theologians, scientists with historians, students with Hell's Angels, pop-stars with IRA supporters, Maoists with Trotskyites, family-planning doctors with dropouts who sleep under the pier'. The description of his preparations for the party offers a clue to what will emerge as one of Bradbury's main objectives in the novel, treated humorously yet with an underlying seriousness, namely his suspicion concerning the academic integrity of the sociology now being cultivated on these campuses, a discipline that had taken over the function of what used to be termed history. Howard, a recognized expert on social interchange, supposedly dedicated to objectively recording and analysing human events, is really, we learn, a manipulator, organizing and, in effect, provoking the political clashes and inter-personal outbursts that he will then be able to document in support of preconceived theories to be posited in his future publications. At first, such activity seems merely amusing. On the evening of what he terms an 'unstructured' party,

> he goes upstairs, to pull beds against the walls, adjust lights, shade shades, pull blinds, open doors. It is an important rule to have as little forbidden ground as possible, to make the house itself the total stage. And so he designs it, retaining only a few tiny areas of sanctity; he blocks, with chairs, the short corridor that leads to the children's rooms, and the steps that lead down to his basement study. Everywhere else the code is one of possibility, not denial. Chairs and cushions and beds suggest multiple forms of companionship. Thresholds are abolished; room leads into room. There are speakers for music, special angles for lighting, rooms for dancing and talking and smoking and sexualizing. The aim is to let the party happen rather than to make it happen, so that what takes place occurs apparently without hostly intervention, or rather with the intervention of that higher sociological host who governs the transactions of human encounter (p. 71).

The care he takes to create dark corners and to place mattresses in strategic positions is not merely for the convenience of his guests. Those elements are lures, temptations to sexual activity, to adventures (or misadventures) calculated to produce the kind of marital disruptions or extra-marital complications that serve as grist for his academic mill. One notes Howard's care that what takes place should occur 'apparently without hostly intervention'. He is, ultimately, creating the statistics and social events that he will later cite as fortuitously emergent phenomena.

There is in such manipulative activity, especially in Bradbury's presentation of it, a modern equivalent to the practice of 'outwitting' that had typified comedy in the past. Conventional comedy had presented the young lover as exploiting some weakness in the symbol of authority – Nicea's desire for a son or Pinchwife's disguising his wife as a man – in order to achieve precisely what the *senex* had hoped to prevent. Here, Howard, in planning the party as a means of furthering his career, cleverly circumvents the requirements of sociology not falsifying facts but ensuring in advance that the facts will occur in a manner supportive of his theories. Amusingly, he has 'outwitted' the requirements of objectivity. Only gradually are his actions perceived in the novel to be unethical, the dubious morality of his professional career being paralleled in his personal life. Hence his interference with his old-fashioned friends, the Beamishes. When a distraught Myra, encouraged by the model the Kirks have provided, informs him in the strictest confidence that she plans to leave her husband, he calms her, offering sympathetic counsel. But that does not prevent him from imperturbably breaking the confidence a little later, when he unabashedly informs her husband Henry of her intention – not in order to preserve or heal the marriage, but in order to mould that essentially conservative couple into his own image, to 'liberate' the pair, urging both parties with the newly coined jargon to defy marital constrictions: 'You've withdrawn too far. You've closed in on yourselves, you've lost touch with everything, you've no outside contacts, and so when anything goes wrong you blame it on each other. What you're doing is trapping each other in fixed personality roles. You can't grow, you can't expand, you can't let each other develop. You're stuck out there, in your little nest, out of time, out of history, and you're missing out on possibility' (p. 170). That he should try to persuade them to adopt his own principles is, perhaps, justified, damaging though it proves for the pair, but the fact that Bradbury includes in that incident a blatant betrayal of a confidence provides a further hint that in the author's view there is something seriously amiss in these new liberal concepts.

Sexual freedom applies not only to the guests invited to Howard's party, but also to his relationship with his wife, Barbara. They both have side-affairs, as it were on principle, and grimly tolerate each other's liaisons, sometimes separating for a while and then returning – the fact that they return winning them, as Bradbury entertainingly states, the reputation of having according to the new standards a stable marriage. But apart from the underlying unhappiness that we are made to perceive in Barbara herself, culminating in her act at the end of the novel, when like Henry she slashes her arms on broken glass to draw attention to her melancholy condition, that freedom from marital restrictions spills over into academic life when Howard, as he has obviously done many times before, beds one of his students, a pimply female who is just emerging from a lesbian relationship. On being challenged by a colleague, his blithe justification is that he is thereby fulfilling his responsibility for the welfare of the students placed under his supervision. It is a witty and lively rejoinder, highlighting the difference from the policy of the more staid universities, but, as becomes apparent later in the novel, it is a principle in patent violation of academic integrity, the prohibition aimed at preventing exploitation of the confidence generated in teacher–student relations, as well as obviating the danger of students bartering their favours in return for improved grades.

What perhaps does not emerge from these brief quotations, which inevitably lose much of their humour when cited out of context, is the lively and entertaining depiction of Howard's immense self-confidence and professional slickness, as he breezes along brilliantly manipulating everything in his path, the more sombre aspects of such activities only slowly emerging as the novel develops. Any adverse criticism of his actions, as in the above instance concerning the bedding of students, is made not by Bradbury, since that would spoil the humorous effect. In general, it comes instead from Howard's mistress, or his equally liberated and somewhat unhappy wife, Barbara. The latter, after reading the typescript of his new book, remarks caustically that it reveals the true nature of its author: 'Do you know what it says?' asked Barbara. 'It says you're a radical poseur. It tells how you've substituted trends for morals and commitments.' 'You've not read it properly,' said Howard. 'It's a committed book, a political book.' 'But what are you committed to?' asked Barbara. 'Do you remember how you used to say "maturity" all the time? And it never meant anything? Now it's "liberation" and "emancipation". But it doesn't mean any more than the other thing. Because there's nothing in you that really feels or trusts, no character.' 'You're jealous,' said Howard, as usual deflecting the criticism by neatly attributing the fault to her, a comment that leads her not only to drop her criticism but henceforth to accept the book as a valid academic study.

Howard's ability to turn everything to his advantage, to win each skirmish, to manoeuvre others in the direction he wants, is perceived acutely by Flora, his colleague and current mistress who is herself effectively parodied, as in Bradbury's description of her debating tactics – cleverly employed at conferences (like Stephen Potter's one-upmanship) to cut the ground from beneath the speaker irrespective of the value of the lecture: 'She habitually sits in a left-hand aisle seat near the front and, the paper over, rises first, a pencil held high for attention, to ask the initial and most devastating question ("I'd hoped to bring evidence to show the entire inadequacy of this approach. Happily the speaker has, presumably unconsciously, performed the task for me in the paper itself …")'. As regards Howard, her own tactics make her sensitive to his. In discussing the psychological reasons that have prompted the unhappy Henry to make the suicidal gesture of smashing a window and deliberately cutting his arm upon the broken glass, Howard asks rhetorically whether she really believes that he pushed Henry. She replies appropriately enough: 'If you wanted someone through a window, you wouldn't push him yourself. You'd get someone else to do it. Or persuade the man he should do it himself, in his best interests' – a comment that Howard seems to relish.

As these instances reveal, the reader is made to perceive that Howard's awesome success in everything he attempts emanates from a disturbing arrogance that needs to be taken down a peg, and the reduction is gradual, usually effected by the teasing humour of the narration. The book he has just completed, *The Defeat of Privacy*, argues impressively on Marxist principles that, in the post-bourgeois society which the modern world is now experiencing, there are to be no more private selves, no more private properties, no more private acts (to which Barbara remarks tartly, 'No more private parts'). However, it is not she who catches him out but Felicity Phee, the female student mentioned above, whom he finds to his annoyance ensconced in his study, reading his manuscript without permission. 'You had no business to do that,' he says sternly. 'It's not quite finished. It's private'; to which she replies aptly enough by quoting from his own manuscript: 'The attempt to privatise life is a phenomenon of narrow historical significance.' For once, Howard has no answer; nor can he produce an effective response when discovering somewhat later that she has been listening on an extension to a highly confidential telephone conversation: 'You were listening,' he says. 'That was private, Felicity.' Felicity smiles at him, appearing not to grasp the point. 'Oh, Howard, darling, what's private?' she asks. 'Private is doing business in my own house without it being interfered with,' says Howard. 'Isn't that rather a bourgeois attitude?' responds Felicity. Once again, a character hoisted with his own petard.

The only person who seems capable of standing up to Howard is the attractive Miss Callendar, newly appointed to the English department, impervious to his blandishments and to his attempts to seduce her. Moreover, she repeatedly outsmarts him in her replies. Accused of having no social conscience, she replies sarcastically that she does indeed possess one: 'I use it a lot. I think it's a sort of moral conscience. I'm very old-fashioned.' He assures her that he can help her modernize it. 'I think I know just how you'd go about that,' she responds, proceeding to quote against him the axiom of his own New Left: 'No, I'm afraid you're too old for me. I never trust anyone over thirty.' Yet by the end of the novel, even she has succumbed to his charms and has allowed herself to be seduced by him.

Howard's calculated manoeuvres and manipulations reach their high point in the incident concerning Mangel, where Bradbury tackles more openly, although again in a manner softened by humour, his reservations concerning the moral integrity of the new sociology, at least as Howard represents it. The incident (recalling a contemporary controversy concerning the Stanford physicist, William Shockley) concerns a geneticist whose scientific research has led to conclusions that stamp him, in the view of radicals, as racist. Howard, realizing that even the suspicion of an invitation to Mangel to speak at the university will ignite violent student and faculty protests which he could then record and analyse for future publication, sees it as it is an opportunity not to be missed. Discreetly, he initiates a rumour (totally unfounded) that a lecture invitation is about to be extended. In the secretary's temporary absence from the office, he adds a message to that effect on the department's dictaphone, and is then able to sit back enjoying the scene when, to the astonishment of the chair, the proposed invitation appears on the agenda at the next committee meeting.

The meeting is, in Bradbury's description, a delight. As sophisticates of the dynamics of interaction, the members of the department choose their places with care, ensuring angles of vision effective for creating dysphoria. Professor Marvin then calls them to order for discussion of the first item on the agenda, an item which is, as he declares, entirely uncontentious, merely approval of the names of two external examiners for the end-of-year finals. Split into rival groups, they raise objection after objection, their dissents founded on such radically different premises that no other names can be agreed upon. A working party is suggested, to bring names to the next meeting, but no one can agree on the membership of the working party. Eventually they approve a compromise motion, that Professor Marvin be allowed to make his own choice of external examiners. 'Professor Marvin promptly indicates that he will recommend to Senate the two names originally mentioned an hour before' (p. 155).

The subsequent discussion concerning Mangel is as acrimonious as Howard had hoped, the bewildered Marvin unable to explain how the matter had appeared on the agenda. Howard takes care discreetly to preserve silence, his only comment occurring when the motion seems about to be lost, and Marvin proclaims firmly that Mangel is neither a racist nor a sexist. Neatly turning the tables, Howard asks innocently whether, since Mangel is neither racist nor sexist, there would be any objection to inviting him if his name were to be proposed. Eventually, the motion to invite Mangel is passed on the grounds that dissenting views should be tolerated, and the decision produces in due course the requisite screaming posters plastered over the campus, student sit-ins, riots, cries of 'Fascist' and 'Histerectomise Mangel', followed by the ravaging of a lecturer's office, just as Howard had visualized.

The final episode in the novel is potentially the most damaging to Howard. He manages once again to emerge unscathed, although the incident leaves its mark upon the reader – namely, his hounding of Carmody for possessing views different from his own. A serious if not brilliant student in Howard's course, conscientiously researching his seminar papers yet invariably being awarded by Howard a failing grade because he refuses to adopt his tutor's radical views, Carmody at last, in a passionate outburst in class, complains with considerable justice: 'Do I have to agree with you, Dr. Kirk, do I have to vote the way you do, and march down the street with you, and sign your petitions, and hit policemen on your demos, before I can pass your course?' When Carmody, in despair, takes the matter to the department chair, Howard's position is seriously threatened, since he has so obviously discriminated against a student on political grounds. But he weathers the storm, skilfully transforming the incident from the potentially crippling charge of faculty prejudice into a matter of academic freedom, the inviolable right of a lecturer to determine student grades. The result is Carmody's eventual flight from the university, thereby ending his academic career. Peace returns, and with the end of the year it is time for the Kirks to organize another party.

These quotations from the novel may seem to have taken us away from our central theme, but they were necessary in leading us to the final assessment. Technically, the victory in that last incident is Howard Kirk's, but, as the reader cannot fail to recognize, the Carmody affair is in blatant contradiction to the freedom of expression and the encouragement of independent thought among students that had formed one of the basic aims of these new academic institutions. It functions as a warning of the ways in which educational experimentation can seriously backfire. Although the humour seems at times to be directed at Howard, it is really aimed beyond him at a larger target. While Bradbury admired the aims of the experimental British universities, in one of which he served for many years as a distinguished professor, that did not prevent him from lampooning their lofty imperviousness to the hazards inherent in the radical sociology flourishing on their campuses, and the absurdities to which their experiments could lead. Yet the criticism remains convivial, with Howard and Barbara as essentially likeable characters, exploring their newfound political and sexual liberation, eager to apply the new principles to others, and providing in their successes and failures a vastly entertaining picture of the new academic generation and the dangers besetting these innovative campuses. Nor do Bradbury's gibes at the pretentiousness of the new institutions disqualify the ideals they had adopted. Like most successful humour, the comedy pokes fun at their weaknesses, suggesting that their ideology needs to be tempered to suit reality, that such principles as academic freedom of thought, egalitarianism and sexual liberation, noble though they may be in themselves, can lead to results diametrically opposed to their aim, unless they are carefully monitored.

It is a brilliant novel, full of humorous situations and witty repartee, of which only a few specimens could be offered here. Moreover, it illustrates perfectly the genial deflating of excessive confidence and authoritative rulings that constitutes true humour. Those new campuses, Bradbury suggests, were not wrong in their aims and innovative ideas, but they needed, like Socrates, to descend from the clouds and modify their principles to suit the requirements of life upon terra firma.

f) Helen Fielding, *Bridget Jones's Diary*

Invited by the British newspaper *The Independent* to contribute a weekly column on her experiences as a single girl living in London, Helen Fielding was hesitant because of the self-exposure it would involve. She chose instead to create a fictional character placed in that situation, the success of her column leading to the publication of *Bridget Jones's Diary*, a book selling over 15 million copies worldwide.

Bridget, a 33-year-old unmarried career girl holding down with trepidation a minor job in a publishing concern and possessing an irrepressible sense of humour that bubbles up even in the most trying conditions, struggles to live up to the roles assigned to her by modern society while acknowledging, with comic self-disparagement, her woeful inability to do so. Her diary is headed each day by a record of her weight as reported by the unforgiving bathroom scales, a painful admission of her dietary backslidings, usually accompanied by a cheerful decision to reform:

> I feel ashamed and repulsive. I can actually feel the fat splurging out from my body. Never mind. Sometimes you have to sink to a nadir of toxic fat envelopment in order to emerge, phoenix-like, from the chemical wasteland as a purged and beautiful Michelle Pfeiffer figure. Tomorrow new Spartan health and beauty regime will begin (p. 15).[212]

The humour of course arises in such passages from the gap between Bridget's confident determination that she will begin the diet next day and her inevitable surrender to temptation when the time comes. Mentally she determines to restrict herself to a half-grapefruit for breakfast, while her hand covertly reaches out for a chocolate croissant, the hand proving the victor. But the first-person confessional narrative, recording with uninhibited mirth and candour her longings, frustrations, failures and (more rarely) her achievements, creates a sense of intimacy and fellow-feeling, a sympathy that, after the initial laughter, directs the ridicule away from her supposed inadequacies to those elements in contemporary society responsible for transforming a potentially normal healthy being into a bundle of neurotic self-condemnations. The process of watching those socially approved directives lampooned forms a primary delight of the book.

The reference to Michelle Pfeiffer in the above passage, with Bridget's mournful recognition of the unlikelihood that she will ever attain to such pulchritude, suggests that the ultimate cause of her torment derives from an illusion imposed upon the females of her generation, the chimera created by the barrage of diet programmes bombarding her from newspaper advertisements, magazine articles and street hoardings assuring her with unassailable confidence that plumpness is a scourge and guaranteeing that adherence to their specific regime will transform her into a gorgeously attractive young woman able to compete with the willowy figures held up as ideals in fashion plates and the movie industry. The suspicion that such promises are baseless is soon confirmed. Delighted to discover on one occasion that she has, by some miracle, lost a few pounds, Bridget goes eagerly to meet her friends, happily expecting a round of applause and fervent expressions of admiration, only to be told that the loss of weight has made her look tired and drawn (a consequence of dieting carefully ignored by the advertisers). Ruefully, she looks back at the orgies of self-indulgence she has so pointlessly sacrificed in the past:

> I feel empty and bewildered – as if a rug has been pulled from under my feet. Eighteen years – wasted. Eighteen years of calorie- and fat-unit-based arithmetic. Eighteen years of buying long shirts and sweaters and leaving the room backwards in intimate situations to hide my bottom. Millions of cheesecakes and tiramisus, tens of millions of Emmenthal slices left uneaten. Eighteen years of struggle, sacrifice and endeavor – for what? Eighteen years and the result is 'tired and flat.' I feel like a scientist who discovers that his life's work has been a total mistake (p. 59).

Even more damaging to the diet-programmers is her eventual discovery that her plumpness, so far from being the dreadful impediment she has been led to believe, is in fact an attraction to men. As Daniel informs her in a phrase that was to become proverbial among admirers of the new 'chic-lit' genre that Fielding inaugurated: 'Nobody wants legs like a stick insect – they want a bottom they can park a bike in, and balance a pint of beer on.'

No less prominent is her battle with two polarized social imperatives concerning her marital (or immarital) status, the second to be discussed a little later. On the one hand, there is the traditional pressure from family and wedded friends that she find a husband before it is too late, spinsterhood being regarded as an unmitigated disaster. In their company, as she wrily comments on one occasion, she feels like Miss Haversham. The clock, they keep reminding her, is ticking, women's charms being subject to an inexorable 'sell-by date'. Tiresomely, aunts and uncles introduce her to supposedly eligible divorcees, while married males infuriate her by the complacent remark that the best male candidates have already been snapped up, leaving for her only a miserable residue. Despite her anguish, her ripostes are at times effective, such as the bland query: 'Is it one of three marriages that end in divorce or one of two?' But the pressure is on. Even the assumption by some that as 'a Singleton' she must be enjoying a promiscuously exciting life she finds distasteful, again responding effectively when repeatedly asked, 'How is your sex life?', although in this instance in unspoken retaliation:

> Why can't married people understand that this is no longer a polite question to ask? We wouldn't rush up to *them* and roar, 'How's your marriage going? Still having sex?' Everyone knows that dating in your thirties is not the happy-go-lucky free-for-all it was when you were twenty-two and that the honest answer is more likely to be, 'Actually, last night my married lover appeared wearing suspenders and a darling little Angora crop-top, told me he was gay/a sex addict/a narcotic addict/a commitment phobic and beat me up with a dildo (p. 12).

As the assumption that singles have a more exciting sex life implies, the prospect of being married is notably flawed for her generation. It no longer carries with it the vision of lifelong bliss, of 'living happily ever after'. Widespread divorces and infidelities have swept away that illusion. Sure enough, Magda, the exemplar of the 'Smug Marrieds', is fated to her horror to discover her husband in pursuit of a younger and more attractive woman. The twentieth-century collapse of the marriage ideal is risibly caricatured in Bridget's previously staid mother. Suddenly realizing the years she has wasted as a mere housewife, she dashes off in exuberant search of new liaisons, determined to rectify the error of her ways, leaving Bridget, after a momentary shock, with strangely mixed emotions – joy at the prospect of the post-menstrual delights revealed to be awaiting her in the future, coupled with a gloomy recognition of her own deplorably cheerless condition:

Awake, alone, to find myself imagining my mother in bed with Julio. Consumed with repulsion at vision of parental, or rather demi-parental sex; outrage on behalf of father; heady, selfish optimism at example of another thirty years of unbridled passion ahead of me (not unrelated to frequent thoughts of Goldie Hawn and Susan Sarandon); but mainly extreme sense of jealousy of failure and foolishness at being in bed alone on Sunday morning while my mother aged over sixty is probably just about to do it for the second .... Oh my God. No. I can't bear to think about it (p. 36).

What, then, is the modern alternative to the married state? – and here we confront the second problem of her unmarried status. The rise of feminism had, of course, created a new concept in direct opposition to the traditional approval of marriage – the liberated woman happily freed from the pressures of wedlock and motherhood, a careerist financially independent, coolly and efficiently taking her place as the director of a highly successful commercial institution and, in her leisure hours, now that she is absolved of marital obligations, casually using men to satisfy her needs while assiduously keeping clear of any commitment. The femininist ideal is now burlesqued in its turn as Bridget, the supposedly self-reliant careerist of the modern age, presents a less sanguinary picture of the situation, her devotion to professional duties swamped by a desperate longing for a lover as she waits neurotically for the phone call that fails to come:

Cannot believe I convinced myself I was keeping the entire weekend free to work when in fact I was on permanent date-with-Daniel standby. Hideous, wasted two days glaring psychopathically at the phone, and eating things. Why hasn't he rung? Why? What's wrong with me? Why ask for my phone number if he wasn't going to ring, and if he was going to ring surely he would do it over the weekend? Must centre myself more. Will ask Jude about appropriate self-help book, possible Eastern-religion-based (p. 20).

The avoidance of commitment authorized by the new mode can, it seems, be adopted only too easily by the male. Alex, entering with his girlfriend, disarmingly declares: 'We're not going out, we're just sleeping together.'

As Bridget's reference to the self-help book indicates, it is now the turn of the purveyors of such advice to be exposed, with the glib assurance in such articles and manuals that following their directives will bring an end to guilt complexes, create perfect psychological adjustment, inner tranquillity and (from the cosmeticians) a complexion free from spots, warts and wrinkles. Such is the counsel indigenous to women's magazines, blandly offering instructions for every aspect of contemporary living and holding out to their readers the glowing picture of happiness, career advancement, health, charm and a satisfying sex life. Bridget, following the guidance of the beauticians, dutifully performs the assigned aerobic exercises, obediently scrapes her body with a stiff brush, and compliantly waxes her legs, only to find that her back aches, her head is sore and her legs, now bright red, are covered by ugly lumps of wax. Sadly she admits that the women's magazines have browbeaten her into becoming 'a child of *Cosmopolitan* culture', that she has been traumatized by supermodels and subjected to too many quizzes. Their demands, she concludes, are excessive:

> Being a woman is worse than being a farmer there is so much harvesting and crop spraying to be done: legs to be waxed, underarms shaved, eyebrows plucked, feet pumiced, skin exfoliated and moisturized, spots cleansed, roots dyed, eyelashes tinted, nails filed, cellulite massaged, stomach muscles exercised. The whole performance is so highly tuned you only need to neglect it for a few days for the whole thing to go to seed. Sometimes I wonder what I would be like if left to revert to nature – with a full beard and handlebar moustache on each shin … Is it any wonder girls have no confidence? (p. 22)

She spends the rest of the evening eating doughnuts and wearing a cardigan with egg on it.

One chapter of the diary is devoted to 'Inner Poise', a day on which Bridget strives to follow the counsel proffered in a recently read article. The encouraging phrase in the title she keeps repeating to herself as a kind of mantra in the hope that it will produce the desired effect. As commanded, she strives to imagine herself immaculately dressed in white linen, wearing an air of dignified hauteur, when her natural impulse is to '… lie fully dressed and terrified under the duvet, chain-smoking, glugging cold *sake* out of a beaker and putting on make-up as a hysterical displacement activity'. The inner poise fails, of course, to materialize. On another occasion, having to appear at a book-launching party, she is relieved to discover all she needs to know in an article (in this instance, an actual article) by Tina Brown in *The New Yorker*. From it she learns the correct techniques for attaining self-confidence, improving social skills and making participation at such a gathering into a brilliant success, only to find when she attempts to apply the approved techniques their disastrous inapplicability to the situation. The instruction to glide charmingly from group to group, spending only two minutes with each, then moving on with the polite explanation that she is required to circulate, turns out somewhat differently in practice. Attaching herself to a group earnestly talking together, she is greeted with the rude query what it is she wants, and finding the polite excuse for having to circulate totally irrelevant, panics and asks idiotically where the toilets are.

Bridget's total freedom from self-aggrandizement and her ability to confront her failings with disarming candour allow her to become both the object of the humour and its creator, but behind the seemingly realistic account of her daily misfortunes so obviously embedded in the late twentieth century, there is throughout the book a patent parallel to Austen's *Pride and Prejudice*, a parallel that might seem to militate against the postmodern aspects of the work. Mark is conspicuously assigned the surname Darcy, so that, by association, Daniel emerges as a modern-day Wickham, Natasha, with her designs on Darcy, substitutes for Miss Bingley, and various events in their lives echo those of the earlier novel.[213] In fact, the parallels contribute little to the humour, and the *Diary* could have functioned very effectively without that shadowy background, but the transcoding does contribute in one important way. For, unlike the characters listed above, Bridget herself is a striking contrast to the sedate Elizabeth Bennett. Where her predecessor was refined, cool, self-assured and morally impeccable, her counterpart is hilariously obsessive, congenitally unsure of herself, tending to wild exaggeration, and sexually uninhibited. Times have indeed changed, as the reader is reminded whenever the parallels are drawn. But the two characters do have one trait in common, their ability to laugh at folly, both in others and in themselves, even though the targets of the comedy have, with the change in eras, come to differ significantly. Where Austen had burlesqued primarily the contemporary notion of marriage as a stepping stone for financial and social advancement, Fielding shoots her darts more broadly, exposing with lively humour the unwarranted imperiousness of contemporary diet-programmers, of guru-like purveyors of Feng Shui or other obscure oriental rituals guaranteed to create an ineffable harmony in spirit and body, the supposed expertise of women's magazines, the feminist insistence on career advancement, and the unattainable standards of slimness and beauty imposed by the movies. In brief, the modern world, however different the conditions, proves to be as vulnerable as any previous era to the comic deflation of those two main targets – individual pretentiousness and the imperious imposition of socially approved standards.

NOTES

1 INTRODUCTION

1 Harold Nicolson, *The English Sense of Humour and Other Essays* (London: Constable, 1956), p. 4.

2 Robin A. Haig, *The Anatomy of Humor* (Springfield: Charles C. Thomas, 1988), p. 9, and John Morreall, *Taking Laughter Seriously*, (Albany: State University of New York, 1983). A similar view is expressed by Harry Levin, *Playboys and Killjoys: An essay on the theory and practice of comedy* (New York: Oxford University Press, 1987), and Andrew Stott, *Comedy* (London: Routledge, 2005), p. 16, while Scott C. Shershow, *Laughing Matters* (Amherst: University of Massachusetts Press, 1986), p. 3, in offering an interesting definition based on the paradox involved in humour, admits neverthless that the process is like attempting to catch a slippery eel. Willibald Ruch, ed., *Sense of Humor: Explorations of a Personality Characteristic* (Berlin: Mouton, 1998) is primarily psychological in approach, focusing upon the influence of personality traits and gender elements in the the person who laughs, whereas this present study, restricted to literary humour, is concerned with factors within a text that produce laughter and not with the characteristics of the receptor. For the linguistic approach, see Victor Raskin, *Semantic Mechanisms of Humor* (Dortrecht: Reidel, 1985) and Walter Nash, *The Language of Humour* (London: Longman, 1985); and, for the social aspect, Sharon Lockyer and Michael Pickering, eds, *Beyond a Joke: The limits of humour* (Basingstoke: Palgrave, 2005), and Michael Billig, *Laughter and Ridicule: Toward a social critique of humor* (London: Sage, 2005). Allan Rodway, *English Comedy: Its role and nature from Chaucer to the present day* (Berkeley: University of California Press, 1975), after an interesting discussion of comic theory in the opening section, provides a survey of humorous works which disappointingly avoids all discussion of the nature of the humour. He offers instead brief, unsubstantiated statements, such as, 'Wycherley hasn't quite the insolent ease of Etherege, or his imperturbable detachment' (p. 138). A valuable reference guide and bibliography is provided by Don F. Nilsen's three-volume *Humor in*

British Literature (London: Greenwood Press, 1997–2000). The collection of essays edited by Jan Bremmer and Herman Roodenburg, *A Cultural History of Humour* (Cambridge: Polity Press, 1977) provides a stimulating study of humour as a means of discerning cultural change, applying the principle internationally. I am grateful to Dr Orley Marron for her comments on this introductory chapter.

3   In addition to those cited above, helpful investigations include Jan Walsh Hokenson, *The Idea of Comedy: History, theory, critique* (Madison: Farleigh Dickinson University Press, 2006), Jerry Palmer, *Taking Humour Seriously* (London: Routledge, 1994), pp. 94f., T. G. A. Nelson, *Comedy: An introduction* (Oxford: Oxford University Press, 1990) and an interesting earlier study, Morton Gurewitch, *Comedy: The irrational vision* (Ithaca: Cornell University Press, 1975). For collections of essays, see Morreall, ed., *The Philosophy of Laughter and Humor* (Albany: State University of New York Press, 1987), and Michael Cordner, Peter Holland and John Kerrigan, eds, *English Comedy* (Cambridge: Cambridge University Press, 1995). The most recent publication, Eric Weitz, *The Cambridge Introduction to Comedy* (Cambridge: Cambridge University Press, 2009), provides a lively and informative study directed mainly to performance features, emphasizing the 'framing' by means of bodily movement, stage setting or situation that establishes the genre and prepares the audience to expect humour. However, those aspects, interesting as they are, function only as warning signals for the audience, creating an appropriate ambience and are not the source of the humour itself. Moreover, those preparatory factors are not always present, laughter often being invoked unexpectedly, as in the instance of a nervous clergyman declaiming during a marriage service: 'Will you take this woman as your awful wedded wife?' For gender investigation, see Regina Barreca, ed., *New Perspectives on Women and Comedy* (Philadelphia: Gordon & Breach, 1992).

4   Morreall, *Taking Laughter Seriously*, pp. 5–6.

5   Thomas Hobbes, *English Works* ed. W. Molesworth (London: Bohn, 1839) 4:8:§13.

6   Francis Hutcheson, *Reflections Upon Laughter* (New York: Garland, 1971, orig. 1750).

7   Thomas Wilson, *The Art of Rhetorique* (London: R.Graftonus, 1553), pp. 135–6.

8   Hobbes, *English Works* 3:1:§6.

9   William Congreve, *Concerning Humour in Comedy* in *Critical Essays of the Seventeenth Century* ed. J. E. Spingarn (London: Oxford University Press, 1957) 3:245.

10 John J. O'Connor, 'Physical Deformity and Chivalric Laughter in Renaissance England' in Maurice Charney, *Comedy High and Low: An introduction to the experience of comedy* (New York: Oxford University Press, 1978) p. 60. He also cites as comic the dwarf in Jonson's *Volpone*, but the play's text contradicts that view, since Volpone treats Nano and his companions with affection and admiration, as I have argued in '*Volpone*, Comedy or Mordant Satire?' in *The Ben Jonson Journal* 10 (2003), 1–21.

[11] Henri Bergson, *An Essay on the Meaning of the Comic* trans. C. Brereton and F. Rothwell (New York: Macmillan, 1911), chapter 3. For an application of this theory to modern literature, see Fred M. Robinson, *The Comedy of Language: Studies in modern comic literature* (Amherst: University of Massachusetts Press, 1980).

[12] From the 'Humour' entry in the *Encyclopaedia Britannica.*

[13] Maurice Charney, ed., *Comedy: New perspectives* (New York: New York Literary Forum, 1978), p. 171, which deals only with stage comedy.

[14] Emanuel Kant, *Critique of Judgment* trans. J. H. Bernard (London: Macmillan, 1892) 1:1:64.

[15] Michael Clark, 'Humour and Incongruity' in *Philosophy* 45 (1970), 243–54, Mike W. Martin, 'Humour and the Aesthetic Experience: enjoyment of incongruities' in *The British Journal of Aesthetics* 23 (1983), 74–85, John Morreall, 'Humor and Emotion' in *The American Philosophical Quarterly* 20 (1983), 297–304, and Elliot Oring, *Engaging Humor* (Urbana: University of Illinois Press, 2003).

[16] Herbert Spencer, *The Physiology of Laughter*, first published in Macmillan's Magazine, March 1860. Wallace Chafe, *The Importance of Not Being Earnest* (Amsterdam: John Benjamin Press, 2007) follows the safety-valve concept, although he devotes most of his analysis to the physical aspects of laughter.

[17] His theory is, of course, based on the *élan vital* which is shared by all creatures.

[18] Robert R. Provine, *Laughter: A scientific investigation* (New York: Viking, 2000).

[19] Sarah's later statement, when her son was born, is ambiguous, the text either meaning, 'God hath made me a laughing stock so that all that hear will laugh at me' or, as the Authorized Version translates the verse more generously, 'God hath made me to laugh, so that all that hear will laugh with me'; but even in the latter version, the word 'laugh' indicates joy at the birth of her son, with no hint of response to a comic situation. There is a similar usage of the word as joy in Job 8.21.

[20] The most ambitious attempts have been J. William Whedbee, *The Bible and the Comic Vision* (Cambridge: Cambridge University Press, 1998) and Conrad Hyers, *And God Created Laughter: The Bible as divine comedy* (New York: Pilgrim Press, 1981). Barry Sanders, *Sudden Glory* (Boston: Beacon Press, 1995), pp. 41–8, on the other hand, denies the existence of humour in the Bible.

[21] Cf. *Joseph Andrews* 4:8 where Parson Adams confidently lectures Joseph on the need to bear misfortunes with equanimity, only to burst into agonized laments a moment later when informed that his son has fallen into the river.

[22] George Meredith, *An Essay on Comedy and the Uses of the Comic Spirit*, first published in *The New Quarterly Magazine*, April 1877.

[23] Aristophanes, *The Clouds*, in the anonymous translation in Internet Classic Archives on the Web.

[24] The Socrates appearing in Plato's dialogues may not have conformed always to Socrates as he was in real life, but there is sufficient confirmation

in Xenophon's account of the man for us to perceive how his button-holing of leading figures in order to lead them into philosophical traps annoyed many of his victims.

[25] Herbert J. Lebovitz, 'Smiles and Laughter: some neurological, developmental, and psychodynamic considerations' in Maurice Charney, ed., *Comedy: New perspectives*, p. 111, confirms this view: 'The earliest smiles from the newborn are often related to satiation and relaxation of oral muscles after sucking. Later when this same facial expression is seen on the mother's face, the child associates and interprets it as a pleasurable state.'

[26] Dryden, *Absalom and Achitophel*, 7–10, and a stanza from the folksong beginning 'Young folks, old folks ...'

[27] The final picture in Hogarth's series, *The Rake's Progress*.

[28] Translation by Benjamin Jowett.

[29] Quoted in Enid Welsford, *The Fool: His social and literary history* (London: Faber, 1968), p. 43.

[30] Aristotle, *The Poetics* in the translation by S. H. Butcher (London: St Martin's Press, 1951), p. 13.

[31] Longfellow, *The Song of Hiawatha* xi, the parody from *Comic and Curious Verse* ed. J. M. Cohen (London: Penguin, 1952), p. 273.

[32] Sigmund Freud, *Jokes and their Relation to the Unconscious* trans. James Strachey (New York: Norton, 1964, orig. 1905), p. 75. The work has also been translated under the title, *Wit and its Relation to the Unconscious*. Dana F. Sutton, *The Catharsis of Comedy* (Boston: Rowman and Littlefield, 1994) has taken Freud's theory further by suggesting that the releasing of psychic energy is a form of Aristotelean 'purgation'.

[33] Noel Carroll, *Beyond Aesthetics: Philosophical essays* (Cambridge: Cambridge University Press, 2001), p. 323.

[34] Delia Chiaro, *The Language of Jokes: Analysing verbal play* (London: Routledge, 1992) aims to examine the interface between wordplay and linguistics, but the book suffers from the drawback – at least in this present author's opinion – that the jokes analysed are generally far from amusing. One of the first instances offered is of a surgeon informing the parents of a seriously injured youngster that he is going to survive, but adding: '... I'm afraid your son's going to remain a vegetable for the rest of his life' (p. 9). It is listed as an example of 'verbal humour'. Richard J. Alexander, *Aspects of Verbal Humour in English* (Tubingen: Gunter Narr, 1997), a sociolinguistic study, states specifically that he will make no attempt to offer any theory, his work being descriptive (p. 18).

[35] Freud, p. 55, and Robert B. Martin, *The Triumph of Wit* (Oxford: Clarendon Press, 1974), p. 44. For an interpretation of comedy in line with Saussure's theory of language, see Susan Purdie, *Comedy: The master of discourse* (Toronto: University of Toronto, 1993).

[36] Samuel Johnson, *A Preface to Shakespeare*; and, on the metaphysical poets, the section on Cowley in his *Lives of the Poets*. On this genre, see Walter Redfern, *Puns* (Oxford: Blackwell, 1984) and Jonathan Culler, ed., *On Puns: The foundation of letters* (Oxford: Blackwell, 1988).

[37] Pope, *Dunciad* 4:201–2.
[38] Charles R. Gruner, *The Game of Humor* (London: Transaction Publishers, 1997), p. 25.
[39] Thomas Sprat, *History of the Royal Society* (London: J. R. for J. Martyn, 1667), section xx.
[40] Addison, *Spectator* No. 61.
[41] Although insistent upon precision in word usage, Johnson could occasionally make fun of his own profession as lexicographer, as in his definition of a net as a 'reticulated, decussated fabric with interstices at intersections'.
[42] Wylie Sypher, *Comedy* (Baltimore: Johns Hopkins University Press, 1956), pp. 206–8.
[43] Freud, pp. 97–8.
[44] M. M. Bakhtin, *Rabelais and his World* trans. H. Iswolsky (Bloomington: Indiana University Press, 1984), p. 21. By the seventeenth century, largely because of Puritan opposition, the attitude to carnival had become ambivalent, as Leah Marcus records in *The Politics of Mirth* (Chicago: University of Chicago Press, 1986).
[45] E. K. Chambers, *The Medieval Stage* (Oxford: Clarendon Press, 1909), 1:294.
[46] 'Whatever Venus commands is sweet labour, as she never inhabits idle hearts' – from the twelfth-century poem, '*Aestuans intrinsecus ...*' in *The Oxford Book of Medieval Latin Verse* (Oxford: Clarendon Press, 1946), p. 123. Helen Waddell, *The Wandering Scholars* (New York: H. Holt & Co., 1934) offers the best account of the Goliardic poets, identifying Abelard as a leading member.
[47] Al Capp, 'The Comedy of Charles Chaplin' in Corrigan, p. 219.
[48] Welsford, p. 310.
[49] See W. Moelwyn Merchant, *Comedy* (London: Methuen, 1972) for the view that comedy is always on the edge of tragedy.
[50] John Durant and Jonathan Miller, *Laughing Matters: A serious look at humour* (Harlow: Longman, 1988), p. 15.
[51] Northrop Frye, *The Anatomy of Criticism* (Princeton: Princeton University Press, 1957), pp. 163f.
[52] Oscar Wilde, *The Importance of Being Earnest* in *Works* (London: Collins, n.d.), p. 858.
[53] Stephen Potter, *Three-Upmanship* (New York: Holt, Rinehart and Winston, 1962), p. 169.
[54] Sir Philip Sidney, *Defence of Poesy* probably written around 1579.
[55] In general, Hamlet is free from the kind of superciliousness that needs puncturing, as in his warm welcome of the socially inferior players and his insistence that Polonius treat them with due respect. But Shakespeare carefully inserts at this point a remark making him vulnerable, his haughty complaint concerning the clown's wit: 'By the Lord, Horatio, this three years I have taken note of it, the age is grown so picked that the toe of the peasant comes so near the heel of the courtier he galls his kibe.'
[56] For this reading of *Hamlet*, see my *Tradition and Subversion in Renaissance Literature* (Pittsburgh: Duquesne University Press, 2007).

[57] James Boswell, *Life of Johnson* (London: Oxford University Press, 1946), 1:604.

[58] Lord Chesterfield, *Letters to his Son* (London: J. M. Dent, 1942), p. 49. The letter is dated 1748.

[59] Roger B. Henkle, *Comedy and Culture: England 1820–1900* (Princeton: Princeton University Press, 1980) p. 4, rightly claims that abstract declarations about the function of the comic – as a means of undermining the social fabric, or conversely, as an accommodation to the prevailing social order – are relatively insubstantial unless we can watch the writer at work, manoeuvering among the shibboleths and sacred assumptions of his day.

2 LATE MEDIEVAL

[60] The term 'mystery' was probably a corruption of the Latin '*ministerium*'.

[61] Quotations are from the modernized text in *The Wakefield Mystery Plays* ed. Martial Rose (New York: Doubleday, 1963). The Towneley manuscript obtains its name from the family that owned it.

[62] See T. M. Parrott, 'Mak and Archie Armstrang' *Modern Language Notes* 59 (1944), 297.

[63] Cf. A. P. Rossiter, *English Drama from Early Times to the Elizabethans* (London: Hutchinson, 1950), p. 78, and Eleanor Prosser, *Drama and Religion in the English Mystery Plays* (Stanford: Stanford University Press, 1961), pp. 82–6.

[64] Chris Holcomb, *Mirth Making: The rhetorical discourse on jesting in Early Modern England* (Columbia: University of Southern Carolina Press, 2001), p. 3, sees the central theme of such jesting as being 'always a flirting with disorder'.

[65] Derek Pearsall provides a informative discussion of these sexually amusing tales in his essay in *The Cambridge Companion to Chaucer* eds Piero Boitani and Jill Mann (Cambridge: Cambridge University Press, 2003), pp. 160–77. Alfred David, 'The Comedy of Innocence' in Jean E. Jost, *Chaucer's Humor: Critical essays* (New York: Garland Press, 1994), 187, provides a sophisticated analysis of the contrast between the animalistic and the ascetic within the work.

[66] See note 68 below.

[67] D. W. Robertson Jr, *A Preface to Chaucer: Studies in medieval perspectives* (Princeton: Princeton University Press, 1962). For his discussion of 'gloss', see pp. 74f.

[68] There is an entertaining yet serious summary of the conflict, written by a critic who admires Robertson but admits to certain failings in the thesis, in Alan T. Gaylord, 'Reflections on D. W. Robertson, Jr., and "Exegetical Criticism"', *Chaucer Review* 40 (2006), 311. The article's publication in 2006 indicates the persistence of the controversy some 40 years after the appearance of Robertson's book.

[69] Seymour Chatman, *Story and Discourse* (Ithaca: Cornell University Press, 1978), p. 151.

[70] Helen S. Corsa, *Chaucer, Poet of Mirth and Morality* (Notre Dame: University of Notre Dame Press, 1969), p. 138.

71 Alistair Minnis, *Fallible Authors: Chaucer's Pardonner and Wife of Bath* (Philadelphia: University of Pennsylvania Press, 2008) has interestingly argued that she was intended as a satire on the Lollards' encouragement of women preachers.

72 There did exist the Wycliffe translation of the Bible (1382), but since reading it was prohibited by the church we can assume she would not have consulted it even were she able to read.

73 Sir Thomas More, *English Works* (London: Rastell, 1557), p. 136.

74 Kirby Olson, *Comedy after Postmodernism* (Lubbock: Texas Tech University Press, 2001), p. 14.

75 Chaucer's *Retraction* following the Parson's tale in which he humbly prays for divine forgiveness for his 'enditynges of worldly vanitees' has been seen by most editors as a late addition by him, paralleling Boccaccio's deathbed repentance for his lubricious writings.

76 Quotations from the modernized text in *Five Pre-Shakespearean Dramas* ed. F. S. Boas (Oxford: Oxford University Press, 1970).

77 George Puttenham, *The Art of English Poesie* [1589] (Menton: Scolar facsimile, 1968), p. 25.

78 Louis Kronenberger, *The Thread of Laughter* (New York: Hill & Wang, n.d.), notes correctly that this distinction does not apply to Restoration drama, where all the main characters, including the Witwouds, belong to the upper class.

79 William Roper, *The Mirrour of Vertue in Worldly Greatnes, or the Life of Sir Thomas More, Knight* (London: Gollanz, 1902: orig. 1555 although not printed until 1626).

3 THE RENAISSANCE

80 Karl Young, *The Drama of the Medieval Stage* (Oxford: Oxford University Press, 1933) 2:14 and 412.

81 R. W. Maslen, *Shakespeare and Comedy* (London: Arden Shakespeare Press, 2005), p. 142.

82 Bertrand Evans, *Shakespeare's Comedies* (London: Oxford University Press, 1967), pp. 37–8.

83 In John Palmer's classic study, *Political and Comical Characters of Shakespeare* (New York: Macmillan, 1962), p. 440. For examples of the wide range of interpretations, see *A Midsummer Night's Dream: A collection of essays* ed. Dorothea Kehler (New York: Garland, 1998); and for a broader perspective, Indira Ghose, *Shakespeare and Laughter: A cultural history* (Manchester: Manchester University Press, 2008).

84 Arthur Schopenhauer, *The World as Will and Idea* trans. R. B. Haldane and J. Kemp (London: Routledge, 1964), p. 76.

85 Frye, pp. 182–3.

86 Leo Salingar, *Shakespeare and the Traditions of Comedy* (Cambridge: Cambridge University Press, 1976), p. 309.

87 In a long-neglected article, Ernest Schanzer, 'The Central Theme of *A Midsummer Night's Dream*', University of Toronto Quarterly 20 (1951),

233, did perceive this unifying theme, although he saw it as focused upon Demetrius' misguided subjection to 'fancy', not as Shakespeare's warning against inconstancy in love.

88 Produced by Michael Hoffman, with Kevin Kline as Bottom.

89 Denis de Rougement, *Love in the Western World* trans. M. Belgion (New York: Doubleday, 1957), especially pp. 23f.

90 Maurice Morgann, *An Essay on the Dramatic Character of Sir John Falstaff* (New York: AMS 1970 [orig. 1777]), pp. 10–11.

91 J. Dover Wilson, *The Fortunes of Falstaff* (Cambridge: Cambridge University Press, 1964), pp. 18–19, citing the text from C. F. Tucker, *Tudor Drama* (Boston: Houghton Mifflin, 1911), p. 333.

92 A. C. Bradley, 'The Rejection of Falstaff' in his *Oxford Lectures on Poetry* (New York: Macmillan, 1962 [orig. 1911]), pp. 247f. More recently, Harold Bloom ed. *Falstaff* (New York: Chelsea House, 1992) p. 4., has argued that he attracts by his exuberance and his freedom from superego.

93 See Roland H. Bainton, *Here I Stand: A life of Martin Luther* (New York: New American Library, 1959), pp. 49–50. Calvin mentions his own experience of a sudden conversion in the preface to his *Commentary on the Book of Psalms*.

94 From Donne's *Death's Duel* and the sermon preached at Whitehall, 8 March 1621.

95 C. L. Barber, *Shakespeare's Festive Comedy* (Cleveland: Meridian Books, 1963), p. 207.

96 Cf. Malcolm Evans, 'Deconstructing Shakespeare's Comedies' in *Alternative Shakespeares* ed. John Drakakis (London: Methuen, 1985), 67. Stephen Greenblatt, *Shakespearean Negotiations* (Berkeley: University of California Press, 1988), pp. 41f., while admitting that Hal represents 'an ideal image', proceeds to define him nonetheless as a hypocrite and falsifier, but as I have suggested here, the brilliant complexity of the play lies primarily in the subversion of traditional values by Falstaff.

97 It may seem strange to have omitted from this book discussion of one of the great comedies of English literature, Ben Jonson's *Volpone*, but my own view of that work, which differs from the usual critical reading, involves detailed discussion, too lengthy for insertion here. It forms a chapter in my *Tradition and Subversion*.

98 S.Schoenbaum, *Shakespeare's Lives* (Oxford: Clarendon Press, 1991), p. 51, gives credence to the tradition, first recorded in the prefatory epistle to John Dennis' play, *The Comical Gallant: or the Amours of Sir John Falstaff* (1702).

99 Cf. Ann Barton's valid comment in her introduction to the Riverside edition of the *Merry Wives*, that Falstaff is less effective there because '… he inhabits and is subject to a world of comedy, as opposed to representing a comic viewpoint in the alien but vulnerable world of historical event'.

100 Text from *The Elegies and Songs and Sonnets of John Donne* ed. Helen Gardner (Oxford: Clarendon Press, 1965), p. 53.

101 There may have been a Renaissance belief that the act of sexual intercourse involved a mingling of two drops of blood; but a reading of this

passage on those terms produces essentially the same logical elision as I
have described here. See Don Cameron Allen, 'John Donne's Knowledge
of Renaissance Medicine' in the *Journal of English and Germanic Philology*
42 (1943), 334.

[102] Blundeville, 'The Learned Prince' in his *Three Moral Treatises* (London,
1580), and Richard Hooker, *The Laws of Ecclesiastical Politie* Bk 1, as
well as Francis Bacon's preface to his *Novum Organum*.

[103] Montaigne, *Apology for Raymond Sebond* in *Complete Essays* trans.
Donald M. Frame (Stanford: Stanford University Press, 1966), p. 405.

[104] From Donne's sermon delivered at St Paul's on Christmas Day 1621 and
from the sonnet, 'Batter my heart'.

[105] From a sermon preached at Hanworth in 1622.

[106] T. S. Eliot's two essays, appearing in 1921 and 1922, were republished in
his *Selected Essays* (London: Faber, 1934); William Empson's appeared
in *Scrutiny* 1 (1932), and Frank Kermode's 'The Argument of Marvell's
"Garden"' in *Essays in Criticism* 2 (1952).

[107] Recommended on the *Luminarium* website, the summary quoted from a
2006 college syllabus by Professor Arnie Sanders.

[108] Text from *The Poems of Andrew Marvell* ed. Hugh Macdonald (London:
Routledge and Kegan Paul, 1956).

[109] *Toil* in its secondary meaning of netting, as in the phrase, 'caught in its
toils'.

[110] Cf. the flippancy in the opening lines of Donne's solemn poem 'The Relique'.

[111] Rosalie Colie, *My Ecchoing Song: Andrew Marvell's poetry of criticism*
(Princeton: Princeton University Press, 1970), p. 166.

[112] The poem, entitled, 'To His Excellent Friend, Mr.Andrew Marvell' which
was published in 1678 is cited in the introduction to *Marvell: modern
judgements* ed.Michael Wilding (Nashville: Aurora, 1970), p. 11.

[113] Marvell's 'On Milton's *Paradise Lost*', 23f.

4 THE RESTORATION AND EIGHTEENTH CENTURY

[114] Cf. 1 Sam. 25.42–4.

[115] *Selected Works of Dryden* ed. William Frost (New York: Rinehart, 1959),
lines 1–10 and 150–7.

[116] *Spectator 23.*

[117] Thomas Shadwell, *The Virtuoso* 3.3.134.

[118] Ann Righter, 'Heroic Tragedy' in *Restoration Theatre* eds John Russell
Brown and Bernard Harris (New York: Capricorn, 1967), p. 142.

[119] Nathaniel Lee, *The Rival Queens* 2:1:258–9 and *The Man of Mode* 2:2.

[120] Sir Philip Sidney, *A Defence of Poesie* (London: Cassell, 1891), p. 52.

[121] Preface to *Volpone* in *Works* ed. C. H. Herford and Percy Simpson
(Oxford: Oxford University Press, 1925–50), vol. 5.

[122] Thomas Rymer, *Tragedies of the Last Age* in *Critical Essays of the
Seventeenth Century* ed. J. E. Spingarn (Oxford: Oxford University Press,
1977) 2:188.

[123] John Dryden, *Essays* ed. W. P. Ker (Oxford: Oxford University Press,
1926) 1:143 and 2:93.

NOTES

[124] Ben Ross Schneider, Jr, *The Ethos of Restoration Comedy* (Urbana: University of Illinois Press, 1971), p. 50.

[125] The prologue, in Wycherley, *The Country Wife* ed. James Ogden (New York: Norton, 2000), subsequent quotations being from this edition.

[126] Marvell, 'A Dialogue Between the Soul and Body', 1–6.

[127] Thomas H. Fujimura, *The Restoration Comedy of Wit* (New York: Barnes & Noble, 1968). See also, Harold Weber, *The Restoration Rake-hero* (Madison: Wisconsin University Press, 1986).

[128] Rose A. Zimbardo, *Wycherley's Drama* (New Haven: Yale University Press, 1965), citing the 'harshness of tone' in these plays, claimed that Wycherley was writing formal satires and not comedies. That statement does not conform to my own experience in attending the production of *The Country Wife* with Albert Finney as Horner, which had the audience (and myself) rocking with laughter.

[129] Thomas Hobbes, *Leviathan* xi, in *The English Philosophers* ed. Edwin A.Burtt (New York: Random House, 1939), p. 159.

[130] Norman N. Holland, *The First Modern Comedies* (Bloomington: Indiana University Press, 1967) takes the view that Pinchwife and Horner represent the 'wrong way' and Alithea and Harcourt the 'right way'. That reading, I believe, oversimplifies the situation, since Harcourt belongs to the group of rakes and Horner is himself an amusing character, but Holland is correct in seeing the importance of Alithea in the play.

[131] See W. B. Carnochan's comment in the introduction to his Regents edition of *The Man of Mode* (Lincoln: University of Nebraska, 1966) p. xiii.

[132] Kathleen Lynch in the introduction to her Regents edition of *The Way of the World* (Lincoln: University of Nebraska, 1965), p. xv, and Alexander Leggatt, *English Stage Comedy 1490–1990* (London: Routledge, 1998), pp. 132–6. For similar readings, see Virginia O. Beardsall, *Wild Civility: The English comic spirit on the Restoration Stage* (Bloomington: Indiana University Press, 1970), pp. 244–5, and Fujimura, p. 66.

[133] In a well-known essay, Arnold Stein argued that the War in Heaven in *Paradise Lost* is intended to be comic. I can see no basis for that view, and have presented a counter-argument in chapter 4 of my *Milton and the Baroque* (London: Macmillan, 1980).

[134] Quotations from *The Poems* ed. John Butt (New Haven: Yale University Press, 1970) which is the Twickenham text in a more available and less cumbersome form.

[135] Quoted in P. Hall, *Sermons and Other Remains of Robert Lowth* (London: Rivington, 1834), p. 40.

[136] Details of her response are recorded in Geoffrey Tillotson's introduction to his edition of the *Poems* (New Haven: Yale University Press, 1962) 2: 90–3.

[137] As a Catholic, Pope did not attend school but was educated privately.

[138] Wordsworth, Preface to *The Lyrical Ballads*.

[139] Quoted in James Sutherland, *A Preface to Eighteenth Century Poetry* (Oxford: Clarendon, 1948), p. 89.

[140] Pope, *Peri Bathous: The art of sinking* ed. Edna L.Steeves (New York: King's Crown Press, 1952).

[141] For the two meanings of *sentiment* and the changes during the century, see R. F. Brissenden, *Virtue in Distress: Studies in the novel of sentiment* (London: Macmillan, 1974), pp. 96–140.

[142] For a general examination of eighteenth-century attitudes to humour, see Stuart M. Tave, *The Amiable Humorist* (Chicago: Chicago University Press, 1960).

[143] Paul E. Parnell, 'The Sentimental Mask' PMLA 78 (1963), 529–35.

[144] Quotations from Samuel Richardson, *Pamela* (London: J. M. Dent, 1938).

[145] Johnson, *Rambler* 117.

[146] A. C. Bradley, *A Miscellany* (London, 1929), p. 32. See also F. B. Pinion, *A Jane Austen Companion* (New York: St Martin's Press, 1975), p. 160.

[147] Quotations are from Jane Austen, *Pride and Prejudice* (New York: New American Library, 1961).

[148] Elizabeth modestly includes herself in that category in order to soften the criticism, but Darcy at once acknowledges its inapplicability to her: 'This is no very striking resemblance of your own character, I am sure,' said he. 'How near it may be to mine, I cannot pretend to say.'

[149] Quotations from Lawrence Sterne, *The Life and Opinions of Tristram Shandy, Gentleman* ed. Ian Campbell (Oxford: Oxford University Press, 1983).

[150] Tobias Smollett, *The Adventures of Roderick Random* (New York: J. M. Dent, 1960), pp. 219–20.

[151] Sir Joshua Reynolds, *Discourses on Art* (London: Collier, 1969), p. 58.

[152] Adam A. Mendilow, *Time and the Novel* (London: Peter Nevill, 1952), pp. 158–99.

[153] Wilbur L. Cross, *The Development of the English Novel* (New York: Macmillan, 1905), pp. 69–76, John Traugott, *Tristram Shandy's World* (Berkeley: University of California, 1954), pp. 6 and 29–61, and Alastair Fowler, *A History of English Literature* (Cambridge MA: Harvard University Press, 1987), p. 195.

[154] John M. Stedmond, *The Comic Art of Lawrence Sterne* (n.p.: University of Toronto Press, 1995), pp. 95–6, wonders whether Locke is being laughed at here, but leaves the question unanswered on the grounds that the problem 'dissipates in clouds' as the brothers nod off to sleep.

[155] Henri Fluchère, *Lawrence Sterne: From Tristram to Yorick* trans. Barbara Bray (London: Oxford University Press, 1965), pp. 102–3.

[156] The fourth volume in most present editions was the third in the original text.

5 THE NINETEENTH CENTURY

[157] Letters from Austen to James Stanier Charles, 1 April 1816 and 11 December 1815.

[158] John Wiltshire's essay in *The Cambridge Companion to Jane Austen* eds Edward Copeland and Juliet McMaster (Cambridge: Cambridge University Press, 1997).

[159] See Audrey Bilger, *Laughing Feminisms: Subversive comedy in Frances Burney, Maria Edgworth, and Jane Austen* (Detroit: Wayne State University Press, 1998), Deborah Kaplan, *Jane Austen Among Women* (Baltimore: Johns Hopkins University Press, 1994), Margaret Kirkham, *Jane Austen: Feminism and fiction* (London: Athlone University Press, 1997) and Janet Todd, *The Cambridge Introduction to Jane Austen* (Cambridge: Cambridge University Press, 2006). There is a brief, but well-written section on Austen's comic genius in J. David Grey, ed., *The Jane Austen Handbook* (London, Athlone Press, 1986).

[160] Lionel Trilling's introduction to the Riverside edition, and Austen H. Wright, *Jane Austen's Novels* (Harmondsworth: Penguin, 1964), p. 137.

[161] Robert M. Polhemus, 'Jane Austen's Comedy' in *The Jane Austen Handbook* ed., pp. 60–9. Polhemus' *Comic Faith: The great tradition from Austen to Joyce* (Chicago: University of Chicago Press, 1982) was, in its section on Austen, less concerned with humour than with the restraints she placed on her wit in order to respect moral and religious principles.

[162] Arnold Kettle, *An Introduction to the English Novel* (London: Hutchinson, 1951).

[163] Samuel Richardson, *Pamela* (London: J. M. Dent, 1938) 1:228.

[164] Henry Fielding, *Tom Jones* (London: J. M. Dent, 1934). For convenience in consulting other editions, references are to chapter rather than page.

[165] From Darcy's letter, Elizabeth learns that Wickham's attempt to seduce Georgiana was only one event in a 'life of idleness and dissipation'.

[166] Cf. Marvin Mudrick, *Jane Austen: Irony as defense and discovery* (Berkeley: University of California Press, 1952), p. 185.

[167] Quotations from Jane Austen, *Emma* (London: J. M. Dent, 1961).

[168] Mark Schorer, 'The Humiliation of Emma Woodhouse', *The Literary Review* (Summer, 1959).

[169] James Edward Austen-Leigh, *A Memoir of Jane Austen* (Oxford: Oxford University Press, 1926), p. 157.

[170] *Dickens and the Twentieth Century* eds John Gross and Gabriel Pearson (London: Routledge and Kegan Paul, 1966), p. xii.

[171] James R. Kincaid, *Dickens and the Rhetoric of Laughter* (Oxford: Clarendon Press, 1971), p. 35.

[172] Quotations from Charles Dickens, *Pickwick Papers* (Harmondsworth: Penguin, 1999).

[173] G. K. Chesterton, *Charles Dickens* (London: Methuen, 1913), p. 75.

[174] W. H. Auden, 'Dingley Dell and the Fleet' in his *The Dyer's Hand* (London: Faber & Faber, 1962).

[175] George Eliot, *Scenes of Clerical Life* 1:8.

[176] The reprimand concerning irreverence is in *Letters* ed. Morton N. Cohen (London: Macmillan, 1979), 2:1116, the rebuke to William Boyd Carpenter, Bishop of Ripon appears on 2:677, and the remark concerning his dislike of religious discussion in 2:618. On the genesis of the poem, see Morton N. Cohen, 'Hark the Snark', published in Edward Guiliano, ed., *Lewis Carroll Observed: a collection of unpublished photographs, drawings, poetry and new essays* (New York: C. N. Potter, 1976), p. 95.

177 See Henkle, p. 189.
178 The Gordon Riots did cause a number of deaths, but the entire affair was swiftly suppressed.
179 Recorded in R. C. Trench, ed., *Letters and Memorials* (London: Kegan Paul, 1897) 1:84. On the general situation at that time, see Walter E. Houghton, *The Victorian Frame of Mind, 1830–1870* (New Haven: Yale University Press, 1972), pp. 54–61, and E. P. Thompson, *The Making of the English Working Class* (New York: Vintage, 1966).
180 Collier, *Op. Cit.* 3:263.
181 From *Iolanthe*, in W. S. Gilbert, *The Savoy Operas* (London: Macmillan, 1930), pp. 212–13. Subsequent quotations are from this edition.
182 In Wilkie Collins' *Moonstone*, Superintendent Seegrave of the local police proves such 'an ass' that the brilliant Sergeant Cuff has to be called in to replace him, while in Trollope's *Phineas Finn Redux* of 1873, Madame Goesler, despairing of the police, travels herself to Prague to solve the mystery. Mr Bucket in Dickens' *Bleak House* is an exception to such negative portrayal.
183 Cited in W. B. Furlong, *Shaw and Chesterton: The metaphysical jesters* (London: Penn State University Press, 1970), p. 42 which provides an enightening account of the debates between the two.
184 Recorded in *The Oxford Book of Literary Anecdotes* ed. James Sutherland (New York: Pocket Books, 1976), p. 383.
185 Wilde, p. 794.
186 Rodway, p. 211.
187 Samuel Butler, *The Way of All Flesh* (New York: Modern Library, 1950), p. 106, Thomas Carlyle, *On Heroes and Hero-Worship* (New York: Scribner, 1898), p. 54, the *Edinburgh Review* No.217, p. 183, and Charles Kingsley's 1862 preface to *Alton Locke*.
188 George R. Drysdale, *The Elements of Social Science* (London: E. Truelove, 1872), p. 357.
189 Mark Girouard, *Life in the English Country House* (Harmondsworth: Penguin, 1980), p. 285.
190 Mark Girouard, *The Victorian Country House* (New Haven: Yale University Press, 1985), p. 29.
191 Quotations from Jerome K. Jerome, *Three Men in a Boat* (London: Dent, 1966).

6 THE TWENTIETH CENTURY

192 Dickens, *The Uncommercial Traveller*, chapter 4.
193 There is a representative collection of such plays in *Victorian Melodramas* ed. James L. Smith (London: Dent, 1976).
194 The excerpt is from *Nineteenth Century Plays* ed. George Rowell (London: Oxford University Press, 1960), p. 374. Other instances of the melodramas that Shaw was parodying in this play are provided in Martin Meisel, *Shaw and the Nineteenth Century Theater* (New York: Limelight Press, 1984), pp. 186–94.

[195] Shaw, *Our Theatres in the Nineties* (London: Constable, 1932, 3 vols) 3:166–7.

[196] Fred Mayne, *The Wit and Satire of Bernard Shaw* (New York: St Martin's Press, 1967), and R. J. Kaufmann, ed., *G. B. Shaw: A collection of critical essays* in the series 'Twentieth Century Views' (Englewood Cliffs: Prentice-Hall, 1965).

[197] The performance is now available on disc.

[198] Meisel, p. 128.

[199] Noted in Louis Crompton, *Shaw the Dramatist* (London: Allen & Unwin, 1971), p. 22.

[200] St John Ervine, *Bernard Shaw: His life, work and friends* (New York: Wm Morrow, 1956), p. 459.

[201] For details, see Nicola Humble, *The Feminine Middlebrow Novel 1920s–1950s* (Oxford: Oxford University Press, 2001).

[202] It was customary to allow members of the upper classes to visit country homes without charge and to be guided around by the housekeeper, but *Strawberry Hill* became so popular that Walpole was compelled to issue free advance tickets to avoid congestion.

[203] Quotations from Stella Gibbons, *Cold Comfort Farm* (Harmondsworth: Penguin, 1951).

[204] There is a useful study of this aspect in Faye Hammill, '*Cold Comfort Farm,* D. H. Lawrence, and English Literary Culture Between the Wars' in *Modern Fiction Studies* 47 (2001), 831.

[205] Samuel Beckett, *Proust* (New York: Grove Press, n.d.), p. 46.

[206] See Anthony Cronin, *Samuel Beckett: The last modernist* (New York: Da Capo Press, 1999) p. 392, as well as Martin Esslin's seminal study *The Theatre of the Absurd* (Doubleday: New York, 1961) and J. L. Styan, *The Dark Comedy* (Cambridge: Cambridge University Press, 1968).

[207] Kingsley Amis, *Lucky Jim* (Harmondsworth: Penguin Books, 1965), pp. 14–15.

[208] Ihab Hassan, *Radical Innocence: Studies in the contemporary American novel* (Princeton: Princeton University Press, 1971), p. 21. Cf. also, Ruth Wisse, *The Schlemiel as Modern Hero* (Chicago: Chicago University Press, 1971), and David Galloway, *The Absurd Hero in American Fiction* (Austin: University of Texas Press, 1981).

[209] Somerset Maugham in *The Sunday Times*, 23 December 1955.

[210] In the United States, Mary McCarthy's *The Groves of Academe* (1952) had preceded this interest in the campus, but that novel, like her later *The Group*, was not comic. In Evelyn Waugh's *Brideshead Revisited* (1944) the brilliant and often amusing evocation of student life at Oxford in the years before the Second World War served as a prelude to the serious story that followed.

[211] Quotations from Malcolm Bradbury, *The History Man* (Harmondsworth: Penguin Books, 1985).

[212] Quotations from Helen Fielding, *Bridget Jones's Diary* (London: Picador. 1997).

[213] Cf. John Wiltshire, *Recreating Jane Austen* (Cambridge: Cambridge University Press, 2001).

WORKS CITED - ON THE COMIC

Alexander, Richard J. *Aspects of Verbal Humour in English.* Tübingen: Gunter Narr, 1997.

Apte, Mahadav L. *Humor and Laughter.* Ithaca: Cornell University Press, 1985.

Attardo, Salvatore. *Linguistic Theories of Humor.* Berlin: Mouton de Gruyter, 1994.

Barber, C. L. *Shakespeare's Festive Comedy.* Cleveland: Meridian Books, 1963.

Barreca, Regina, ed. *New Perspectives on Women and Comedy.* Philadelphia: Gordon & Breach, 1992.

Beardsall, Virginia O. *Wild Civility: The English comic spirit on the Restoration Stage.* Bloomington: Indiana University Press, 1970.

Berger, Peter L. *Redeeming Laughter: The comic dimension of human experience.* Berlin: De Gruyter, 1997.

Bergson, Henri. *An Essay on the Meaning of the Comic* trans. C. Brereton & F. Rothwell. New York: Macmillan, 1911.

Bilger, Audrey. *Laughing Feminisms: Subversive comedy in Frances Burney, Maria Edgworth, and Jane Austen.* Detroit: Wayne State University Press, 1998.

Billig, Michael. *Laughter and Ridicule: toward a social critique of humor.* London: Sage, 2005.

Bremmer, Jan and Roodenberg, Herman, eds, *A Cultural History of Humour.* Cambridge: Polity Press, 1977.

Cavaliero, Glen. *The Alchemy of Laughter: Comedy in English fiction.* Basingstoke: Macmillan, 2000.

Chafe, Wallace. *The Importance of Not Being Earnest.* Amsterdam: John Benjamin Press, 2007.

Charney, Maurice ed. *Comedy: A geographic and historical guide.* Westport, Conn.: Praeger, 2005.

— *Comedy High and Low: An introduction to the experience of comedy.* New York: Oxford University Press, 1978.

— ed., *Comedy: New perspectives.* New York: New York Literary Forum, 1978.

Chiaro, Delia. *The Language of Jokes: Analysing verbal play.* London: Routledge, 1992.

Clark, Michael. 'Humour and Incongruity' in *Philosophy* 45 (1970), 243–54.

Congreve, William. *Concerning Humour in Comedy* in *Critical Essays of the Seventeenth Century* ed. J. E. Spingarn. London: Oxford University Press, 1957.

Cook, Albert, *The Dark Voyage and the Golden Mean: A philosophy of comedy.* Cambridge Mass.: Harvard University Press, 1949.

Cordner, M., Holland, P., and Kerrigan,J., eds, *English Comedy*. Cambridge: Cambridge University Press, 1994

Corrigan, Robert W. ed. *Comedy: Meaning and form.* San Francisco: Chandler, 1965.

Critchley, Simon. *On Humour.* London: Routledge, 2002.

Davies, Christie. *Ethnic Humor around the World.* Bloomington: Indiana University Press, 1990.

— *Jokes and their Relation to Society.* Berlin: Mouton de Gruyter, 1998.

Davis, J. M. and Farina, Amerigo, 'Humour Appreciation as Social Communication' *Journal of Personality and Social Psychology* 15 1970, 175.

Donaldson, Ian. *The World Upside Down: Comedy from Jonson to Fielding.* Oxford: Oxford University Press, 1970.

Durant, John, and Miller, Jonathan. *Laughing Matters: A serious look at humour.* Harlow: Longman, 1988.

Elliot, Oring. *Engaging Humor.* Urbana: University of Illinois Press, 2003.

Evans, Bertrand. *Shakespeare's Comedies.* London: Oxford University Press, 1967.

Fischler, Alan. *Modified Rapture: Comedy in W. S. Gilbert's Savoy operas.* Charlottesville: University of Virginia Press, 1991.

Freud, Sigmund. *Jokes and their Relation to the Unconscious* trans. James Strachey. New York: Norton, 1964.

Fujimura, Thomas H. *The Restoration Comedy of Wit.* New York: Barnes & Noble, 1968.

Ghose, Indira. *Shakespeare and Laughter: A cultural history.* Manchester: Manchester University Press, 2008.

Gruner, Charles R. *The Game of Humor.* London: Transaction Publishers, 1997.

Gurewitch, Morton. *Comedy: The irrational vision.* Ithaca: Cornell University Press, 1975.

Haig, Robin A. *The Anatomy of Humor*, Springfield: Charles C. Thomas., 1988

Heilman, Robert B. *The Ways of the World: Comedy and society*. Seattle: University of Washington Press, 1978.

Henkle, Roger B. *Comedy and Culture: England 1820–1900.* Princeton: Princeton University Press, 1980.

Hill, Carl. *The Soul of Wit: Joke theory from Grimm to Freud.* Lincoln: University of Nebraska Press, 1993.

Hokenson, Jan Walsh. *The Idea of Comedy: History, theory, critique.* Madison: Farleigh Dickinson University Press, 2006.

Holcomb, Chris. *Mirth Making: The rhetorical discourse on jesting in Early Modern England*. Columbia: University of Southern Carolina, 2001.

Holland, Norman N. *The First Modern Comedies*. Bloomington: Indiana University Press, 1967.

Hutcheson, Francis. *Reflections upon Laughter*. New York: Garland, 1971 (orig. 1750).

Hyers, Conrad. *And God Created Laughter: The Bible as divine comedy*. New York: Pilgrim Press, 1981.

Jost, Jean E. *Chaucer's Humor: Critical* essays. New York: Garland Press, 1994.

Kincaid, James R. *Dickens and the Rhetoric of Laughter*. Oxford: Clarendon Press, 1971.

Kronenberger, Louis. *The Thread of Laughter*. New York: Hill & Wang, n.d.

Leggatt, Alexander. *English Stage Comedy 1490–1990*. London: Routledge, 1998.

Levin, H *Playboys and Killjoys: An essay on the theory and practice of comedy*, New York: Oxford University Press, 1987.

Lewis, Paul. *Comic Effects: Interdisciplinary approaches to humor in literature*. Stonybrook: SUNY Press, 1989.

Lockyer, Sharon, and Pickering, Michael, eds, *Beyond a Joke: The limits of humour*. Basingstoke: Palgrave, 2005.

Lowe, John. 'Theories of Ethnic Humor' in *American Quarterly* 38 (1986), 439.

Marcus, Leah. *The Politics of Mirth*. Chicago: University of Chicago Press, 1986.

Martin, Mike W. 'Humour and the Aesthetic Experience: Enjoyment of incongruities' in *The British Journal of Aesthetics* 23 (1983), 74–85.

Martin, Robert B. *The Triumph of Wit*. Oxford: Clarendon Press, 1974.

Maslen, R. W. *Shakespeare and Comedy*. London: Arden Shakespeare Press, 2005.

Mayne, Fred. *The Wit and Satire of Bernard Shaw*. New York: St Martin's Press, 1967.

Merchant, W. Moelwyn. *Comedy*. London: Methuen, 1972.

Morreall, J. *Taking Laughter Seriously*. Albany: State University of New York, 1983.

— 'Humor and Emotion' in *The American Philosophical Quarterly* 20 (1983), 297–304.

—, ed., *The Philosophy of Laughter and Humor* (Albany: State University of New York Press, 1987).

Nash, Walter. *The Language of Humour*. London: Longman, 1985.

Nelson, T. G. A. *Comedy: The theory of comedy in literature, drama, and cinema*. Oxford: Oxford University Press, 1990.

Nicolson, H. *The English Sense of Humour and Other Essays*. London: Constable.

Nilsen, Don F. *Humor in British Literature*. London: Greenwood Press, 3 vols 1997–2000.

Olson, Elder. *The Theory of Comedy*. Bloomington: Indiana University Press, 1968.

Olson, Kirby. *Comedy, After Postmodernism.* Lubbock: Texas Tech University Press, 2001.

Palmer, Jerry. *Taking Humour Seriously.* London: Routledge, 1994.

Palmer, John. *Political and Comical Characters of Shakespeare.* New York: Macmillan, 1962.

Pfister, Manfred, ed., *A History of English Laughter: Laughter from Beowulf to Beckett and beyond.* Amsterdam: Rodopi, 2002.

Polhemus, Robert M. *Comic Faith: The great tradition from Austen to Joyce.* Chicago: University of Chicago Press, 1982.

Potts, L. J. *Comedy.* London: Hutchinson, 1957.

Provine, Robert R. *Laughter: A scientific investigation.* New York: Viking, 2000.

Purdie, Susan. *Comedy: The master of discourse.* Toronto: University of Toronto Press, 1993.

Raskin, Victor. *Semantic Mechanisms of Humor.* Dortrecht: Reidel, 1985.

Robinson, Fred M. *The Comedy of Language: Studies in modern comic literature.* Amherst: University of Massachusetts Press, 1980.

Rodway, Allan. *English Comedy: Its role and nature from Chaucer to the present day.* Berkeley: University of California Press, 1975.

Ruch, Willibald, ed., *Sense of Humor.* Berlin: Mouton, 1998.

Salingar, Leo. *Shakespeare and the Traditions of Comedy.* Cambridge: Cambridge University Press, 1976.

Sanders, Andrew. 'Dickens and the Idea of the Comic Novel', *Yearbook of English Studies* 36 (2006), 51.

Sanders, Barry. *Sudden Glory.* Boston: Beacon Press, 1995.

Schneider, Ross Ben, Jr. *The Ethos of Restoration Comedy.* Urbana: University of Illinois Press, 1971.

Segal, Erich. *The Death of Comedy.* Cambridge: Harvard University Press, 2001.

Shershow, Scott C. *Laughing Matters.* Amherst: University of Massachusetts Press, 1986.

Stedmond, John M. *The Comic Art of Lawrence Sterne.* n.p.: University of Toronto Press, 1995.

Stott, Andrew. *Comedy.* London: Routledge, 2005.

Styan, J. L. *The Dark Comedy.* Cambridge: Cambridge University Press, 1968.

Sutton, Dana F. *The Catharsis of Comedy.* Boston: Rowman and Littlefield, 1994.

Sypher, Wylie. *Comedy.* Baltimore: Johns Hopkins University Press, 1956.

Tave, Stuart M. *The Amiable Humorist.* Chicago: Chicago University Press, 1960.

Weitz, Eric. *The Cambridge Introduction to Comedy.* Cambridge: Cambridge University Press, 2009.

Whedbee, J.William. *The Bible and the Comic Vision.* Cambridge: Cambridge University Press, 1998.

Ziv, Avner, ed., *National Styles of Humor.* New York: Greenwood Press, 1988.

WORKS CITED – GENERAL

Aristotle. *The Art of Rhetoric* ed. and trans. J. H. Freese. London: Heineman, 1926.

Auden, W. H. *The Dyer's Hand.* London: Faber & Faber, 1962.

Bakhtin, M. M. *Rabelais and his World* trans. H. Iswolsky. Bloomington: Indiana University Press, 1984

Bloom, Harold, ed., *Falstaff.* New York: Chelsea, 1992.

Boitani, Piero and Mann, Jill, eds, *The Cambridge Companion to Chaucer.* Cambridge: Cambridge University Press, 2003.

Brissenden, R. F. *Virtue in Distress: Studies in the novel of sentiment.* London: Macmillan, 1974.

Brown, John Russell and Harris, Bernard, eds, *Restoration Theatre.* New York: Capricorn, 1967.

Carroll, Noel. *Beyond Aesthetics: Philosophical essays.* Cambridge: Cambridge University Press, 2001.

Chambers, E. K. *The Medieval Stage.* Oxford: Clarendon Press, 1909.

Chatman, Seymour. *Story and Discourse.* Ithaca: Cornell University Press, 1978.

Colie, Rosalie L. *My Ecchoing Song: Andrew Marvell's poetry of criticism.* Princeton: Princeton University Press, 1970.

Copeland, Edward and McMaster, Juliet, eds, *The Cambridge Companion to Jane Austen.* Cambridge: Cambridge University Press, 1997.

Corsa, Helen S. *Chaucer, Poet of Mirth and Morality.* Notre Dame: University of Notre Dame Press, 1969.

Crompton, Louis. *Shaw the Dramatist.* London: Allen & Unwin, 1971.

Cronin, Anthony. *Samuel Beckett: The last modernist.* New York: Da Capo Press, 1999.

Cross, Wilbur L. *The Development of the English Novel.* New York: Macmillan, 1905.

Culler, Jonathan, ed., *On Puns: The foundation of letters.* Oxford: Blackwell, 1988.

Daleski, H. M. *Dickens and the Art of Analogy.* New York: Schocken, 1970.

De Rougement, Denis. *Love in the Western World* trans. M. Belgion. New York: Doubleday, 1957.

Drakakis, John, ed. *Alternative Shakespeares.* London: Methuen, 1985.

Elyot, Thomas. *The Book Named Governor*, ed., S. E. Lehmberg. London: Dent, 1970.

Ervine, St John. *Bernard Shaw: His life, work and friends.* New York: Wm Morrow, 1956.

Esslin, Martin. *The Theatre of the Absurd.* Doubleday: New York, 1961.

Fluchère, Henri. *Lawrence Sterne: From Tristram to Yorick* trans. Barbara Bray. London: Oxford University Press, 1965.

Fowler, Alastair. *A History of English Literature.* Cambridge MA: Harvard University Press, 1987.

Frye, Northrop. *The Anatomy of Criticism.* Princeton: Princeton University Press, 1957.

Furlong, W. B. *Shaw and Chesterton: The metaphysical jesters.* London: Penn State University Press, 1970.

Galloway, David. *The Absurd Hero in American Fiction.* Austin: University of Texas Press, 1981.

Gaylord, Alan T. 'Reflections on D. W. Robertson, Jr, and "Exegetical Criticism"', *Chaucer Review* 40 (2006), 311.

Goad, Caroline M. *Horace in English Literature of the Eighteenth Century.* New Haven: Yale University Press, 1918.

Greenblatt, Stephen. *Shakespearean Negotiations.* Berkeley: University of California Press, 1988.

Gross, John and Pearson, Gabriel, eds, *Dickens and the Twentieth Century.* London: Routledge and Kegan Paul, 1966.

Hammill, Faye. '*Cold Comfort Farm*, D. H. Lawrence, and English Literary Culture Between the Wars' in *Modern Fiction Studies* 47 (2001) 831.

Hassan, Ihab. *Radical Innocence: Studies in the contemporary American novel.* Princeton: Princeton University Press, 1971.

Hobbes, Thomas. *English Works* ed. W. Molesworth. London: Bohn, 1839.

Humble, Nicola. *The Feminine Middlebrow Novel 1920s–1950s.* Oxford: Oxford University Press, 2001.

Kant, Emanuel. *Critique of Judgment* trans. J. H. Bernard. London: Macmillan, 1892.

Kaplan, Deborah. *Jane Austen among Women.* Baltimore: Johns Hopkins University Press, 1994.

Kaufmann, R. J., ed., *G. B. Shaw: A collection of critical essays.* Englewood Cliffs: Prentice-Hall, 1965.

Kehler, Dorothea, ed., *A Midsummer Night's Dream: A collection of essays.* New York: Garland, 1998.

Kermode, Frank. 'The Argument of Marvell's "Garden"', *Essays in Criticism 2* (1952).

Kirkham, Margaret. *Jane Austen: Feminism and fiction.* London: Athlone University Press, 1997.

Koestler, Arthur. *The Act of Creation.* Harmondsworth: Penguin Arkana, 1989.

Kolve, V. A. *The Play Called Corpus Christi.* Stanford: Stanford University Press, 1966.

Meisel, Martin. *Shaw and the Nineteenth Century Theater.* New York: Limelight Press, 1984.

Mendilow, Adam A. *Time and the Novel.* London: Peter Nevill, 1952.

Minnis, Alistair. *Fallible Authors: Chaucer's Pardonner and Wife of Bath.* Philadelphia: University of Pennsylvania Press, 2008.

Morgann, Maurice, *An Essay on the Dramatic Character of Sir John Falstaff.* New York: AMS 1970 [orig. 1777].

Mudrick, Marvin. *Jane Austen: Irony as defense and discovery.* Berkeley: University of California Press, 1952.

Parnell, Paul E. 'The Sentimental Mask' PMLA 78 (1963), 529.

Parrott, T. M. 'Mak and Archie Armstrang' *Modern Language Notes* 59 (1944), 297.

Plato. *Philebus*, in *Dialogues* trans. Benjamin Jowett. Boston: Scribner, 1871.

Pollack, Ellen. *The Poetics of Sexual Myth.* Chicago: University of Chicago Press, 1985.

Prosser, Eleanor. *Drama and Religion in the English Mystery Plays.* Stanford: Stanford University Press, 1961.

Rabelais, François. *Gargantua and Pantagruel* trans. T. Urquart and P. Mottreux. London: Lawrence and Bullen, 1892.

Redfern, Walter. *Puns.* Oxford: Blackwell, 1984.

Robertson, D. W. Jr. *A Preface to Chaucer: Studies in medieval perspectives.* Princeton: Princeton University Press, 1962.

Rossiter, A. P. *English Drama from Early Times to the Elizabethans.* London: Hutchinson, 1950.

Schanzer, Ernest. 'The Central Theme of *A Midsummer Night's Dream*' *University of Toronto Quarterly* 20 (1951), 233.

Schopenhauer, Arthur. *The World as Will and Idea* trans. R. B. Haldane and J. Kemp. London: Routledge, 1964.

Spencer, Herbert. *Essays Moral, Political, and Aesthetic.* New York: D. Appleton, 1871.

Sprat, Thomas. *History of the Royal Society.* London: J. R. for J. Martyn, 1667.

Todd, Janet. *The Cambridge Introduction to Jane Austen.* Cambridge: Cambridge University Press, 2006.

Toliver, Harold E. *Marvell's Ironic Vision.* New Haven: Yale University Press, 1965.

Traugott, John. *Tristram Shandy's World.* Berkeley: University of California, 1954.

Waddell, Helen. *The Wandering Scholars.* New York: H. Holt & Co.,1934.

Weber, Harold. *The Restoration Rake-hero.* Madison: Wisconsin University Press, 1986.

Weinbrot, Howard D. *Augustan Caesar in 'Augustan' England.* Princeton: Princeton University Press, 1978.

Welsford, Enid. *The Fool: His social and literary history.* London: Faber, 1968.

Wilson, J. Dover. *The Fortunes of Falstaff.* Cambridge: Cambridge University Press, 1964.

Wilson, Thomas. *The Art of Rhetorique.* London: R. Graftonus, 1553.

Wiltshire, John. *Recreating Jane Austen.* Cambridge: Cambridge University Press, 2001.

Wisse, Ruth. *The Schlemiel as Modern Hero.* Chicago: Chicago University Press, 1971.

Wright, Austen H. *Jane Austen's Novels.* Harmondsworth: Penguin, 1964.

Young, Karl. *The Drama of the Medieval Stage.* Oxford: Oxford University Press, 1933.

Zimbardo, Rose A. *Wycherley's Drama.* New Haven: Yale University Press, 1965.

INDEX

Addison, Joseph 20–1, 109, 124, 129
Alleyn, Edward 67, 82
Amis, Kingsley 226–33
animal laughter 5, 9–10
animated cartoons 50
anti-hero 228–30
Aristophanes 7–8, 215
Aristotle 1, 14, 21
Armin, Robert 56
Arnold, Matthew 191
Auden W.H. 168
Austen, Jane 137–9, 155–66, 218–9, 250

Bakhtin, Mikhail M. 24–6
Barber, C.L. 87
Beckett, Samuel 222–6
Belloc, Hilaire 180
Bentley, Richard 20
Bergson, Henri 3–5
Bible 6, 10–11, 48, 103, 107
Bilger, Audrey 155
Blundeville, Thomas 95
Boy Bishop 26–7
Bradbury, Malcolm 233–44
Bradley, A.C. 77–8, 137
Brontë, Emily 219–21
burlesque 8, 10, 15–16, 73–5, 129, 142, 174, 186, 191, 218, 230–1, 234–6, 148, 250, 227
Butler, Samuel 191
Byron, Lord 141

Calvin, John 83
Capellanus, Andreas 74

Capp, Al 26
Carlyle, Thomas 191, 194
carnival 24–26
Carroll, Lewis 19–20, 176–9
Carroll, Noel 18
Castiglione, Baldassare 52
changes in humour 35
Chaplin, Charles 26–8
Charney, Maurice 4
Chatman, Seymour 45
Chaucer 27, 42–51, 198
Chesterfield, Lord 34
Chesterton, G.K. 167, 188–9, 212–13
Cibber, Colley 128–9
Cicero 21
circumlocution 124–6
Clark, Michael 4
clowns 26
Colie, Rosalie 104
Collier, Jeremy 128, 182
comic relief 5, 32–4
Congreve, William 3, 115, 118–21, 128
Corsa, Helen 48
Coward, Noël 222
Cross, Wilbur L. 145

Dali, Salvador 4
Darwinism 185, 223
De Rougement, Denis 74
Dickens, Charles, 166–76, 183, 205
Donne, John 85, 90–7
Dryden, John 11, 20, 107–9, 112, 123
Du Maurier, George 185

Eliot, George 194
Eliot, T.S. 97
Empson, William 98
Etherege, George 115, 117–8
Evans, Bertrand 68–9

Feast of Asses 26–7
Feast of Fools 26–7
Fenton, Elijah 125
fertility 28–9, 70, 116–9
Fielding, Helen 245–51
Fielding, Henry 6, 45, 75, 130–3,
    156–7
Fluchère, Henri 151
Fool, the 14
Fowler, Alastair 145
Freud, Sigmund 4, 16–18, 23, 223,
    228–9
Frye, Northrop 28–9
Fujimura, Thomas 114

Garrick, David 123, 134
Gaskell, Elizabeth 183
Gerhoh of Reichesberg 63
Gibbons, Stella 217–22
Gilbert W.S. 183–8
Goldsmith, Oliver 56, 75, 133–6
Goliardic poets 25–6
gothic novels 218–9
Graham, Harry 180
Gray, Thomas 137
green world 70
Gross, John 166–7
Gruner, Charles R. 20

Haig, Robin 1
Hallam, Arthur 181
Hassan, Ihab 229
Hobbes, Thomas 2, 4, 12, 114
Hogarth, William 12
Homeric laughter 10
Hood, Thomas 180
Hooker, Richard 95

Horace 108, 111–112
Hutcheson, Francis 2

iconoclastic humour 50
implied author 45
incongruity 4, 69
indecent jokes 23–4, 42
infant laughter 5–6, 10

Japonisme 185–6
Jerome, Jerome K. 197–203
Johnson, Samuel 19–21, 34–5,
    137–9, 142
Jonson, Ben 110, 254, 260, 97n
Julius II, Pope 84
Juvenal 50, 107–8,123

Kant, Immanuel 4
Kaplan, Deborah 155
Keats, John 185
Kempe, William 56
Kermode, Frank 98
Keystone Kops 184
Killham, John 167
Kincaid, James R. 167
Kingsley, Charles 191
Kirkham, Margaret 155

Lee, Nathaniel 109–110
Leggatt, Alexander 118
Locke, John 145–153
Lodge, David 233–4
Longfellow, Henry W. 15–16, 217
Luther, Martin 83
Lyly, John 22
Lynch, Kathleen 118

Machiavelli, Niccolo 29
Marlowe, Christopher 67–8
Martin, M.W. 4
Martin, Robert 19
Marvell, Andrew 97–106, 113–4,
    198

Maslen, R.W. 68
Maugham, Somerset 233
Mayne, Fred 207
Medwall, Henry 52–9
Meisel, Martin 208
melodrama 205–7
Meredith, George 6
Miller, Jonathan 27
Milton, John 105, 121–2, 219
Montaigne, 95–6
More, Thomas 49, 52, 57
Morgann, Maurice 75–6
Morreall, John 1, 4
Morton, John 52
mystery cycles 37–42, 63, 65

Newman, John 191
Nicolson, Harold 1

O'Connor, John J. 3
Olson, Kirby 50
Oring, Elliot 4

Palmer, John 69
Park, Bruce R. 207
Parnell, Paul E. 130
parody 15–16, 25, 54, 66–8, 74–5,
        83, 132, 187–8, 217–9
Pasquier, Etienne 91
Patmore, Coventry 194
Peel, Sir Robert 184
Plato 13, 110
Plautus 29, 55
Polhemus, Robert 156
political cartoons 26
Pope, Alexander 15, 121–7, 136, 219
Potter, Stephen 31, 241
Provine, Robert 5
Prynne, William 128, 182
psychologist viewpoint 1
Punch 35, 185
puns 18–24, 81–2, 95, 100, 124, 177,
        180

Puritans 83, 105–6, 182
Puttenham, George 55

Rabelais 24
Rattigan, Terence 222
Reynolds, Joshua 142
Richardson, Samuel 130–3, 156
Righter, Ann 110
Robertson, D.W. Jr. 44–5
Robertson, T.W. 206–7
Rodway, Allan 191
Rossiter, A.P. 39
Russian humour 181–2
Rymer, Thomas 111

sadistic humour 3, 13, 26, 50
Salinger, J.D. 229
Salinger, Leo 70
satire 9, 50, 107–9, 123–4
Schneider, Ben Ross 112
Schopenhauer, Arthur 4, 69
Schorer, Mark 160
Sennett, Mack 184
sentiment 128–139
Shadwell, Thomas 110
shaggy-dog stories 28, 46
Shakespeare, William 3, 14, 21–3,
        30–4, 55–6, 61–90, 109,
        119–20, 182, 208
Shaw, G.B. 56, 188–9, 205–17
Shelley, Percy B. 141
Sheridan, Richard, B. 2, 12,
        136–7
Sidney, Sir Philip 32, 110
slapstick 50, 53
Smollett, Tobias 141
Socrates 7–8, 13, 215
Spencer, Herbert 4, 16
Sprat, Thomas 20
Steele, Richard 56, 124, 129–130
Sterne, Lawrence 140–153
Swift, Jonathan 155
Sypher, Wylie 23

Tate, Nahum 112
Terence 55
Tertullian 97
Thurber, James 11
Todd, Janet 155
tragicomedy 223–6
Traugott, John 145
Trilling, Lionel 156

Wain, John 226
Walpole, Horace 218
Watts, Isaac 177
Webb, Sidney 212

Welsford, Enid 13–4
Wilde, Oscar 31, 187–197, 205, 212
Wilson, J.Dover 76–7
Wilson, Thomas 2, 21
Wiltshire, John 155
wit 15, 17, 93–6, 105, 113–4, 126, 136
wordplay, *see* puns
Wordsworth 125
Wright, Austen 156
Wycherley, William 113–17

Yeats, W.B. 185, 285